GREENWOOD's *Contributions in Economics and Economic History* is an open-ended series of original monographs, treatises, and upper-division texts in economics, economic history, business, and finance. Titles in the series are selected by distinguished academic consultants and advisors on the basis of originality and scholarly significance. The chief consultant for the program is *Robert Sobel,* New College, Hofstra University, who also serves as the series editor of the Greenwood Press reprint program entitled *The Money Markets.*

American Financing of
World War I

Contributions in Economics and
Economic History

American Financing of World War I

CHARLES GILBERT

Contributions in
Economics and Economic History

NUMBER 1

Greenwood Publishing Corporation
Westport, Connecticut

Library of Congress Catalog Card Number: 73–79060
SBN: 8371–1496–9

Greenwood Publishing Corporation
51 Riverside Avenue, Westport, Conn. 06880

Greenwood Publishers Ltd.
42 Hanway Street, London, W.1., England

Printed in the United States of America

*To the Memory of
my Father*

Contents

The stock market. The money market recovery. Federal finance.

The House Ways and Means Committee bill. Debate in the House of Representatives. Senate Finance Committee hearings. The Senate Finance Committee. The debate in the Senate. War Revenue Act of 1918.

List of Tables

Preface

There is a great deal of difference between a study of war finance and a study of the normal financing of government expenditures. A war period is a period of emergency and requires the performance of many activities by both the government and the nongovernment sectors of the economy which are not generally undertaken at other times. Furthermore, a war period is one in which an enormous expansion takes place in government activity, for war is a governmental rather than a private enterprise. During a war period this expansion of government activities and expenditures creates a need for receipts not only in far greater volume than in the prewar period, but also in a steady, dependable flow. This need sets up the problem that is the concern of this book — the ways in which the government financed the war expenditures during World War I and the effects on the economy of the financing methods which were used.

A war period does not exist in a vacuum, but rather is part of a continuous span of time containing both a past and a future, of which the war period is the present. Just as life in the immediate present is influenced by what has gone on in the past and in turn has an influence on the future, so is a war period affected by past action and in turn influences future events. It is therefore important when discussing or evaluating the war period to consider both the limitations of the past and the effects on the future.

So far as World War I was concerned, the immediate past which exerted a direct effect on wartime policies and practices was the period from July 1914 to June 1916. In this period the United States expanded its production to provide arms, ammunition, food, and other war materials for the European nations at war. The achievements of the economy in these prewar years influenced to a large extent the potential achievements during the actual war years. In a similar vein, practices and policies put into effect during the war period had some repercussions in the immediate postwar years, and in various degrees in the future.

This study is divided into three interrelated parts. The first part deals with the immediate prewar years 1914 to 1916. In this period occurred the panic at the outbreak of war, the recovery shortly afterward, and the prosperity of the neutrality period. An attempt is made to show the ways in which the war period was influenced by prewar activities.

The second part deals with the financing of the war, and includes the years 1916–1920. These years cover the period of preparedness, the period of belligerency, and the immediate postwar period when some war measures were still in effect.

The third part of this study discusses the effects of war finance on the economy both during and after the war period itself.

There are several reasons why World War I is appropriate for a study of war finance. It was the second of the major wars in which the United States took an active part, and so allows a comparison with both the past and the future insofar as the available data will allow. It was a period in which the power of government on the Federal level received an enormous impetus which was more or less retained in the near future and greatly expanded from the 1930's on. During World War I the Federal Reserve System was molded into a tool of the Treasury, thereby greatly influencing the future development of the System. The Great War lends itself to study from still another point of view. Between the Civil War and World War I great changes had taken place in the industrial life of the country — much greater changes than those that took place between the two World Wars. World War I was the first major war in which the United States participated as a truly industrialized nation. The new industrial economy thus presented a far different situation to the Treasury than that existing in the Civil War period. It might well serve as a model or proving ground for the financing of World War II and later wars.

In addition to the descriptive material, an effort has been made to set forth criteria by which a war-finance program can be evaluated. These criteria, while heavily weighted with fiscal theory, also recognize the importance of psychology and political expediency when dealing with the human element. Above all, the finance program of World War I should be evaluated as much by the standards and knowledge which existed at that time as by those of the present day.

In conclusion I would like to express my gratitude to the staffs of the New York Public Library and the *Commercial and Financial Chronicle*, who fetched and carried in my behalf, and to Professor Herman E. Krooss of the New York University Graduate School of Business, who gave so generously of his time and advice.

I

Basic Problems in War Finance*

The fundamental problem in a war economy is the choice of the methods by which the diversion of productive resources from peacetime production to war production can be best attained. Because this diversion must be involuntary, and not a result of consumer choice, the methods by which it is accomplished are of extreme importance.

National Resources

The resources which a nation possesses consist of mental and physical manpower, stocks of capital equipment, natural resources, claims on foreign nations, and organizational ability. Within this structure lies the economic potential, and only from it can the government take the resources necessary for the operation of the war. These resources, taken and used by the government for war purposes, are the real costs of the war.[1] These costs cannot be postponed to the future, for the resources used must be taken from stockpiles of goods produced in the past or must be currently produced. There are two exceptions to this rule: (a) goods supplied by foreign nations either as a loan or gift, and (b) a greater than normal depletion of natural resources. Goods supplied by foreign nations, if sent in the form of a loan, will be repaid out of future production; if sent as a gift, they are paid for by foreign producers. If the foreign goods are sent in repayment of a past loan, they represent part of the stockpile of goods built up by past producers. A greater than normal depletion of natural resources pushes the nonconsumption of these resources far into the future when the last possible users will be forced to forgo their consumption.

Waging a war in a democracy presents entirely different problems from those of a totalitarian state. In a totalitarian state materials and manpower can be commandeered with no thought to the desires and reactions of the citizens. There might be no need for either borrowing or taxation. A section of the population could be shifted to war production, and given whatever the ruling group decided to give,[2] so that fiscal decisions might never present a problem. In a democracy, the desires and reactions of the citizens must necessarily be considered, or the war program will fail, for a democracy wages war by voluntary effort. This does not mean that citizens will sacrifice cheerfully, but it does mean that they will understand that sacrifice is necessary in wartime and that they will not rebel against the tools used in the conduct of the war. In other words, war in a democracy does not require eagerness, but it does require willingness to cooperate. The decisions made by those in authority must therefore be acceptable to the citizens of the nation.

Financing the War

In an exchange economy the diversion of resources is attained by the transfer of money claims to resources from consumers to the government. This transfer process may be either permanent or temporary. If permanent, the government effects the transfer through compulsion in the form of taxation. If the transfer is to be a temporary one, it is effected by loans with a promise of repayment of the money claim at some future date. The real costs of the war are represented by money expenditures and real income by money receipts. Government war expenditures represent payments to persons engaged in providing war materials. Government money receipts represent the claims to goods given up by the persons paying their money to the government either as taxes or loans. These transactions therefore represent the transfer of claims from the nonwar sector to the war sector with the accompanying shift of resources. These costs, when represented by money, are known as the money costs or the financial costs of the war.

Because the financing of a war consists mainly in financing a shift of resource utilization from current nonwar production to current war production, the importance of the decision regarding taxation and borrowing might seem somewhat obscure. On the contrary, the decision is one of primary importance. While the shift of physical resources must take place, the use of taxes and loans to meet the war expenditures determines which groups will suffer the loss of these resources, the degree to which each group will contribute to the war effort, and whether this contribution will be a permanent or a temporary one. Before proceeding with the examination of the practices followed in financing World War I, it would be worth while to examine the implications and relative merits of taxation and borrowing.

Taxation versus Borrowing

In the last analysis the financial cost of the war can only be paid in one way—through taxation. This is true regardless of the method used by the Treasury during the actual period of conflict, for if borrowing is resorted to, the debt must eventually be repaid through tax receipts.[3] The decision regarding the relative amounts of taxation and borrowing is therefore a decision regarding the time element in taxation and the distribution of the burden of war costs within the economy. It is a decision concerning who shall bear the burden, rather than when it shall be borne. Current tax payments represent a permanent transfer of purchasing power by the taxpayer to the government. Bond purchases involve a temporary sacrifice of purchasing power by the bond buyer in exchange for a claim to future purchasing power which may be greater than, equal to, or less than the purchasing power currently sacrificed. In either case present purchasing power is shifted from the taxpayer to the government, but the methods used to achieve this transfer will have different effects on the economy.

Three criteria by which government wartime fiscal policy can be evaluated are (a) its ability to control inflationary pressures, (b) the effect of the policy on production incentives, and (c) the postwar effects. Interrelated with the above criteria are psychological effects and questions of political expediency and equitability, all of which are extremely important in war finance.

Taxation and Inflation

A shift of resources from nonwar production to war production during a war period does not change the payments to the factors of production. Whether the money payments are for war or nonwar production cannot alter the fact that all money payments represent purchasing power which can be used only for the purchase of the nonwar production. To the extent that more resources go into war production there will be fewer resources which can be utilized for the production of consumer goods. This gap between purchasing power and goods available for purchase is the primary cause of inflation.[4] If the money is translated into demand for goods, prices will rise until the amount of purchasing power is equated with the volume of goods for sale. To the extent that part of the money gap is saved, the rise in the price level will be mitigated.

To illustrate this concept, let us take an economy producing $50 billion in consumer goods, and making payments of $50 billion to the factors of production. Here the payments are equal to the amount of production and if no savings take place the market will be cleared at the price level of, let us say, $1 per unit of goods. When war is declared the government uses $20 billion for waging war. The economy may merely transfer $20 billion of resources to the government or expand production by $20 billion by putting into production idle resources. In either case there will be the danger of inflation. If there are no idle resources, factor incomes will remain at $50 billion but available consumer goods will decrease to $30 billion. If the $20 billion excess is allowed to enter into the demand for goods, prices will rise until the $50 billion can purchase the existing goods for sale. The tendency will be for the price level to increase by about 66 per cent. If idle resources are available to produce the $20 billion of war goods, the output of consumer goods will remain the same but factor payments will increase to $70 billion. Again the tendency will be for prices to rise, but not as high as they did in the previous example. The tendency will be for a 40 per cent increase in prices due to the relatively smaller money gap. The inflationary pressure could be removed by the government if the war were put on a pay-as-you-go basis, and the total excess income were removed through taxation. It should be mentioned that to the extent that consumers draw upon past savings or reduce their current rate of savings, the inflationary pressures will be increased.

Taxation and Incentives to Produce

The effect of taxation on production incentives is not easily ascertained. There is a point where incentives become endangered by taxation, but this point differs for each individual, and precisely when it affects the nation as a whole is difficult to determine. The taxable capacity of a nation in wartime is the limit beyond which production would suffer, and since production is a voluntary activity, the tax limit becomes the point beyond which additional net income is less desirable than additional leisure. A country's taxable capacity, if incentives are to be retained, is not the level which the economy *can* sustain,[5] but the level which the economy *decides* to sustain, and the higher the tax rate, the quicker will this limit be reached. Tax rates are within the desired level if they do not reduce real output. This implies that taxes must come out of surplus income, income which is not required by the producer to motivate his production.

A tax program based on this principle would be extremely difficult to impose. First of all, there can be only a vague idea of where this surplus income may be found and the extent of the surplus. Secondly, it would be impossible to collect surplus incomes without hitting individual nonsurplus incomes, especially among groups whose wartime incomes remained fairly equal to their prewar incomes. A tax on nonsurplus incomes would have the same effect as a cut in wages or salaries. If the supply curve of human effort has a positive slope, with less effort offered for less remuneration, there would be a reduction in the amount of human effort offered in production of both war goods and nonwar goods. However, if the tax rate is extremely high, the supply curve of effort may be a negative one as producers are willing to work longer so that some semblance of a standard of living may be maintained. This might lead to an increase in output caused by a situation in which the producer must work longer merely to subsist.

To the extent that high taxes reduce the investment incentive there would be a reduction in private investment expenditures. This presents no problem during a war period and may in fact be beneficial for it may divert more resources to war production.

But if the war period extends far enough into the future so that the current stock of capital goods is consumed and must be replaced, the production of war goods will suffer.

The effect of a wartime tax policy in the postwar period will depend to a great extent on the height of the tax rates and the distribution of the tax burden. If the wartime taxes are so high that replacement of capital is sacrificed to the war effort, a larger part of the postwar production will be devoted to capital goods than would otherwise be necessary. This would increase capital expenditures in the postwar period and act as a bulwark against unemployment and falling prices. A tax which would decrease cash balances and savings would make the postwar readjustment more difficult since there would be a smaller backlog of effective demand.

The postwar impact of the distribution of the wartime tax burden among the various income groups cannot be ascertained in an absolute manner, for this will depend to a large extent upon the consumer pattern during the war. A tax program falling predominantly on the upper-income groups and leaving the lower-income groups relatively free of the tax burden may result in a surge of consumer demand during the war period as consumers translated their increased wartime incomes into current purchasing power. On the other hand, if the increased wartime incomes were saved a backlog of postwar purchasing power would be built up to sustain consumption during the transition to a peacetime economy. If the surplus wartime income were to be translated into demand for goods, it would be equal to an increase in the money supply, and would tend to raise prices. If the surplus income were to be saved, there would be little pressure on prices, and cash balances of consumers would be increased. These cash balances could sustain the necessary demand in the postwar period. On the other hand, a tax program falling predominantly on low-income groups would be deflationary during the war period but would not create a backlog of potential consumer demand in the postwar period.

There is then no "absolute value" in a policy of total tax financing. Taxation as a rule will divert purchasing power from consumers to the government, but to properly divert the purchasing power, it would be necessary to tax the lower-income groups which have a higher propensity to consume than do the upper-income groups. In diverting purchasing power from consumers, however, there is a possible danger of lessening production incentives, and also of sacrificing the backlog of potential demand so necessary in a period of postwar adjustment.

In addition to and interrelated with the economic implications of taxation, there are also political and psychological limitations to be considered. One limitation is the unwillingness of legislators to pass a high tax bill for which they will be held accountable by their constituents. Another is the inability of the average taxpayer to understand the necessity for taxation, and his preference for a government bond rather than a tax receipt. An astute tax policy, therefore, involves a careful evaluation of the various possible economic and psychological effects. It should be high enough to discourage inflation, but not so high that it will diminish incentives, crush morale, and prevent postwar economic readjustment.

Borrowing

The policy of borrowing to finance a war cannot be any better evaluated in an absolute sense than the policy of taxation. The success or failure of a borrowing program depends mostly upon the manner of its administration. Such phases of borrowing as interest rates, maturities, methods of borrowing, and the relative amount of the borrowing will be considered more fully in later chapters which will discuss these subjects as they were handled during World War I. Here, a general borrowing policy will be subjected to the criteria used in evaluating a tax program.

Financing a war by borrowing is usually an inflationary

process, although it does not necessarily need to be. If the Treasury borrows money from consumers which they would otherwise have spent for goods, the effect on the economy from the point of view of inflation will be the same as a policy of taxation. In either case, purchasing power equal to the amount of government spending will be diverted from consumers to the government, and there will be no surplus demand tending to raise the general price level. However, tapping this excess demand would be a Herculean task—one that has never been accomplished in any war period. Even if there were no bank borrowing, it would be unlikely that there would be a diversion only of surplus demand, and not a diversion of past or present savings. There would be a strong tendency on the part of consumers to regard a government bond as a substitute for, instead of an addition to, cash balances. To the extent that consumers drew on savings for bond purchases, inflationary tendencies would exist, with the amount of diverted savings acting as an increase in the money supply. Therefore, the inflationary or deflationary effect on the economy of nonbank borrowing depends upon the source of the money which consumers use to purchase government debt.

Bank borrowing usually is, although it need not be, a government instigated inflationary process. Banks having ample reserves can extend loans to either the public or the private economy. To the extent that loans to the government are substituted for private loans, there will be no greater addition to the money supply than that which would have otherwise occurred. When added to private borrowing, government borrowing serves to further increase the money supply. This additional purchasing power, when placed in the hands of consumers, and translated into demand for goods, inevitably results in a higher price level. When the government resorts to bank borrowing, the necessary reserves are usually made available, so that government borrowing is added to rather than substituted for private borrowing, and thus results in inflationary pressures.

Unlike taxation, borrowing to finance a war is an ideal means of motivating production. Whether the borrowing is from consumers or from the banking system, the penalties associated with taxation will not be present to dampen motivation for production. Borrowing from consumers, while diverting part of the demand for goods, will at the same time place rights to future purchases in consumer hands. These rights, or evidences of government debt, are accepted by the consumer as liquid assets, although for the economy as a whole they represent no such thing. A total of $25 billion of government bonds in the hands of consumers merely represents a further tax bill which must be paid. Since the debt is eventually repaid out of tax receipts, the purchasing power of the nation will remain unchanged. All that will occur will be a redistribution of purchasing power from the taxpayers to the bondholders. Nevertheless ownership of a bond in the eyes of the wartime taxpayer is a desirable alternative to ownership of a tax receipt. Where, for example, leisure might be preferred to overtime work under a program of heavy taxation, the receipt of a bond under similar circumstances would tend to lessen the disutility of the additional burden.

Borrowing also enables the government to partly synthesize the conflicting demands of politics and economics, for under a borrowing program the low-income groups may be relieved of their surplus incomes without resort by the legislature to the political inexpediency of taxation. Borrowing becomes a process by which the surplus income is painlessly extracted.

Bank borrowing, with its accompanying increase in the money supply, will increase consumer cash balances, which can then be used for the purchase of government securities. With a decreasing marginal propensity to consume, the ratio of saving to spending would increase in the form of either time deposits or government debt. Under this concept, an increase in bank borrowing in relation to taxation and nonbank borrowing would either directly or indirectly increase sales of government debt to noncommercial bank investors. To the consumer the production incentive in bank borrowing would be the same as that in non-bank borrowing, since his payment to the government would in either case be rewarded with a government bond.

In the postwar period the impact of a government borrowing policy will depend on the height and distribution of the debt. Furthermore, the debt for the most part affects individuals rather than the total economy. As previously suggested in the present chapter, the effect of a nonbank held debt on the total economy is a redistribution of income when the interest is paid, and when the bonds are redeemed. But it must be remembered that this is true only if the debt is held by nonbank investors. When part of the debt is held by the commercial banking system, the redemption of the debt can become a potent tool of fiscal policy. On the assumption that the debt is held jointly by the banking system and by nonbank investors, the redemption of the bank-held debt will reduce both investments and deposits, and consequently reduce the money supply by an amount equal to the bank-held bond redemptions. This occurs through the tax payment which reduces either bank deposits or money in circulation, and the purchase of the bonds from the banks by the government, which reduces the volume of bank investments. In the same fashion a transfer of the debt from the banking system to nonbank investors will decrease the money supply, while the money supply would be increased by a transfer of debt to the banking system.

To elaborate further on the effects of the debt when held by nonbank investors, the payment of interest or the redemption of the debt would merely transfer deposits or currency in circulation from taxpayers to bondholders. Here both the distribution of the debt and the distribution of the tax burden is of primary importance. If the tax burden was distributed in the same ratio as the debt distribution there would be no change in individual positions. Each taxpayer would, in effect, be paying himself that part of his tax bill which was allocated for debt reduction and interest charges. The bondholders might without loss destroy their bonds, cancel the debt, and consider the original bond purchase in its true light — as a form of taxation. This admittedly exaggerated illustration serves to demonstrate the real implication of government borrowing. However, it is extremely unlikely that the burden of taxation and the distribution of the debt will correlate to any great degree. The effect of the wartime debt on the postwar public will depend on the ratio of debt ownership to tax liability of the individuals within the economy. Those persons with a greater than 1:1 ratio will be net income receivers, while those with a ratio of less than 1:1 will be net payers. If the nonbank held debt is held primarily by the high-income group, a progressive tax policy will tend to equalize the ratio, while a regressive tax policy will tend to widen the ratio. That is, while the height of the debt will determine the extent of taxation, it is the relative distribution of debt and taxes that measures the debt impact.

Conclusions

The problem of war finance should be approached with the intention of creating a balance between taxation and borrowing which will divert the necessary purchasing power to the government and at the same time control inflationary pressures, maintain production incentives, and create a basis for postwar readjustment.

To attain these ends, the tax policy should be aimed at the taxation of surplus incomes, and the borrowing policy should be directed toward noninflationary borrowing. If these policies are carried out successfully, the postwar readjustment should present a minimum of problems.

NOTES

*Among the discussions of problems of war finance various views will be found in A. C. Pigou, *The Political Economy of War;* E. R. A. Seligman, *Essays in Taxation;* C. Shoup, M. Friedman, and R. P. Mack, *Taxing to Prevent Inflation;* C.R. Noyes, "Fallacies of War Finance," *Yale Review,* October 1918, pp. 72–89; C. J. Bullock, "Financing the War," *Quarterly Journal of Economics,* May 1917, pp. 357–379; F. F. Anderson, "Fundamental Factors in War Finance," *Journal of Political Economy,* November 1917, pp. 857–887; L. W. Crum, J. F. Fennelly, and L. H. Seltzer, *Fiscal Planning for Total War;* Jules Backman, ed., *The Economics of Armament Inflation;* Irving Fisher, *The Right and Wrong Way of Financing the War;* and Seymour Harris, *The Economics of America at War,* Chapters 9, 10.

[1] Other costs (loss of life, injury, property damage, human suffering, fatigue) are just as real and perhaps more important, but they cannot be objectively measured.

[2] Subsistence would be a necessary minimum or production would be in danger of falling.

[3] If the debt is refunded, the taxation is merely extended further into the future.

[4] Henry C. Murphy, *National Debt in War and Transition,* p. 73.

[5] This concept is expressed by Richard A. Musgrave, "Fiscal and Monetary Problems in a High-Level Defense Economy: A Study in Taxable Capacity," *American Economic Review,* May 1950, p. 210 (italics added).

2

The Effect of the Outbreak
of the War on the
American Economy

When the war broke out, the initial effects were depressing on the American economy. This initial period brought about an almost complete halt to exports, a breakdown of the credit structure, and a fall of 18 per cent in the index of industrial production, between August and November of 1914.[1]

As the war continued, it was inevitable that the American industrial potential would be used to supply the European belligerents. Not only did the United States expand its productive capacity to meet this challenge, but it emerged from the war as the world's major financial power. The achievement of this latter result was due to a combination of financial statesmanship and fortunate past legislation which enabled the United States to meet and conquer the emergency.

The Financial Market

On Monday, July 27, 1914, the principal European stock exchanges started closing down. The threat of war had become a reality and each country tried desperately to halt the inevitable avalanche of security liquidation. The London exchange remained open until Friday, July 31, when it too decided to close. During the preceding week prices had fallen disastrously as a result of liquidation by British and Central European investors. British Consols were at $69\frac{1}{2}$ as against $74\frac{15}{16}$, a drop of more than 7 per cent during the week; London and Northwest Railroad fell more than 11 per cent, from $136\frac{3}{4}$ to 121; while, strangely enough, German Imperials 3's fell from 75 to 72, a loss of only 4 per cent.[2]

As each of the European exchanges closed, the result was reflected in increased trading in New York, and it was feared that if the New York Stock Exchange remained open, the entire impact of world liquidation would cause a panic on the New York market, as an unprecedented amount of selling orders had been piling up in brokers' offices since the close on Thursday. Between July 25 and July 30, sales on the New York Stock Exchange increased from 203,956 shares to 1,298,818 shares, and each daily increase in trading brought lower prices. Starting with a 3- to 6-point drop on Tuesday, the decline was extended on the following two days. In the railroad group, Reading fell 17 points; Lehigh Valley, 12 points; and New York Central, 6 points. Among the industrials, General Motors lost more than 30 points; International Harvester, 23 points; and United States Steel, 6 points. The oils were hit equally hard with Texas dropping 21 points; Atlantic Refining, 80 points; Prairie Oil and Gas, 74 points; and South Penn Oil, 41 points.[3]

Throughout the preceding week the Dow Jones averages had fallen sharply with a $9.10 loss in the industrials and a loss of $8.54 in the rails. It was feared that if the market remained open, there would be further panic selling. Accordingly, the board of governors of the New York Stock Exchange decided on the morning of July 31, 1914 to follow London's example and close down, and it did not open for unrestricted trading until April 1915.

For a few days the financial community ceased activities. But gradually the demand for a securities market created an outlaw market started by a group of brokers not connected with the New York Stock Exchange. Here the prices kept falling as country after country joined the European conflict. While this was going on, frequent meetings were held by the board of governors of the New York Stock Exchange, and on August 12, 1914 the Exchange Clearing House Committee announced that restricted trading would be resumed at prices not lower than those at the closing on July 30. A list of bids and offers was to be sent to the Committee which would clear those orders priced not below the July 30 price.[4] When the plan went into effect on December 15 it was not satisfactory as the outlaw market prices were lower than the restricted prices, and it was not until the price minimums were lowered that any active trading took place.

Unrestricted trading in municipals commenced on November 13, 1914, and unrestricted trading in all other bonds on November 28. Meanwhile, on the unofficial exchange, prices had started to firm in February 1915 and many were above their July closing prices. When the New York Stock Exchange opened for unrestricted trading in April 1915, stocks resumed the upward trend which had started the previous February. The Dow Jones Averages showed that between July and December 1914 the industrials lost $16.70 while the rails gained $.80, but from the July close to the April 1915 opening, the loss in the industrials was only $10.37 while the rails actually gained $3.43.

The Gold Situation

While the closing of the New York Stock Exchange had halted the danger of an enormous European liquidation of American securities and a concomitant drain on a diminishing gold supply, there still remained a short-term debt of $530 million owed by banks and merchants to creditors in London

Table 1

Dow Jones Averages, July 1914–April 1915

Date	Industrials	Rails
July 30, 1914	71.42	89.41
December 12, 1914	54.72	90.21
April 1, 1915	61.05	92.84

Source: Barron's, The Dow Jones Averages.

and Paris. This included $80 million owed by the City of New York to creditors in London and Paris, falling due on January 1, 1915.[5] Normally a great part of this payment would be made by exporting goods, but the export market in August 1914 was undergoing a drastic decline so that a further decline in American gold holdings seemed to be in prospect. During the early part of 1914, until the outbreak of war, about $117 million in gold had been shipped abroad. The New York Clearing House statement showed that on August 1, 1914, there was a deficiency of $17,425,750 in the gold reserves of the New York banks and by August 8 this deficiency had more than doubled to $43,116,000.[6] The entire gold reserve of all banks reporting to the Comptroller of the Currency was less than double the maturing foreign obligations.[7] From July to November 1914 net gold exports amounted to $115,975,441. There was keen bidding for sterling, which had risen above $7.00, so that unless sterling exchange could be reduced to $4.87 gold would continue to be shipped. It was evident that the United States had to choose between following the example of the European countries by halting gold payments, or suffering the consequences of a depleted gold supply. Neither alternative was attractive. If gold payments were stopped the prestige of the United States as a financial power would fall; if gold payments continued there was the danger of an almost complete loss of bank reserves.

The bankers were divided in their opinion as to what policy to pursue. At first they were in favor of suspending gold payments in order to protect their reserve positions. There seemed to be little chance of gold imports from Europe and the bankers looked forward only to further depletion of their gold stock.[8] On the other hand, great emphasis was given to the necessity of paying the $80 million New York City loan. In the absence of other means of payment, it would have to be paid in gold. If it were not paid, the largest city in the United States would default on its debts and cause a loss in prestige that would be difficult to overcome.

Accordingly, in September 1914 there was a conference between the Secretary of the Treasury, the members of the Federal Reserve Board, and representatives of the clearing houses of all the reserve cities. This conference worked out a plan for raising a gold fund of $100 million by allotting pro rata to each clearing house district a sum sufficient to meet the emergency. About $108 million was actually subscribed, but only $27 million was called, and only $10 million was shipped to Canada because shortly after the fund was formed the rate for sterling exchange fell, and an upward swing in exports started to take place. By the time the Federal Reserve banks opened on November 16, 1914, the danger had passed.

By deciding to meet its gold obligations, the United States greatly increased its financial prestige. Not only were Europe's fears put to rest, but the United States became a haven for gold shipments from the nonbelligerent countries in South America. In December 1914 the gold flow had turned and for the first month since the war had been declared the United States had a gold import balance of almost $4 million. From December 1914 to June 1915 $141,320,048 of gold was imported,[9] and for the entire year of 1915 the inflow was $420,529,000.[10] By November 1914 sterling exchange was again at parity.

The Banking Crisis

While the gold export situation was being solved, an internal problem of money hoarding developed because of the uncertainties brought about by the sudden outbreak of war in Europe and the fears of individuals regarding the economic prospects of the United States. As individuals increased their cash balances, bank reserves fell. To solve this problem the bankers resorted to the same solution used on other occasions—the clearing-house loan certificates. These certificates were used to discharge balances owed by one bank to another. The New York Clearing House Association started to issue clearing house certificates early in August 1914. By October 15, $124,695,000 in certificates had been issued with the maximum amount outstanding at any one time being $109,185,000.[11] All were cancelled by November 28, 1914 or in 118 days. This was 36 days less than similar certificates had been outstanding during the 1907 crisis.[12]

Congress, at the suggestion of Secretary McAdoo, also came to the aid of the banks by amending both the Aldrich-Vreeland Act of 1908, and the Federal Reserve Act which had not yet started active operation. On August 4, 1914 the Federal Reserve Act was amended so as to authorize the Secretary of the Treasury to allow national banks to issue an amount of circulating currency equal to 125 per cent of their unimpaired capital and surplus instead of the legal 100 per cent. The immediate result of this action was to increase national bank notes from $852 million in August to $1,051 million in September, an increase of more than 23 per cent in this type of currency.[13] In addition, the emergency currency provisions of the Aldrich-Vreeland Act were reactivated and amended. Under the original Act interest on the emergency notes was to be 5 per cent the first month and an additional 1 per cent each month until a total of

10 per cent had been paid. As amended, the Act called for interest payments of 3 per cent the first month and $\frac{1}{2}$ per cent each additional month with a limit of 6 per cent as the maximum payment.[14]

The entire country was divided into 44 currency districts with each district representing the banks in the area. The requests for the emergency currency were to be made by the banks to the currency associations and by the associations to the Treasury. In the 44 national currency associations were 2,102 banks with total capital of $687,494,910 and surplus of $510,276,091.

On August 1, 1914 New York Clearing House statements showed a drop in reserves of $43,599,500 from the preceding week.[15] By the middle of August actual reserves of New York banks had decreased by about $83 million, nearly all of it in gold. Whereas on July 25 there were excess reserves of $25,127,000, by August 15, three weeks later, there was a reserve deficit of $47,992,000.[16] McAdoo announced on August 3 that the department was ready to issue to the national banks in New York $100 million in emergency currency.[17]

The emergency currency was finally issued to 1,363 banks through 41 currency associations in 40 states. The amounts

Table 2
Issues of Emergency Currency

Month Ending	Emergency Currency Issued (Cumulative)
August 31, 1914	$208,810,790
September 30, 1914	326,789,380
October 31, 1914	369,558,040
November 30, 1914	383,301,305

Source: U.S. Treasury Department, Annual Report, 1914, pp. 481–482.

issued during the four months of issue totaled $383,301,305.[18]

After the first month the demands for the currency slackened appreciably, only 15 per cent of the total amount being distributed during the last two months. Of the total approved circulation, $309,308,210 went to banks in reserve cities. Retirement of the emergency currency was very rapid. It started when the Federal Reserve banks opened and by January 15, 1915 less than $100 million was still in circulation.[19] On February 25, 1915 McAdoo announced that the Treasury would keep on hand $500 million of Federal Reserve notes in lieu of the emergency currency which was to be retired by June 30.[20] By April 20 less than $9 million remained outstanding.

The Cotton Loan Fund

During the first month of the war American exports had virtually vanished, and the situation in the cotton market was a serious one. About 60 per cent of the cotton crop was normally exported and the 1914 crop was expected to be a large one. The crop was approaching maturity and the cotton exchanges both in England and the United States were closed. Prices collapsed and quotations were unobtainable, although sales were made sporadically at five cents a pound and lower.[21]

On August 26, 1914 Secretary McAdoo called a conference of representatives of cotton producers, manufacturers, bankers, merchants, railroad men and the Federal Reserve Board. To alleviate the situation it was proposed to issue emergency currency to southern banks for cotton and tobacco loans. Collateral was to be warehouse receipts with the amount of the loan at 75 per cent of face value.[22] About $68 million of emergency currency was so issued, in addition to which $27 million of government funds was deposited in banks in the South. However, by September cotton was only bringing $8\frac{1}{2}$ cents a pound in the interior points in the South, while cost per pound was

Table 3
Cotton Loan Fund Subscriptions

New York	$ 50,000,000.
Other cities	47,292,000.
Kuhn, Loeb, and Co.	2,000,000.
Bernard Baruch	1,000,000.
Total	$100,292,000.

estimated at $9\frac{1}{2}$ cents. Although the price was above the 5–$6\frac{1}{2}$ cents range in August, it was far below the price needed by the cotton grower.[23]

A proposal was made by Festus J. Wade of St. Louis that a fund be raised to aid the cotton growers. The fund was to be in the amount of $135 million of which $50 million was to be raised by the New York banks and financiers, $50 million by banks in other large cities, and $35 million by banks in the South. This was agreed to by the banks and on October 24, 1914 the Cotton Loan Fund received the official sanction of the Federal Reserve Board. The total fund subscriptions were $100,292,000.[24]

This fund was pledged to be loaned against cotton at six cents per pound but before that price was reached the situation had changed, cotton moved at higher prices, and the immediate danger was over.

Industry

During this period of financial panic, as was to be expected, industrial production and employment also suffered.

Production of steel ingots dropped from the 2,561,000 tons produced in March 1914 to a low point of 1,646,000 tons in November 1914.[25] Pig iron output reached a low of 48,896 tons per day in December 1914 as compared to 75,665 tons per day in April of that year.[26] Employment at the United States Steel Company fell from 228,906 in 1913 to 179,353 in 1914,[27] with unfilled orders dropping from 4,213,331 tons in August 1914 to 2,787,667 tons just one month later.[28] Annual production of pig iron fell from 30,966,152 tons in 1913 to 23,332,244 tons in 1914. Considering that 1913 was not a prosperous year, the outlook in the late summer and fall of 1914 was indeed dismal.

The number of active blast furnaces decreased from 208 on June 30, 1914 to 164 in December 1914. Prices of metals and metal products dropped from an index of 90.8 (1926 = 100) in 1913 to 80.2 in 1914.[29] The Colorado Fuel and Iron Company reported a loss of $334,662 and American Locomotive a loss of $3,241,980 in 1914.[30] Not foreseeing what was to come, *The Iron Age,* on August 6, 1914[31] advised Americans to shift their concentrations from the European to the South American markets.

Exports

So suddenly did the impact of war make itself felt that export trade was, in August 1914, completely demoralized. Trade with our principal European customers, Germany, France, and the United Kingdom was completely cut off by both the collapse of the foreign exchange market and credits, and the lack of ocean transportation. The situation was extremely serious. Agricultural products and manufactured goods were so congested at the leading ports that a temporary embargo was placed by railroads on shipments of grain to New Orleans, Galveston, and Baltimore.[32] Total exports which had averaged $171,654,595 per month from January through July 1914 fell to $110,367,494 in August, a drop of almost 40 per cent. In August 1913 exports had amounted to $187,909,020, 70 per cent more than in August 1914.[33] Pig iron exports fell from 277,648 tons in 1913 to

114,423 tons in 1914.[34] However, exports recovered suddenly in September when they amounted to $156,052,333, and climbed steadily thereafter.

To alleviate the strained situation Secretary McAdoo called a series of foreign trade conferences. He met at the Treasury Department on August 14, 1914 with 62 representatives of business, banking, and transportation. The problems to be considered were the restoration of the market for foreign bills of exchange, provision for transportation of goods to Europe, and war risk insurance.

The first of these problems, the restoration of the foreign exchange market, was solved through the previously mentioned gold fund and the restoration of the par value for the pound sterling which accompanied the restoration of confidence brought about by the gold fund.

The other problems were solved by the establishment of the War Risk Insurance Bureau in the Treasury Department authorized by Congress on August 18, and the Ship Registry Law which provided for the registration of foreign-built ships under United States ownership and permitted the President to suspend certain requirements in the Navigation Laws. Secretary McAdoo had desired an expanded government-owned merchant marine. This desire was embodied in the Shipping Bill presented to Congress in August 1914. However, this seemed to be too much "government in business" for the tenor of the times, and when the bill failed to be enacted a leading financial paper commented that there was occasion for gratitude that the Ship Purchase Bill was definitely shelved due to the evidence that any attempt to pass the bill would lead to renewed filibustering on the part of Republicans in the Senate.[35] It was more than two years later (September 5, 1916) before the Shipping Bill was finally passed in a much modified form. On September 7, 1916 President Wilson signed the measure which created the Shipping Board, giving it $50 million for the construction and purchase of mer-

chant ships suitable for naval auxiliaries and for commerce. The
Federal government had made one more small inroad into the
economic life of the country.

The export crisis, the financial panic, and the sharp decline in
production created a serious problem of unemployment. Average weekly earnings in manufacturing industries fell from $11.20
in June to a low of $10.81 in October,[36] while the Consumers
Price Index rose from 70.7 in 1913 to 72.6 in 1914, bringing real
weekly wages still lower.[37] Wholesale prices declined from 69.8
to 68.1 with greater than average declines in textiles, fuel and
lighting, metal and metal products, and building materials.[38]

Although there were no reliable statistics on unemployment at
the time, a survey made in March and April 1915 by the Bureau
of Labor Statistics and the Metropolitan Life Insurance Company reported that of 401,548 families canvassed, 15 per cent
contained some unemployment. Of 647,394 wage earners canvassed, 11.5 per cent were unemployed and 16.6 per cent worked
on a part-time basis.[39] The Department of Labor held repeated
conferences with state and local officials between August and
December 1914,[40] and plans for unemployment assistance were
being drawn up or going into effect on a local level by the beginning of 1915.

This situation was not destined to continue, and by June 1915
a full recovery was underway with signs of the future boom
showing themselves as early as September 1914 in export trade,
and somewhat later in other fields.

Federal Finance

With the sharp drop in exports and imports following the
declaration of war together with the drop in industrial production, the Treasury faced a decline in ordinary receipts and the
prospect of an operating deficit. That this fear was well grounded
is shown in Table 4.

Table 4

Ordinary Receipts and Disbursements, Year Ending June 30, 1915

Month	Receipts	Expenditures	Deficit (—) Surplus (+)
1914			
July	$ 73,224,173	$ 70,704,496	$+ 2,519,677
August	51,072,898	69,046,272	—17,973,374
September	51,971,395	59,602,779	— 7,631,384
October	44,563,946	62,771,226	—18,207,280
November	44,825,384	60,706,247	—15,880,863
December	51,429,362	56,994,982	— 5,565,620
1915			
January	$ 50,712,626	$ 58,829,053	$— 8,116,427
February	43,636,272	56,137,624	—12,501,352
March	56,398,959	61,308,792	— 4,909,833
April	48,042,077	61,992,174	—13,950,097
May	54,238,901	57,925,408	— 3,686,507
June	127,794,835	55,380,706	+72,414,129
Total	$697,910,828	$731,399,759	$—33,488,931

Source: U.S. Treasury Department, Annual Report, 1915, p. 228.

Emergency Revenue Act of 1914

Ordinary receipts declined rapidly in August while disbursements remained on a high level. A surplus of $2.5 million in July 1914 was followed by ten monthly deficits, starting with a deficit of $18 million in August. In anticipation of the deficit, on October 22, Congress passed the Emergency Revenue Act of 1914. This was a temporary measure supposed to expire on December 31, 1915, but it was later extended to December 31, 1916. The Emergency Revenue Act increased the tax rate on distilled spirits, and imposed special excise taxes on toilet articles; telephone and telegraph messages and chewing gum; special license taxes on tobacco products and dealers, bankers, brokers, and amusements; and stamp taxes on transactions.

The results obtained from the emergency legislation were disappointing as were the initial results from the personal income tax adopted in 1913. Personal income taxes for fiscal 1914 amounted to only $28,253,535, with returns filed by only 357,515 persons for the part of the fiscal year. For the entire fiscal year 1915, personal income taxes amounted to $41,046,162.[41]

The Emergency Revenue Act was expected to produce $100 million additional revenue in 1915 to make up for the decline in customs duties, but it produced only $52 million. Total internal revenue receipts were $415.7 million in 1915 compared to $380 million in 1914,[42] an increase of $35.7 million, but this was not enough to make up for the decrease of $85 million in customs. Total ordinary receipts in 1915 amounted to $37 million less than they had been in 1914. While the new taxes did increase

Table 5
Excise Receipts, 1914–1915

Tax	1914	1915
Distilled spirits	$159,098,177.31	$144,619,699,37
Manufactured tobacco	79,986,639.68	79,957,373.54
Fermented liquors	67,081,512.45	79,328,946.72
Bankers, brokers, etc.		4,967,179.18
Documents, perfume, cosmetics, etc.		23,455,965.34
Total	$306,166,429.44	$332,329,164.15

Source: U.S. Treasury Department, Annual Report, 1915, p. 134.

excise receipts by $26 million, there were decreases in revenues from taxes on distilled spirits of $15 million, and a slight decrease in revenues from manufactured tobacco products (see Table 5).

Impact of Federal Finance

While the Treasury general deficit of $57,442,500 in fiscal 1915 was an indication of the impact of Federal finance on the total economy, it failed to measure the impact on the nonbank economy. To achieve this it is necessary to inspect the changes in bank-held debt. When the banking system increases its holdings of government debt the result is an increase in the money supply, while a decrease is the same as a decrease in the money supply. In other words, the banking system, unlike nonbank investors, does not pay for government debt with cash, but merely expands its total deposits by the amount of the debt which it purchases.

The net Treasury impact showed a slightly different picture from that shown by the budget figures. Although the effect of Treasury operations was inflationary during fiscal 1915, it was tempered by an $8.4 million decrease in total bank-held debt.

Table 6
Federal Impact on the Nonbank Economy, Year Ending June 1915
(thousands of dollars)

Budget deficit[a]	$57,443.
Less decrease in commercial bank–held debt[b]	16,000.
Plus increase in Federal Reserve–held debt[c]	7,601.
Net Treasury increase in nonbank money supply	$49,044.

Source: (a) U.S. Treasury Department, *Annual Report, 1914*, pp. 47–48; *ibid., 1915*, pp. 57–58. (b) Federal Reserve Board, *Banking and Monetary Statistics*, p. 19. (c) Federal Reserve Board, *Annual Report, 1915*, pp. 45–46.

Table 7
Increase in Nonbank-Held Debt, Year Ending June 30, 1915
(millions of dollars)

Public debt receipts	$22.5
Public debt payments	17.3
Net debt receipts	5.2
Add decrease in commercial bank–held debt	16.0
Deduct increase in Federal Reserve–held debt	7.6
Increase in nonbank-held debt	$13.6

Source: U.S. Treasury Department, *Annual Report, 1915*, pp. 57–58.

Inasmuch as total debt receipts exceeded total debt payments by about $5.2 million,[43] nonbank investors bought about $13.6 million net of government debt during the year.

The nonbank public therefore received from the Treasury $62.6 million in ordinary income more than was returned as government revenue, from which it returned $13.6 million in debt purchases for a net increase in money received of $49 million. In part, this may explain why the panic of August 1914 did not continue throughout the year. However, in addition to the increase in the money supply caused by Treasury operations, there was an increase of $348 million in commercial bank loans and $287 million in commercial bank purchases of other securities.[44] In comparison with these figures, the Treasury impact appears indeed small. The cushion for the depression of the latter half of 1914 was primarily a private and not a government cushion, although the Treasury impact should not be completely minimized.

NOTES

[1] Federal Reserve Board, *Index of Industrial Production.*
[2] *Commercial and Financial Chronicle,* August 1, 1914, p. 298.
[3] *Ibid.,* pp. 324–326.
[4] H. G. S. Noble, *The New York Stock Exchange in the Crisis of 1914,* pp. 61–65.
[5] U.S. Treasury Department, *Annual Report, 1914,* p. 17.
[6] *Commercial and Financial Chronicle,* August 15, 1914, p. 432.
[7] U.S. Treasury Department, *Annual Report, 1914,* p. 539.
[8] *Ibid., 1915,* p. 228.
[9] *Ibid.*
[10] Federal Reserve Board, *Banking and Monetary Statistics,* p. 539.
[11] U.S. Treasury Department, *Annual Report, 1914,* pp. 482–483.
[12] *Ibid.,* pp. 484, 535.
[13] Federal Reserve Board, *Banking and Monetary Statistics,* p. 409.
[14] *Commercial and Financial Chronicle,* August 8, 1914, p. 368.
[15] U.S. Treasury Department, *Annual Report, 1914,* pp. 481–482.
[16] A. D. Noyes, *Financial Chapters of the War,* pp. 85–87.
[17] U.S. Treasury Department, *Annual Report, 1914,* pp. 481–482.
[18] *Ibid.*
[19] Federal Reserve Board, *Annual Report, 1914,* pp. 481–482, p. 15.
[20] *Federal Reserve Bulletin,* May 1915, p. 51.
[21] Federal Reserve Board, *Annual Report, 1914,* pp. 14–15.
[22] William G. McAdoo, *Crowded Years,* pp. 298–302.
[23] *Ibid.*
[24] U.S. Treasury Department, *Annual Report, 1914,* pp. 14–17.
[25] American Iron and Steel Institute, *Monthly Production of Steel Ingots in the United States 1901–1940.*
[26] *The Iron Age,* "Pig Iron Output," December 10, 1914.
[27] *Ibid.,* November 23, 1916, p. 1181.
[28] *Ibid.,* November 15, 1914, p. 915.
[29] Bureau of Labor Statistics, *Index Numbers of Wholesale Prices.*
[30] *The Iron Age,* October 19, 1916, p. 912; October 5, 1916, p. 779.
[31] *Ibid.,* August 6, 1914, pp. 354–356.
[32] U.S. Treasury Department, *Annual Report, 1914,* pp. 4–5.
[33] U.S. Department of Commerce, Bureau of Foreign and Domestic Commerce, *Annual Report, 1918,* p. 6–7.
[34] American Iron and Steel Institute, *Annual Statistical Reports.*
[35] *Commercial and Financial Chronicle, Monthly Review,* April 3, 1915, p. 15.
[36] U.S. Department of Labor, Bureau of Labor Statistics, *Bulletin No. 852: War and Postwar Wages, Prices, and Hours, 1914–23 and 1939–44.*
[37] *Ibid., Consumer Price Index.*
[38] *Ibid.. Index Numbers of Wholesale Prices.*
[39] *Ibid., Bulletin No. 195: Unemployment in the United States,* July 1916.
[40] *Ibid., Historical Study No. 2: Labor Relations in the United States.*
[41] U.S. Treasury Department, *Annual Report, 1915,* p. 753.

[42] U.S. Division of Bookkeeping and Warrants, *Combined Statement of Receipts and Expenditures, 1914*, p. 194; *ibid.*, *1915*, p. 194.

[43] U.S. Treasury Department, *Annual Report, 1915*, pp. 57–58.

[44] Federal Reserve Board, *Banking and Monetary Statistics*, p. 19.

3

Prosperous Neutrality

The second phase in the prewar period ended by the summer of 1916—the phase of neutrality when the United States combined a futile dream of neutrality with a willingness, perhaps eagerness, to expand its economy by providing the materials of war to the belligerents. By that time President Wilson had already asked for increased appropriations for the Army and Navy, Secretary McAdoo was proposing increased taxes on both business and individuals, and Congress had passed legislation increasing the Armed Services and creating a council of National Defense.

While the boom proper can be dated from the summer of 1915, the previous year was not without indications that the initial shock of the first few months of the war was over and business was recovering from the depths into which it had fallen. Gradually there were signs of recovery—a slow recovery to be sure—but by January 1915 the signs were there to be seen.

Increased Exports

The first indication that the crisis in exports had passed was a 41 per cent increase in exports in September over August 1914. From $110,367,494 in August exports jumped to $156,052,333 in September. The dollar amount of exports expanded rapidly from that point (see Table 8).

Not only did the value of exports take an upward turn in September, but in the following month the export value exceeded the seven-month prewar average of $171,654,595, and in November exports were greater than in any prewar month in 1914. During the calendar year 1916, exports advanced from

Table 8
Dollar Value of Exports, 1914–1917
(millions of dollars)

Month	1914	1915	1916	1917
January	$204.1	$267.9	$330.0	$613.3
February	173.9	299.8	401.8	467.6
March	187.5	296.6	410.7	554.0
April	162.6	294.7	398.6	529.9
May	161.7	274.2	474.8	549.7
June	157.7	268.5	464.7	573.5
July	154.1	268.5	444.7	372.8
August	110.4	260.6	510.2	488.7
September	156.1	300.7	514.9	454.5
October	194.7	336.2	492.8	542.1
November	205.9	327.7	516.2	487.3
December	245.6	359.3	523.2	600.1

Source: Bureau of Foreign and Domestic Commerce, *Annual Report, 1918,* pp. 6–7.

$330 million in January to $410.7 million in March, went to $474.8 million in May, and reached a maximum amount of $523.2 million in December. In January 1917 exports exceeded the amount in any previous month with a total of $613.3 million. War materials constituted a large part of the increase. According to the Department of Commerce, exports of war materials amounted to $1,163,160,279 in 1916 as compared to only $189,185,589 in 1914.[1] Two things explain this great increase. First, the allies were unable to provide the food and materials needed for the continuation of the struggle. Consequently, they turned to the United States, and by October 1914 the sea lanes had been made safer by the British Navy, enabling the allies to receive American shipments.[2] Second, war risk insurance, started on September 2, 1914 had by November 17, 1916 issued 1,684 policies and written $163,595,687 worth of insurance.[3]

Rise in Business Activity

Business activity was slower to recover than exports, but showed signs of improvement once the initial shock was over. The Federal Reserve Board Index of Industrial Production reached its low point of 39 (1935–1939 = 100) in November 1914, and by May 1915 it reached 54, a gain of almost 40 per cent. By March 1915 it equaled the seven-month prewar average of 49. For the calendar year 1915 the average was 59 compared to 46 in 1914; in 1916 the annual average jumped to 75.[4]

Whereas on June 1, 1915 the Treasury reported that 300,000 railroad cars and a corresponding number of locomotives were still standing idle,[5] by December 6, 1915 there was no idle capacity of railroad rolling stock. In September and October 1915, the railroads placed orders for 683,500 tons of rails, 280 locomotives, 18,000 freight cars, 60 passenger cars, and other material at more than $48 million.

In iron and steel, the number of active blast furnaces rose

after the winter of 1914, and by June 30, 1915 numbered 236 compared to 164 the previous December.[6] Pig iron production in 1915 increased to 29,916,213 tons compared with 23,332,244 tons in 1914, and 30,966,152 tons in 1913.[7] Beginning in May 1915, war orders came pouring in. A British order for $100 million went to the Bethlehem Steel Company which had $175.4 million in unfilled orders at the end of 1915 compared with $46.5 million a year earlier and $24.9 million at the end of 1913. Iron and steel exports in 1915 amounted to 381,317 tons, four times the tonnage exported in 1914, while the value of machinery exports increased from $5.3 million in 1914 to $12.4 million in 1915.[8] Unfilled orders at the United States Steel Corporation increased from 2,787,667 tons in September 1914 to 3,461,097 tons in October and to 4,248,571 tons by January 1915.[9]

Steel ingot production reached its low of 1,646,000 tons in November 1914 and climbed steadily from that date.[10] By March 1915 it exceeded the seven-month prewar average of 2,278,000 tons.

By June 1916 the steel industry had converted losses into profits, employment was rising, and wage rates were slowly following.[11] Average weekly earnings, which had dropped to $10.81 in October 1914 reached $11.07 by the end of the year, and $11.29 by June 1915.[12]

The Stock Market

Conditions in the stock market also foreshadowed the coming boom.

While the initial effect of the war was a sharp drop in stock prices, by the time the New York Stock Exchange reopened in December 1914, the Standard and Poor Averages had leveled off and the prices of stocks had started to move upward. The list in Table 9 shows the price movement of a few representative

Table 9

Prices of Five Selected Stocks—Selected Dates

Stock	7/30/14	9/22/14	1/2/15	6/1/15	6/20/15
U.S. Steel Corporation	$51\frac{3}{4}$	$49\frac{3}{8}$	49	$53\frac{3}{4}$	60
Penna. Rail Road	$106\frac{1}{2}$	$100\frac{3}{4}$	$104\frac{1}{2}$	$106\frac{7}{8}$	$105\frac{7}{8}$
Erie	$20\frac{3}{8}$	19	$21\frac{3}{8}$	$24\frac{3}{4}$	$26\frac{1}{2}$
Amer. Sugar Refinery	99	$102\frac{1}{2}$	102	103	107
Union Pacific	113	$109\frac{1}{2}$	$115\frac{3}{4}$	123	$127\frac{3}{4}$
	$390\frac{5}{8}$	$381\frac{1}{8}$	$392\frac{5}{8}$	$411\frac{3}{8}$	$427\frac{1}{8}$
Average price	$78\frac{1}{8}$	$76\frac{1}{4}$	$78\frac{1}{2}$	$82\frac{1}{4}$	$85\frac{1}{2}$

Source: *Commercial and Financial Chronicle.*

stocks from July 30, 1914 to June 30, 1915. These stocks dropped only 2.4 per cent in value based on the estimate of prices on September 22, 1914, and by the time of the reopening were selling above their average price on July 30. By June 1, 1915 each stock was selling at a higher price than it had sold for on July 30, 1914.

A comparison of the movements of stocks by both the Standard and Poor Averages and the Dow Jones Averages shows that there is some discrepancy between the two for the period between July and December 1914 (Table 10). From December 1914 on, however, the differences were much smaller.

The volume of trading expanded rapidly once the Exchange was reopened. From 2 million shares traded in December 1914, volume rose to 21 million in April 1915,[13] three months before the "official" start of the boom period. Yields of high-grade railroad bonds rose from 4.04 per cent in June 1914 to 4.23 per cent in December.[14] This surely did not denote a flight to safety in fixed income investments. Rather, the entire pattern in the securities markets forecast a coming boom as early as December

Table 10

Stock Prices, Monthly, 1914-1916

(1935–1939 = 100)

Month	Total	Industrial	Railroad	Utilities	Dow-Jones[a]	
1914						
July	63.9	36.9	211.9	82.8	(30)*	71.42
December	61.2	35.3	201.9	82.0	(12)	54.72
1915						
January	62.2	35.9	204.8	83.4	(2)	54.63
February	61.4	35.2	201.3	84.2	(2)	57.26
March	62.9	36.8	205.0	85.4	(2)	55.66
April	67.7	42.0	215.9	88.2	(3)	61.49
May	66.2	41.2	210.1	86.9	(3)	69.54
June	66.9	43.0	208.5	88.0	(2)	65.72
December	80.6	59.4	235.3	95.8	(31)	99.15
1916						
June	79.5	58.3	232.9	95.8		
December	83.3	64.9	232.1	100.2	(31)	95.00

Source: Federal Reserve Board, *Banking and Monetary Statistics,* Table 133, p. 480. (a) Barron's *The Dow Jones Averages.*

*Parentheses denote day of month.

1914 and funds seemed to be already shifting from the sanctuary of high-grade bonds to the profitability of common stocks.

While the Dow Jones Averages showed a fairly large decline from July to December, the Standard and Poor Index dropped only 4.2 per cent. From December on, both sets of figures show a gradual rise up to June 1915, and by December 1915, both averages were about 30 per cent above July 1914, while compared with December 1914 the Standard and Poor Index gained about 32 per cent and the Dow Jones Averages showed a gain of about 80 per cent.

An interesting comparison can be made based on the Standard and Poor Index for the periods between the start of hostilities and the entrance of the United States into the war for World War I and World War II.

During World War I stock prices recovered quickly after their initial fall, and advanced throughout the neutrality and preparedness period, to fall only slightly upon the declaration of war. The total gain for the period was 22 per cent. In World War II the averages fell initially and the loss finally reached 28 per cent for the neutrality period. Taxes and expectation of higher rates evidently affected stock prices in the 1939–1941 period. The drop in stock prices in 1917 came with the expectation of war taxes.

The Money Market Recovery

The money panic, which had expanded the amount of currency in circulation from $3,107 million in July 1914 to $3,457 million in October 1914, and gold coin in circulation from $317 million to $353 million, was over. By the end of 1914 currency and gold coin in circulation had fallen to $3,032 million and $320 million respectively.[15] On January 7, 1915 Secretary McAdoo announced that exchange between the United States and the United Kingdom had become practically normal.[16] By May 1, 1915 all Federal Reserve Districts except Philadelphia reported that business conditions were "good and improving".[17]

On December 4, 1916, the Treasury announced that "the prosperity which set so strongly *during the fiscal year 1915* has grown in strength and volume," and further announced that "we have been transformed from a debtor to a creditor nation."[18]

Whether the coming boom was foreseen or not, there is no doubt that the period starting July 1915 saw a tremendous expansion of all economic and financial activity.

Table 11
Changes in Stock Prices—4 World Wars I and II,
Selected Dates

Time	Date		World War I	Date		World War II
Start of war	July	1914	63.9	Sept.	1939	99.7
6 months	Jan.	1915	62.2	March	1940	96.7
Per cent change			− 2.6%			− 3.%
1 year	July	1915	68.1	Sept.	1940	85.5
Per cent change			6.5%			−14.2%
1½ years	Jan.	1916	79.3	March	1941	80.3
Per cent change			24.0%			−20.0%
U.S. enters the war	April	1917	77.9	Dec.	1941	71.8
Per cent change			22.0%			−28.0%

Source: Federal Reserve Board, *Banking and Monetary Statistics*, Table 133, pp. 480–481.

Between June 1915 and June 1916 private loans and investments of all banks increased by $3,170 million, while net deposits increased by $3,633 million.[19] The American businessman was starting the expansion of capacity to satisfy the demands of the belligerents, the expansion which was later to produce the goods for the American forces when the United States entered the war.

From December 1914 on, gold movements into the United States proceded at a rapid pace. From December 1914 to December 1916 the gold stock increased from $1,526 million to $2,556 million, an increase of $1,030 million; $530 million of this entered in 1916. Included in this amount was $50.6

million from the United Kingdom and $570.7 million from Canada, which was merely re-exporting gold received from the British Commonwealth. Exports of gold from the United States went mainly to Argentina, $27 million; Japan, $25 million; Dutch East Indies, $9.7 million; British West Indies, $19 million; and Spain, $17 million.[20]

This expansion of the gold supply provided a convenient base for the expansion of money and credit. On December 31, 1914, near the beginning of their operations, the Federal Reserve District banks had $229 million of gold reserves among their assets, mainly received from member banks for their subscriptions to Federal Reserve stock. On December 29, 1916, the District banks held $454 million in gold, an increase of $225 million.[21]

Table 12
Money and Banking Operations of Commercial Banks, 1914-1916
(millions of dollars)

	June 30, 1914	June 23, 1915	June 30, 1916
Loans	$13,171	$13,519	$15,768
Nongovernment investments	2,865	3,152	3,891
Total	$16,036	$16,471	$19,659
Annual increase		435	3,188
Deposits—excluding interbank deposits	$14,692	$15,232	$18,616
Annual increase		540	3,384
Currency in circulation[a]	$ 3,172	$ 3,033	$ 3,362
Annual increase		139	329

Source: Federal Reserve Board, *Banking and Monetary Statistics,* Table 3, p. 19. (a) *Ibid.,* Table 110, pp. 409–410.

Between June 30, 1914 and June 30, 1916, nongovernment loans and investments increased by 27.5 per cent, while net deposits increased by 26.7 per cent over the same period, a slightly smaller increase in deposits than in loans (see Table 5). Currency in circulation also increased because of the increased business activity, increasing 6 per cent for the two-year period, and 18 per cent between June 23, 1915 and June 30, 1916.

Bank clearings in 1916 were $224,338,270,000 compared with $152,891,985,000 in 1915,[22] an increase of more than 46 per cent in the one-year period.

Prices rose rapidly during this period as increased foreign demand was reflected in the domestic market. The retail food price index starting from 106 in July 1915, remained fairly stable during the remainder of that year, but rose in 1916, and by September 1916 had reached 120.[23] The wholesale price index, starting from 100 in August 1915, rose to 108 by the end of the year, and to 145 by December 1916. It continued to rise rapidly thereafter.[24]

Federal Finance

During 1916, Federal ordinary receipts amounted to $779.7 million compared with $697.9 million in 1915, despite a drop in customs duties. This was an increase of $81.8 million. Ordinary disbursements amounted to $724.5 million in 1916 compared with $731.5 million in 1915, a decrease of $6.9 million. Total ordinary gain in 1916 over 1915 was therefore $88.7 million.[25]

Tables 13 and 14 show the final results of the financial operations of the government for fiscal 1916. Nondebt receipts exceeded nondebt expenditures by some $40.5 million. Net borrowing amounted to $33.8 million for a total of $74.3 million received by the Treasury and not disbursed. While this included bank borrowing as well as nonbank borrowing, the situation remained virtually unchanged even when bank borrowing was considered, for although the Federal Reserve member banks

Table 13
Treasury Cash Receipts and Expenditures, 1916

Total nondebt receipts	$782,534,547
Total nondebt disbursements	741,996,727
Excess of nondebt receipts	40,537,820
Net increase in debt	33,783,489
Total cash received and not paid out	$ 74,321,309

Source: U.S. Treasury Department, *Annual Report, 1916*, pp. 32–34.

Table 14
Treasury Impact on Nonbank Public, 1916

Total net cash received[a]	$74,321,309
Less increase in Federal Reserve–held government[b]	49,528,000
Plus decrease in commercial bank–held governments[c]	50,000,000
Decrease in nonbank funds	$74,793,309

Source: (a) Table 13. (b) Federal Reserve Board, *Annual Report, 1915*, pp. 45–46; *ibid., 1916*, pp. 56–57. (c) *Ibid., Banking and Monetary Statistics*, p. 19.

increased their holdings of governments by $49.5 million, the commercial banks reduced their holdings by $50 million, and the net decrease in total bank held debt was less than $500,000.

During this prewar prosperity year the Treasury impact on the money supply was deflationary rather than inflationary. Pressures on prices during this year must therefore have come from other sources.

A reexamination of Table 12 will show that commercial bank expansion of loans and nongovernment investments during

Table 15
Increase in Money Supply, 1915–1916
(millions of dollars)

Commercial bank deposits	$3,384.
Currency in circulation	329.
Total nongovernment	$3,713.
Treasury impact	(75.)
Total increase in money supply	$3,638.

Source: Tables 12 and 14.

fiscal 1916 amounted to $3,188 million, more than making up for the $50 million decrease in government debt holdings, while net bank deposits increased by $3,384 million. Currency in circulation increased by $329 million.

The increase in the money supply which formed the base for the pressure on prices came from the private economy which was expanding rapidly to meet the needs of the European nations at war. The impact of government finance, while deflationary, was too small compared with private finance to have much effect on the inflationary trend.

In addition to the increase in the money supply, a larger part of American production was being channeled into the export market. In 1915 net exports of merchandise amounted to $1,796 million and increased to $3,130 million in 1916.[26] This represented goods taken out of domestic production and not available for domestic consumption. Inasmuch as the payments for the goods had entered into domestic purchasing power, the increase in net exports tended also to raise prices.

Looking at the total situation during fiscal 1916, the one outstanding conclusion is that the Federal government had no part in the economic expansion, but on the contrary was a deflationary influence. The expansion in production and the increase in the money supply were both due to the eagerness of the private economy to provide the Allies with the materials of war, and the willingness and ability of the commercial banks to provide the necessary credit.

NOTES

[1] U.S. Department of Commerce, Bureau of Foreign and Domestic Commerce, *Annual Report, 1916*, p. 13.

[2] *Ibid.*

[3] U.S. Treasury Department, *Annual Report, 1916*, p. 6.

[4] Federal Reserve Board, *Index of Industrial Production.*

[5] U.S. Treasury Department, *Annual Report, 1915*, p. 3.

[6] *The Iron Age.*

[7] *Ibid.*

[8] *Ibid.,* November 11, 1915, p. 1152.

[9] *Ibid.*

[10] American Iron and Steel Institute, *Monthly Production of Steel Ingots in the United States.*

[11] *The Iron Age,* November 23, 1916, p. 1181.

[12] Bureau of Labor Statistics, *Monthly Labor Review.*

[13] Federal Reserve Board, *Banking and Monetary Statistics,* Table 135, p. 485.

[14] *Ibid.,* Table 132, p. 478.

[15] Federal Reserve Board, *Banking and Monetary Statistics*, Table 110, p. 409.

[16] *Federal Reserve Bulletin,* May 1, 1915, p. 50.

[17] *Ibid.,* pp. 55–59.

[18] Treasury Department, *Annual Report, 1916*, p. 1 (Italics added).

[19] Federal Reserve Board, *Banking and Monetary Statistics,* Table 2, p. 18.

[20] The large import from Canada which produced only $19 million in 1916 can best be explained by the greater safety in shipping direct to Canada instead of to Great Britain.

[21] Federal Reserve Board, *Annual Report, 1915*, p. 45–46; *ibid., 1916*, p. 56.

[22] U.S. Treasury Department, *Annual Report, 1916*, p. 6.

[23] G. F. Warren and F. A. Pearson, *Prices*, p. 187.

[24] *Ibid.,* p. 13.

[25] U.S. Treasury Department, *Annual Report, 1916*, pp. 32–34.

[26] National Industrial Conference Board, *The International Financial Position of the United States*, p. 39.

4

The Eve of War Finance

In order to understand the economic and financial policies and practices pursued during the actual war period, it is important that an examination be made of the situation at the beginning of the period, for this is the background from which the war policies emerged. There are four factors which are of major significance in determining the character and effect of a war-finance period. These are (1) the extent of resource utilization at the start of the period; (2) bank excess reserves and interest rates; (3) the structure of the national debt, and (4) the tax situation.

Resource Utilization

The ability of a nation to expand its real output depends upon the amount of idle capacity which can be put to work, and the improvement in productivity which can be achieved. In April 1917 idle resources in the United States were at a minimum. A

45

great change had taken place in resource utilization and production between August 1914 and March 1917, the last peacetime month. The Federal Reserve Board Index of Industrial Production rose from 48 in August 1914 to 76 in March 1917 (1935–1939 = 100), an increase of almost 60 per cent. This increase left a lower expansion potential in the physical production of goods and put the Federal government in the position of competing with both the private economy and the Allies for scarce existing resources. Any increase in production for war purposes would have had to be taken from the other sectors unless productivity could be increased at a rate high enough to provide for all. Such an increase in productivity was extremely unlikely, first of all because the time period was too short, and secondly because the shift to war production tended to decrease productivity. Under the circumstances, a decline in total production was likely to take place. This was demonstrated during the period of belligerency. Measured in constant prices, from the first quarter of 1917 to the last quarter of 1918 war production increased by $11.2 billion, but nonwar production decreased by $13.0 billion, resulting in a $1.8-billion decline in the gross national product.[1]

This situation was further reflected in the Federal Reserve Board Index of Industrial Production, which reached a wartime peak of 81 (1935–1939 = 100) in May 1917 and declined thereafter. At the same time wholesale prices advanced continuously throughout the entire war period and well into 1920.[2] This inelasticity of available resources with the consequent rise in prices contributed in no small degree to the cost of the war.

Bank Reserves and Interest Rates

A second factor influencing the character of war finance is the ability of the banking system to extend the necessary credit to the private and public economy in the form of loans and investments. The Treasury, when it borrows, becomes a competitor for loanable funds, and the ease of obtaining the funds will depend to a large degree on the credit expansion potential of the banking system. This credit-expansion potential is limited by the amount of credit expansion which has taken place during the preceding period, and by the amount of reserves which the banking system is required to maintain. The amount of reserves also affects the structure of interest rates with low rates predominating during periods of large excess reserves and high rates predominating during periods of low excess reserves. When there are no available reserves a "tight" money market exists and short-term interest rates rise rapidly while bond prices fall as liquidation takes place.

The American banking system entered World War I with greatly expanded reserves. Under the Federal Reserve Act, member banks were required to keep a 12 per cent reserve against demand deposits if they were country banks, 15 per cent if they were city banks, and 18 per cent if they were central reserve city banks. This was a large reduction from the reserve requirements under the National Banking Act,[3] which required 15 per cent from the country banks, 25 per cent from the city banks, and 25 per cent from the reserve city banks. Consequently, the adoption of the Federal Reserve Act greatly increased the excess reserves of the commercial banks.

At the start of the operation of the Federal Reserve Act the opportunity for monetary expansion was further enhanced by the regulation covering the reserve requirements of member banks. Until June 1917 all member bank reserves did not have to be deposited with the Federal Reserve District banks. Central reserve city banks were required to transfer directly only $\frac{7}{18}$ of their required reserves to the District Reserve bank, and could carry $\frac{6}{18}$ in their own vaults; the other $\frac{5}{18}$ might be carried either in their own vaults or in the Federal Reserve District bank. For city banks the comparable requirements were $\frac{6}{15}$, $\frac{5}{15}$, and $\frac{4}{15}$, but the $\frac{6}{15}$ might be transferred by semiannual payments extending over three years. The country banks were, over three years, to transfer $\frac{5}{12}$ to the Federal Reserve District bank, $\frac{4}{12}$ could remain in their own vaults, with the remaining $\frac{3}{12}$ being optional.[4] These requirements would by November 16, 1917 have had all the reserves either in the banks' own vaults or in the Federal Reserve banks. Until that time reserve balances could still be carried with correspondent banks in reserve cities. Thus the practice of carrying fictitious reserves was not completely done away with during this period.

After November 1914 bank reserves were increased by net imports of gold. Merchandise export balances increased monthly, and as part payment gold came into the United States. The Federal Reserve Board estimated that from the beginning of the war until the end of December 1916, approximately $870 million in gold had moved into the United States.[5]

Bank expansion was also encouraged by the Federal Reserve rediscount rate which had been lowered almost immediately after the start of operations on November 16, 1914. Commercial paper rates were lowered by $\frac{1}{2}$ to 1 per cent by December 31, 1914,[6] despite the fact that the Board defined as a matter of fundamental importance the "adoption of a discount policy which would prevent dissipation of resources by banks."[7] If by this was meant an overexpansion of credit their actions somewhat belied their words. From the original $5\frac{1}{2}$–$6\frac{1}{2}$ per cent fixed as the starting rates, by January 1, 1915 five Reserve District banks including all the larger ones had reduced their rates to $4\frac{1}{2}$ per cent, and the others to 5 per cent. By January 1, 1916 all Reserve banks except San Francisco had a 4 per cent discount rate on 30- and 60-day paper.[8] During 1916 several Reserve banks increased their rates by $\frac{1}{2}$ per cent because of what the Board called "a strain on the credit mechanism caused by the expanding industrial economy and the ease of rediscounting,"[9] but nevertheless rediscount rates were still 1 to 2 per cent lower than in 1914. Meanwhile, the District banks were also increasing bank reserves by engaging in open-market operations which were far greater in amount than rediscounts of member banks.

The Boston District bank reported desultory operations for the first six months of 1916, with a much more pronounced demand for rediscounts for the latter half.[10] An examination of its profits and loss account shows that $42,303 was earned on rediscounts from member banks while $315,435 was earned from discounts on open-market purchases.[11]

The New York District bank in 1916 reported $22.3 million of member bank rediscounts as against $123.4 million of acceptances bought in the open market.[12]

The Philadelphia Reserve Bank announced that, "By far the largest part of the Federal Reserve Bank's earning assets consists of bankers' acceptances bought in the open market." Cleveland reported that "The increase in revenue... did not come through rediscounting for member banks, but from the reserve bank's open-market transactions." Richmond announced a decrease of $1,000,000 of member bank discounts during the year. Other District banks repeated the same general sentiments.[13] During 1916, total bills on hand at the Reserve banks increased from $53.2 million to $157.7 million,[14] but of this $104.5 million increase only $3.3 million was an increase in discounts for member banks, while $101.2 million represented an increase in bills bought in the open market.[15] Governor W. P. G. Harding noted this light demand for rediscounts in the same report [16] Two years later he was to state that "the only period when the Federal Reserve Board was able to exercise any effective control over the banking situation was during the last two or three months of 1916 and the first quarter of 1917."[17] During this so-called control period member bank rediscounts increased from $20.5 million on November 24, 1916 to $30.2 million on December 29, 1916, and bills bought in the open market increased during the same period from $102.1 million to $127.5

million. In the first two months of 1917 the Federal Reserve Board also took precautions against a shortage of Federal Reserve notes by placing orders with the Bureau of Engraving and Printing through the Comptroller of the Currency for more than $900 million of Federal Reserve notes, and by arranging that new orders be placed as these were withdrawn.[18]

The "ease of rediscounting" as a cause of the strain on the credit mechanism was therefore not substantiated by the facts. The expansion of Federal Reserve credit had taken place primarily through open-market purchases rather than by rediscounting operations of member banks. This policy was pursued for the purpose of enabling the Reserve banks to attain earnings with which to pay the expenses of operation, to pay dividends to member banks, to finance internal development, and to maintain prestige in the eyes of the public.[19]

The steady stream of gold imports, part of which were deposited in the Federal Reserve banks, combined with the installment payments of member bank reserves into the District banks served to cushion any sharp drop in the reserve ratio of the Reserve banks.[20] Although the reserve ratio of the Reserve banks had been decreasing steadily during 1915 and 1916, at the end of 1916 it was still 81.1 per cent and by April 5, 1917 it had increased to 89.0 per cent.[21] Thus despite the expansion which had taken place, a "tight" situation did not exist. This was equally true with regard to the member banks. On November 17, 1916 member bank reserves amounted to $2,536 million of which only $1,510 million was required.[22] At the existing ratio of reserves to deposits, which were $12,893 million on November 17, 1916, the excess reserves of $1,026 million could support an expansion of $8,760 million in member bank deposits. In addition, member banks, by rediscounting with the District banks, could generate an even larger amount of excess reserves.[23]

In contrast to the production potential of the economy on the eve of American participation in the war, the credit expansion potential had far greater elasticity. Both the Reserve banks and the member banks had large amounts of excess reserves and by Federal Reserve policy reserves could be expanded still further by rediscounting by member banks and open-market operations by the Reserve banks.

The effect of this large volume of reserves was to maintain for the most part a low structure of interest rates. Following the money panic in 1914, interest rates fell, and by the end of the year they were only slightly higher than they had been in June. Throughout 1915 and 1916 they changed very little, and on March 30, 1917 interest rates, while somewhat higher than in the previous two years, were not nearly so high as the panic rates of August 1914.

Table 16
Average Rates for Money in New York, Selected Dates

Date	Stock Exchange Call Loans (per cent)	60-Day Paper (per cent)	Prime 4–6- Month Paper (per cent)
June 5, 1914	$1\frac{3}{4}$	2	$3\frac{7}{8}$
August 7, 1914	7	8	$5\frac{3}{4}$
December 31, 1914	3	$3\frac{5}{8}$	$4\frac{1}{8}$
February 5, 1915	2	$2\frac{5}{8}$	$3\frac{3}{4}$
August 6, 1915	$1\frac{3}{4}$	$2\frac{5}{8}$	$3\frac{5}{8}$
January 7, 1916	2	$2\frac{5}{8}$	$3\frac{1}{8}$
March 17, 1916	$1\frac{7}{8}$	$2\frac{3}{4}$	$3\frac{1}{8}$
May 26, 1916	$2\frac{1}{8}$	$2\frac{3}{4}$	$3\frac{1}{8}$
August 4, 1916	$2\frac{3}{8}$	$2\frac{7}{8}$	$3\frac{7}{8}$
October 27, 1916	$2\frac{3}{8}$	3	$3\frac{3}{8}$
December 29, 1916	3	$4\frac{1}{4}$	4
March 30, 1916	$2\frac{1}{4}$	$3\frac{1}{2}$	$4\frac{1}{8}$

Source: Commercial and Financial Chronicle, Monthly Reviews.

The National Debt

From June 30, 1914 to June 30, 1916 the net interest-bearing debt increased by a little less than $4 million, and on June 30, 1916 stood at $971,562,590. During this period the per capita gross debt increased by only 3 cents, from $11.99 to $12.02. In 1861, on the eve of the Civil War, the net interest-bearing debt was $90,423,292 and the per capita gross debt was only $2.80.[24] The total debt remained the same in December 1916 with an increase of $10 million of Treasury notes and a corresponding decrease of Treasury bonds.[25] The annual interest charge of $23 million was equal to a rate of 2.376 per cent and amounted to 29 cents per capita.[26] The $23 million interest charge represented about .05 per cent of the gross national product of $43.6 billion,[27] and the gross debt was about 3 per cent of the gross national product.

Gross per capita debt had been as high as $75.42 in 1866,[28] decreasing steadily until it reached a low of $11.85 in 1915. The current debt could therefore expand more than sixfold before reaching the per capita debt burden of the Civil War. The gross national debt during the Civil War reached an estimated 40 per cent of the gross national product in 1866.[29] There was evidently room for expansion of the debt in 1916 compared to the debt expansion during the Civil War. The amount of expansion which could occur might be $5.4 billion based on the per capita figure, or $16.4 billion based on the percentage of gross debt to the gross national product. If the gross national product increased, the debt could also be increased accordingly.

Within this possible debt expansion lies the danger of inflationary borrowing with the same rise in prices which resulted from the Civil War borrowing. While the total expansion potential in the debt was great, the danger of inflation was ever-present unless the borrowing could be accomplished with a minimum of bank borrowing.

Government Bond Market

The prices of government bonds on the New York Stock Exchange moved narrowly through 1915 and 1916, and in April 1917 were priced to yield from about $2\frac{1}{2}$ per cent to 3 per cent.[30] The 2 per cent bonds were selling at near par, but these carried the circulation privilege. Prices during April 1917 for the government issues were stable and showed no signs of panic selling.[31]

In contrast to the government issues, basic yields of corporate bonds were 4.05 per cent in 1917 for all maturities.[32] Yields of high grade railroad bonds fell during the latter half of 1916 but rose in 1917 and in April 1917 were 4.12 per cent.[33]

The credit position of the Federal government in April 1917 based on prices and yields of government bonds was excellent, but there were some signs of weakening during the early part of 1917. Whereas the Treasury 3's of 1961 sold at $102\frac{3}{4}$, and the Treasury 4's of 1925 sold at 110 in January 1917, they were down to 99 and 107 in April.[34] Sales of future issues would have to be

Table 17
Prices of Government Bonds, April 1917

	Low	High
Consol 2's—1930	$99\frac{3}{4}$	$99\frac{3}{4}$
3's 1908–18	$100\frac{1}{2}$	$101\frac{7}{8}$
3's 1961	99	99
4's 1925	107	109

Source: Commercial and Financial Chronicle, May 1917.

made at slightly higher than current yields, therefore, in order to ensure quick placement.

Taxation

The ability of the Treasury Department to finance a war through taxation depends upon the amount of the national product already being taxed. Beyond a certain point, the tax rate may act as a deterrent to incentives and hinder the productive efforts of the nation. Where this point may be is difficult to determine. The tax potential during the war will be limited by this theoretical top rate, and by the rate in force at the start of the period. Between these points lies the war tax potential.

In 1916 Federal tax revenue consisted chiefly of excise taxes and customs duties which together brought in 74.8 per cent of the total revenue. Income and profits taxes had not yet reached the heights they were to attain later in the war, accounting for only $125 million or 16 per cent of total revenue. Other revenue including Panama Canal tolls and public land sales accounted for the remainder.[35] Ordinary receipts of $780 million represented less than 2 per cent of the $43.6 billion gross national product in 1916.[36] It would seem that there was a relatively large tax potential no matter what point was determined to be the top limit. A 10 per cent limit would make possible almost a fivefold increase in raxes; at a 25 per cent limit, a tenford increase would be possible.

Summary

The situation which faced the Treasury on the eve of war finance can be summarized by the following statements.

1. The resources of the nation were being almost fully utilized. There was little unemployment and prices had ad-

vanced, slowly until 1916 as unemployed resources came into production, but much more rapidly thereafter. Both retail and wholesale prices advanced about 50 per cent from August 1914 to April 1917.[37]

2. Although a large expansion of bank credit had taken place since August 1914, there remained in the banking system sufficient reserves for a great deal of further credit expansion.

3. The Federal debt per capita was almost at its lowest point since 1861. Government bond quotations were steady and priced to yield 3 per cent or less but were selling at lower prices than at the start of 1917.

4. Taxes were a small part of the gross national product and the opportunity for large tax increases was favorable from an economic point of view.

NOTES

[1] Simon Kuznets, *National Product in Wartime*, Table III-4, p. 105.
[2] G. F. Warren and F. A. Pearson, *Prices*, p. 13.
[3] Fictitious reserves existed under the National Banking Act by the use of the same reserves by two or more banks under the redeposit system.
[4] Ray B. Westerfield, *Banking Principles and Practices*, pp. 400–401.
[5] Federal Reserve Board, *Annual Report, 1916*, pp. 1–3.
[6] *Ibid., 1914*, pp. 203–205.
[7] *Ibid.*, p. 7.
[8] *Ibid., 1916*, pp. 36–37.
[9] *Ibid.*, pp. 5–6.
[10] *Ibid., 1916*, p. 197.
[11] *Ibid., 1914*, pp. 203–205.
[12] *Ibid., 1916*, pp. 226, 228.
[13] *Ibid.*, pp. 263, 277, 296.
[14] *Ibid.*, pp. 56–57.
[15] *Ibid.*
[16] *Ibid.*, pp. 2–4.
[17] *Federal Reserve Bulletin*, January 1919, p. 2.
[18] Federal Reserve Board, *Annual Report, 1917*, p. 2.
[19] Harold L. Reed, *The Development of Federal Reserve Policy*, p. 247.

[20] Federal Reserve Board, *Annual Report, 1916*, pp. 1, 22–23.

[21] *Ibid., 1917*, p. 2.

[22] *Ibid., 1916*, p. 23.

[23] Federal Reserve Board, *Banking and Monetary Statistics*, p. 72. $1,510 ÷ $12,893 = 11.7 per cent.

[24] U.S. Treasury Department, *Annual Report, 1949*, p. 397.

[25] Federal Reserve Board, *Banking and Monetary Statistics*, p. 509.

[26] U.S. Treasury Department, *Annual Report, 1949*, p. 480.

[27] Kuznets, *National Product in Wartime*, p. 139.

[28] U.S. Treasury Department, *Annual Report, 1949*, p. 397.

[29] Henry C. Murphy, *National Debt in War and Transition*, p. 16.

[30] *Commercial and Financial Chronicle*, Monthly Review.

[31] *Ibid.*, May 1917.

[32] David Durand, *Basic Yield of Corporate Bonds, 1900–1942*, pp. 5–6.

[33] Frederick R. Macauley, *The Movements of Interest Rates, Bond Yields, and Stock Prices in the United States Since 1865*, pp. A 141–161.

[34] *Commercial and Financial Chronicle*, February 1917.

[35] Tables 20 and 24, U.S. Treasury Department, *Annual Report, 1916*, pp. 32–34.

[36] *Ibid.*; Kuznets, *National Product in Wartime*, p. 139.

[37] Warren and Pearson, *Prices*, pp. 13, 187.

5

Taxation and War Finance*

In Chapter 1 the relative merits of taxation and borrowing were discussed from a theoretical point of view. Before proceeding with a discussion of the actual World War I revenue measures, it is desirable to go somewhat more deeply into the theoretical aspects of taxation as a method of war finance.

While the purposes of taxation may be many and varied in peacetime, during a war period the major purpose to be achieved by taxation, aside from that of paying the actual war cost, should be the diversion of purchasing power from potential consumers to the government. This would not only reduce the war costs and the tax revenue needed by the government, but would at the same time temper the rise in the general price level and make more money available for tax payments. On the other hand, it would not take into account the effect of high tax rates on the production incentives of taxpayers in their activities as pro-ducers. Thus not only the size of the tax revenues, but their distribution and effects as well, are important elements in a wartime tax policy.

If all of these factors are taken into consideration, the planning of a wartime tax program becomes a formidable task requiring knowledge, judgment, and discrimination. Each type of tax produces both desirable and undesirable results. The use of taxes as a method of war finance involves juggling a complex mixture of ingredients, each of which must be used in its proper proportion if the desired results are to be achieved. This chapter discusses the theoretical aspects involved in the use of five of the major types of taxes, and their specific effects during a war economy.

The five types of Federal taxes which will be studied are individual income taxes, corporation income and profits taxes, excises, estate taxes, and customs duties. Each of these will be classified as to its shiftability and incidence, its relative progressive or regressive tendencies, and its desirability as a wartime tax measure. Shiftability and incidence in taxation may be defined as the ability of the initial taxpayer to shift the tax either forward (as in price increase) or backward (as in lower wage rates), and the final resting place of the tax burden. Progression and regression in taxation refer to the income group which bears the burden of the tax payment, the progressive tax being one that bears more heavily percentagewise on upper-income groups.

Excise Taxes

Excise taxes are taxes imposed on the manufacture or sale of commodities. To the seller they appear as added costs of production and are customarily included in the base for the resale markup. Since this raises the price of the commodity to the buyer it acts as a deterrent to consumption. Whether the price increase will be lower than, equal to, or greater than the tax will depend on the ability of the seller to increase the price to the consumer. Since the seller desires to sell as large a quantity as he can at as high a price as possible the consumers' reaction to the price change will be an important factor influencing his decision. Where there is a relative shortage of goods it is quite probable that the entire tax will be shifted forward in the form of higher prices. Whether an excise tax is progressive or regressive will depend on the commodity taxed. A tax on a commodity customarily purchased only by the upper-income groups may be regarded as a progressive tax while a tax on such things as bread, whisky, beer, and cigarettes would be a regressive tax. An excise tax levied on those commodities purchased by upper-income groups, however, would do little to divert purchasing power, since the upper-income groups would not be as likely to restrict their consumption as would the lower-income groups. It would, on the other hand, provide the Treasury with revenue to meet its expenditures.

The excise tax can accomplish either of two things. It can divert resources to the government by restricting consumption, or it can raise revenue for the government but sacrifice all or part of the resource diversion. If the tax deters consumption there will be no revenue, yet if consumption is not deterred revenue will be received but the resources will be used for non-war rather than for war purposes.

The excise tax in a war period should therefore be imposed heavily (to attain resource diversion) on those commodities needed in the war effort, and not too heavily (for revenue) on the resources not needed in the war effort. If this is done both purposes can be achieved. In wartime general excises are desirable because of their ability to achieve diversion of both revenue and resources to the government without penalizing production as might a direct tax on income.

Customs Duties

In general, the effects of the customs duty are quite similar to those of the excise tax. In addition, the customs duty, or tariff, may be imposed for the purpose of protecting American industry from foreign competition, in which respect it tends to raise prices not only on imports, but on the domestic product as well. During a war period, however, customs duties tend to fall as the amount of imports drops off, so that it becomes less important as a revenue producer for the government.

Estate Taxes

Estate taxes are taxes imposed upon the estates of deceased persons. These taxes cannot be shifted and the incidence falls upon the heirs of the deceased. Their chief effect is a redistribution of wealth as large estates are made smaller by taxation. During any particular period the amount of revenue from an estate tax cannot be depended upon since it is contingent upon unpredictable occurrences. It is therefore not too reliable a tax medium through which to achieve the objectives of war taxation as the amount of revenue is unpredictable and diversion of purchasing power is not attained.

Personal Income Taxes

During a war period the personal income tax is an ideal medium for raising revenue. With heavy government expenditures, the money income stream is expanded with all income groups sharing in the expansion, although not in the same proportion. This tax is the most difficult to shift and the incidence falls wholly on the initial taxpayer.[1] In addition to raising revenue, the personal income tax determines the disposable personal income, bringing into play consumer decisions regarding consumption and saving, and possibly affecting the production incentives as mentioned earlier. Whether the income tax will depress the rate of consumption or savings and the degree to which each will be depressed will depend to a large extent on the consumption and savings patterns of the groups affected by the tax. As the bulk of savings ordinarily comes from high-level incomes, a tax imposed on this group will depress savings rather than consumption.

In order to achieve a diversion of purchasing power by means of the personal income tax, it should be imposed on those who would actively compete with the public economy for the limited resources—the low- and middle-income groups. While a steeply progressive personal income tax might seem desirable from the point of view of welfare and equitability, it will not produce as great a diversion of purchasing power as would a tax on low-income groups which have a relatively higher consumption propensity. Although the tax would tend to lower the amount of disposable personal income and savings, it is the distribution of the tax burden which will accomplish the necessary diversion of purchasing power from consumers to the government.

A direct tax on low-income groups, while achieving the desired diversion of purchasing power, is not the most expedient one from the psychological and political points of view. The legislators theoretically attempt to transform the "willingness to be taxed" of their constituencies into legislation. This "willingness to be taxed," or psychological limit of taxation, may be estimated erroneously by Congress, with the resulting tax rates either too low or too high. If the rates are too low the government leaves some purchasing power undiverted. If the rates are too high there may be a sacrifice of production and possibly a smaller revenue from the tax than would have occurred with lower rates, for if production drops so will the incomes which form the tax base.

A steeply progressive income tax falling heavily on those persons with large incomes may act either as an incentive or a deterrent to investment. The high tax rate tends to lower both the net return from a successful investment and the net loss from an unsuccessful investment. A situation such as this may well lead to an increase in the incidence and size of risk taking. On the other hand, the more conservative investments showing greater promise of profit may understandably be postponed until a later period when the tax rates are lower. It cannot be said with any accuracy that the income tax will either promote or deter investment incentives.[2] To the extent that savings are lowered, the available funds for investment will be lowered, but since the investment decisions are not primarily dependent upon the rate of savings there need be no short-run equality between the two.

Corporation Profits Taxes

A corporation profits tax, like the personal income tax, lends itself to complexities in analysis. Traditional reasoning would liken the profits tax to the personal income tax in respect to shiftability, but this concept is open to question. In the testimony presented before the Colwyn Committee in Great Britain in the 1920s, it was repeatedly stated that the income tax was not borne by the firm or its owners, and in the United States many businessmen have argued that lower corporate income taxes would mean lower prices.[3] This leads to the presumption that part if not all of corporate income and profits taxes are passed along to the consumer. If this is true, then the profits tax can be partly compared in its effects to the excise tax, being shifted as far as is feasible to the buyer. It is doubtful that the total tax is shifted forward as some "stickiness" is present in all taxes, and the farther the tax is removed from the final consumer, the less likely he is to pay the tax in full.[4]

If we assume that the incidence of profits taxes is shared equally by the consumers and the corporations, then one-half of the tax would be similar to an excise, while the other half would be in effect a tax on either dividends or undistributed profits. The part that comes out of dividends might restrict the consumption of the stockholder, but more than likely it would reduce savings as the stockholder group is mostly an upper-income group. The part of the tax that reduces the share of the profits retained by the corporation would reduce the funds available for reinvestment in the business and might seriously retard plant expansion for war production.

The effect of profits taxes on investment incentives might have the same effect as has the personal income tax, since the profits tax also cushions the gain or loss resulting from corporate investment. With a high rate of taxes on corporate profits, a successful corporation could indulge in many activities which were not feasible under lower taxes, since the government will be paying a major share of the expenditure. Such things as heavy expenditures for good-will advertising,[5] large outlays for research and experimentation, and year-end bonuses for employees are typical examples. Although these expenditures may be highly productive in the light of future output, they tend to reduce tax revenues during the war period unless the marginal tax rate of those receiving the payment is equal to or greater than that of the paying corporation. In the ordinary flow of income distribution this would be doubtful.

As a method of attaining revenue during a war period, the profits tax can be used successfully. Corporations share in the wartime income expansion so that the tax base grows larger; the danger of waste expenditures exists only when the rates are very high, and corporation taxes fit well within the political limitation since corporations as such do not vote.

The foregoing discussion attempted to accomplish two things. The first was to present each type of taxation in the perspective of its use as a war revenue measure. The second was to point out the difficulties involved in formulating a war revenue program. The optimum tax program would entail not only the proper proportion of tax revenue to total government receipts, but also the proper distribution of the tax burden. In a war period the objective of income diversion must not be forgotten in a stream of welfare legislation. Nor is taxation to be thought of as an end in itself, but rather as one of the means by which the war expenditures may be successfully financed.

NOTES

*This topic has been discussed by many writers among whom are Lewis H. Kimmel, *Taxes and Economic Incentives*; John K. Butters and John Linter, *Effect of Federal Taxes on Growing Enterprises*; Alfred G. Buehler, ed., "Government Finance in a Stable and Growing Economy," *Annals of the American Academy of Political and Social Science*, November 1949; Arthur C. Pigou, *The Political Economy of War*, Chap. 7; E. R. A. Seligman, *Essays in Taxation*; C. Shoup, M. Friedman, and R. P. Mack, *Taxing to Prevent Inflation*; Harry G. Brown, *The Economics of Taxation*; Harold M. Groves, *Trouble Spots in Taxation*; Sir Josiah C. Stamp, *Fundamental Principles of Taxation*; Council of Economic Advisers, *The Economics of National Defense*, Chapter 8; Seymour Harris, *The Economics of America at War*, chaps. 6–10; and Alfred G. Buehler, ed., "Billions for Defense," *The Annals of the American Academy of Political and Social Science*, March 1941.

[1] If the taxpayer reduces his consumption, the incidence may be thought of as being shifted backward to business and the factors employed.
[2] Lewis H. Kimmel, *Taxes and Economic Incentives*, pp. 32, 40, 108–124; John K. Butters and John Linter, *Effect of Federal Taxes on Growing Enterprise*; Charles C. Abbot, *Business Finance During the Critical Transition from War to Peace*.
[3] E. Gordon Keith, "Repercussions of the Tax System on Business," in Kenyon E. Poole, ed., *Fiscal Policies and the American Economy*, pp. 337–339.
[4] Mabel Newcomer, "Taxation and the Consumer," *The Annals of the American Academy of Political and Social Science*, November 1949, pp. 55–62.
[5] Frank E. Seidman, "Influence of Excess Profits Taxation on Business Policy," in *Financing the War*, a symposium conducted by the Tax Institute, pp. 56–57.

6

War Expenditures and Revenues

During a war period, as during other periods of national emergency, government expenditures increase out of all proportion to their former peacetime level. In the War of 1812 expenditures went from $8 million in 1811 to a peak of $34.7 million in 1814, an increase of 334 per cent. In the Civil War, peak expenditures were $1,297.6 million in 1865, compared with a prewar figure of $66.5 million in 1861, an increase of 1,847 per cent. In World War I expenditures increased from $742.0 million in 1916 to $18,952.1 million in 1919, an increase of 2,454 per cent. During World War II expenditures increased from $9.0 billion in 1940 to $98.7 billion in 1945, an increase of 997 per cent.[1]

War Expenditures

While it is true that all expenditures have a similar effect on the economy, to measure or evaluate the effect of the war expenditures it is necessary to separate from the total volume of expenditures—those undertaken because of the war situation. This requires a dual determination involving the time period to be considered as the war period, and the expenditures to be considered as war expenditures. In order to encompass all war expenditures in the measurement, recognition must be given to the fact that war expenditures neither start nor end with the periods of actual belligerency. There is a period during which defense expenditures are made with the recognition that war is somewhat more than a mere possibility. With World War I, this period started in July 1916 when defense expenditures were made not only because Europe was at war, but also because of the possibility—perhaps the expectation—that the United States would enter the war. As such, these expenditures properly belong in the category of war expenditures.

While the actual conflict was terminated in November 1918, expenditures made because of the war continued well beyond that date. There were the immediate expenditures for troop transportation and supplies under contract. Other expenditures such as interest on the war debt and pensions continued far into the future. Since any exact study would have to await the termination of these expenditures, some value judgment will necessarily be inherent in the selection of the terminal date. While expenditures for war purposes decreased rapidly after December 1918 and may reasonably be thought of as terminating by the end of fiscal 1919, expenditures for the War and Navy departments continued well above the prewar level during fiscal 1920, as did expenditures for the independent bureaus set up during the war, such as the War Finance Corporation, the War Industries Board, the Shipping Board, the Food and Fuel Administration. The exclusion of fiscal 1920 from the computation would also exclude some receipts from the Victory loan, and taxes collected in 1920 under the Revenue Act of 1918. The period from July 1916 to June 1920 would include practically all expenditures pertaining to preparedness, war, and postwar reconstruction with the exception of interest and pension payments made after June 1920.

Types of War Expenditures

The determination of war expenditures as differentiated from peacetime expenditures is a complicated procedure, not easily resolved in any exact manner. Essentially, the volume of war expenditures is influenced by three factors: (a) new types of expenditures caused by the war, (b) the expansion of peacetime types of expenditures because of the war, and (c) the additional expenditures caused by price increases because of wartime inflation. Inflation requires a greater money expenditure for all purchases and therefore increases the money cost of the war with no corresponding increase in the real cost.

Total expenditures for the years 1917 to 1920 amounted to $40,971.8 million. We are concerned, however, not with total expenditures, but with war expenditures. Therefore, an assumption must be made regarding the volume of expenditures which would have existed if the United States had not prepared for and entered the war. The volume of expenditures during the war period consists of expenditures for the peacetime functions, expansion of peacetime functions, new war functions, and the increased expenses due to rising prices. The problem is to abstract from this total a sum assumed to be the normal nonwar expenditure.

During the war period large expenditures were made both for the expansion of normal government functions and for new functions undertaken because of the war. Expenditures for the army, navy, war bureaus, pensions, and debt service were expanded beyond those of any previous period. The expenditures for the purchase of foreign obligations was greater in 1918 than

Table 18
Federal Expenditures, 1916–1920
(millions of dollars)

Expenditure	1916	1917	1918	1919	1920
War	$134.3	$412.5	$5,672.9	$9,240.2	$1,053.6
Navy	155.9	258.2	1,370.4	2,019.1	632.7
Interior	24.8	29.2	35.3	29.1	28.2
Pensions	159.3	160.3	181.1	221.6	213.3
Legislative, executive, etc.	31.3	33.3	49.7	73.5	535.2
Commerce and labor	14.9	15.5	19.2	29.0	41.9
Treasury	73.7	84.9	181.8	289.9	260.5
Agriculture	28.0	29.6	46.8	36.9	66.6
Independent bureaus	7.2	22.7	1,135.8	2,723.5	1,706.5
Rivers and harbors	32.5	30.5	29.6	33.1	49.9
Panama Canal	17.5	19.3	20.8	12.3	6.0
Purchase of foreign obligations	—	885.0	4,739.4	3,477.9	421.3
Interest	22.9	24.7	197.5	615.9	1,024.0
Miscellaneous	39.7	80.2	111.3	150.4	102.0
Total	$742.0	$2,086.1	$13,791.9	$18,952.1	$6,141.7

Source: U.S. Treasury Department, *Annual Reports, 1916–1920.*

the entire budget for any previous year in history, and 6.4 times total expenditures in 1916.

Since the budget figures do not show a division between non-war and war expenditures, two possible methods may be used to abstract war expenditures from total expenditures. The first is to assume that nonwar expenditures during the war years were

Table 19
Expenditures for War Purposes, 1917–1920
(millions of dollars)

Year	Total	Nonwar	War
1917	$ 2,086.1	$ 742.0	$ 1,344.1
1918	13,791.9	742.0	13,049.9
1919	18,952.1	742.0	18,210.1
1920	6,141.7	742.0	5,399.7
Total	$40,971.8	$2,968.0	$38,003.8

Source: Table 18.

the same as those in the nearest prewar year, in this case 1916. The second method is to assume a trend of some sort for each year of nonwar expenditures based on the trend of expenditures in the past. Needless to say, neither method can be considered perfectly accurate. We have no more assurance that expenditures would have stayed the same had the United States remained neutral than we have that expenditures would have continued the trend had one been evident. While it is generally possible to determine a long-term trend, this trend cannot be objectively fitted to a period of four years with any degree of accuracy, and in fact could be more inaccurate than an assumption of the 1916 level of expenditures for each of the war years, which at least has the advantage of compensatory errors. The assumption will therefore be made that the nonwar expenditures during the war period were equal in volume to those of 1916. Using this method, a total of $2,968.0 million as assumed nonwar expenditures is subtracted from total expenditures of $40,971.8 million, with a resulting figure of $38,003.8 million as the money costs of the war.

War Revenues

War revenues, for the most part, reflect the changes in business activity because of the war, the changes in tax rates, and the imposition of new types of taxes. Increases in business activity with no change in tax rates will increase government tax revenues from business taxes. Increases in tax rates will obviously increase revenues if business activity remains the same. New taxes will similarly increase government revenues whether or not an increase occurs in business activity. A combination of new taxes, increased rates, and increased business activity will therefore have a multiple effect on government revenue.

During the war period government revenues increased from $782.5 million in 1916 to an average of $4,165.9 million a year over the 1917–1920 period, as a result of a combination of new taxes, higher rates, and increased incomes. The only type of tax revenue that did not show an appreciable increase was customs duties, due to a decrease in imports and no increase in the tariff rates. Excise taxes were both extended and increased, and income and profits taxes achieved a position of major importance in the tax structure, a position which was never to be relinquished.

To ascertain which part of total revenues can be termed "war revenues," an assumption must be made regarding the volume of nonwar revenues. The measurement of war revenues presents one problem not encountered in the measurement of war expenditures, for if the same period and the same projective technique is used for revenue as was used in the expenditure measurement the result would be a $40.5 million surplus in each of the war years for the nonwar part of the budget. It is quite probable that Congress, in the face of perennial pressures from constituents, would attempt and succeed in reducing tax revenues to the lower expenditure figure. This probability must

Table 20
Federal Nondebt Receipts, 1916–1920
(millions of dollars)

Source	1916	1917	1918	1919	1920
Customs	$213.2	$226.0	$ 182.8	$ 183.4	$ 323.5
Incomes and profits	124.9	359.7	2,839.0	2,600.8	3,956.9
Estates	—	6.1	47.5	82.0	103.6
Capital stock	—	—	25.0	28.8	93.0
Excise taxes:					
Spirits and liquors	241.3	278.3	443.8	483.1	139.9
Tobacco	85.3	102.2	156.2	206.0	295.8
Manufacturers	—	27.7	39.1	82.4	216.1
Dealers	--	—	1.0	6.1	109.2
Sales stamps, playing cards, etc.	38.1	8.3	17.5	33.6	84.3
Transportation	—	—	70.7	237.8	289.3
Oleomargarine	.9	1.2	2.4	2.9	3.8
Insurance	—	—	6.5	14.5	18.4
Admissions to entertainments, dues to occupations	6.9	5.2	31.3	59.7	91.8
Public land sales	1.9	1.9	2.0	1.4	1.9
Panama Canal tolls	2.9	6.2	6.4	6.8	9.0
Other revenue	67.1	101.5	329.2	625.1	969.9
Total	$782.5	$1,124.3	$4,180.4	$4,654.4	$6,704.4

Source: U.S. Treasury Department, *Annual Reports, 1916–1920.*

be taken into consideration in estimating war revenue. In view of this, nonwar revenue during each of the war years will be assumed to equal the 1916 expenditure figure.

War revenue amounted to $13,695.5 million under a balanced budget assumption and $13,533.5 million based on a projection of 1916 receipts, a total difference of $162 million over the four-year period.

Table 21
Federal War Revenue Based on 1916 Revenue
(millions of dollars)

Year	Total Revenue	Nonwar Revenue	War Revenue
1917	$ 1,124.3	$ 782.5	$ 341.8
1918	4,180.4	782.5	3,397.9
1919	4,654.4	782.5	3,871.9
1920	6,704.4	782.5	5,921.9
Total	$16,663.5	$3,130.0	$13,533.5

Source: Table 20.

Table 22
Federal War Revenue Based on a Balanced Budget for 1916
(millions of dollars)

Year	Total Revenue	Nonwar Revenue	War Revenue
1917	$ 1,124.3	$ 742.0	$ 382.3
1918	4,180.4	742.0	3,438.4
1919	4,654.4	742.0	3,912.4
1920	6,704.4	742.0	5,962.4
Total	$16,663.5	$2,968.0	$13,695.5

Source: Table 18 and 20.

Ratio of War Revenue to War Expenditures

The problem of the proper war revenue assumption loses a great deal of its significance upon close examination of the revenue and expenditure figures. The total difference of $162 million amounted to only a .4 per cent difference in the total ratio of war revenues to war expenditures, and a difference of

Table 23

Ratio of War Revenue to War Expenditures, 1917–1920

(millions of dollars)

Year	War Expenditures*	War Revenues+ (1916 Base)	Ratio of Revenue to Expenditures
1917	$ 1,344.1	$ 341.8	.254
1918	13,049.9	3,397.9	.260
1919	18,210.1	3,871.9	.212
1920	5,399.7	5,921.9	1.097
Total	$38,003.8	$13,533.5	.356

Year	War Expenditures*	War Revenue ‡ Balanced Budget	Ratio of Revenue to Expenditures
1917	$ 1,344.1	$ 382.3	.284
1918	13,049.9	3,438.4	.263
1919	18,210.1	3,912.4	.215
1920	5,399.7	5,962.4	1.104
Total	$38,003.8	$13,695.5	.360

Source: Tables 19, 21, and 22.

(*) War expenditures — total expenditures minus $742.0.
(+) War revenue – total revenue minus $782.5 million a year.
(‡) War revenue – total revenue minus $742 million a year.

.7 per cent or less in the three annual ratios from 1918 to 1920. Only in 1917 does the $40.5 million cause as much as a 3 per cent difference. As both revenues and expenditures increased the $40.5 million difference in assumed war revenue resulted in only a minor change in the annual ratios.

Using the balanced-budget assumption for war revenues,[2] there are two factors which indicate the lack of reliance on revenue as a means of financing the war. First, while war revenues financed 36 per cent of war expenditures, in three out of the four years the ratio was less than 29 per cent. It was only due to the budget surplus in 1920 that the 36 per cent ratio was achieved for the four-year period. The budget surplus in 1920 was for the most part the result of the extension of war revenue measures beyond the period of heavy war expenditures, and the quarterly payments in fiscal 1920 of taxes based on 1919 incomes.

Secondly, the ratios of war revenues to war expenditures declined annually from 1917 to 1919, portraying the reluctance of Congress to pass adequate tax legislation in view of expanding national income during the period. While the government was using resources in increasing amounts, until 1920 larger proportions of war expenditures were being financed by borrowing rather than by taxation.

NOTES

[1] U.S. Treasury Department, *Annual Report, 1949*, pp. 356–361, and Table 18 in the present volume.

[2] This appears to be a relatively more valid assumption, and does not change the results of the computation to any significant degree.

7

Defense Revenue and the War Revenue Act of 1917

During World War I the types of tax revenues and their relative importance to Federal revenues underwent a radical change. With the volume of expenditures far exceeding those of any past period, it was not surprising that the structure of the tax system would also change. Wartime tax legislation not only changed the relative importance of the type of taxation for the war period but set the pattern which has been in effect up to the present.

From the Civil War to the period immediately prior to World War I, about 90 per cent of government revenue came from excise taxes and customs duties. As late as 1916 these two types of taxes accounted for 74.8 per cent of total Federal revenue. World War I tax legislation made a drastic change in this distribution.

Revenue from the income and profits taxes, nonexistent from 1878 to 1909 (except in 1881, 1884, and 1895) and accounting for only 16 per cent of total revenue in 1916, became the most important source of Federal revenue during the war period and

Table 24
Percentage Distribution of Federal Revenue, 1916–1920

	1916	1917	1918	1919	1920	1917–1920
Excises	47.6	37.6	17.9	24.3	18.8	21.4
Incomes and profits	16.0	32.0	67.8	55.9	59.0	58.6
Customs	27.2	20.1	4.4	3.9	4.8	5.5
Estates	—	.5	1.1	1.7	1.5	1.4
Capital stock	—	—	.6	.6	1.4	.8
Land sales and Panama Canal tolls	.7	.8	.4	.2	.1	.2
Other revenues	8.5	9.0	7.8	14.4	14.4	12.1
Total	100.0	100.0	100.0	100.0	100.0	100.0

Source: Table 20.

has retained its importance since that time. This type of revenue accounted for 58.6 per cent of the total during the war period.

Customs duties, the most important revenue source in the pre-Civil War period, had been falling in importance since then. World War I saw the end of customs duties as an important source of Federal revenue. Accounting for 27.2 per cent of revenues in 1916, by 1919 customs duties accounted for only 3.9 per cent. For the war period only 5.5 per cent of Federal revenue was due to customs, and since then customs duties have ceased to be regarded as an important element in Federal revenue.

The third major change was in the importance of excise taxes. These taxes had grown in importance since the Civil War period, and by 1916 had become more important than customs duties as a source of Federal revenue. From the 47.6 per cent of total revenue due to excise taxes in 1916, the ratio of excises to total revenues fell to less than half of that figure for the war period.

While the excise taxes did not decline relatively as much as customs duties, they never again reached the 1916 ratio.

The combination of excises, customs, and incomes and profits taxes accounted for 85.5 per cent of total revenue during the war period. The remaining 14.5 per cent was received through taxes on estates and corporation capital stock, sales of public land, Panama Canal tolls and a group of miscellaneous revenue sources, none of which was relatively important in itself, but which in combination accounted for 12.1 per cent of total revenue for the war period.

Revenue Act of September 8, 1916

With the start of the defense period, larger government appropriations gave rise to a need for additional revenue. This problem was promptly taken up by the House Ways and Means Committee, which recommended tax increases because of the "necessity growing out of the extraordinary increase in the Appropriations for the Army and Navy, and the fortification of the country."[1] Chairman Kitchin estimated the excess of disbursements for fiscal 1917 at $266,922,000, as shown in Table 25.[2]

Earlier that year Secretary of the Treasury McAdoo had requested that the entire estimated deficit be raised by taxes with the possible exception of the Panama Canal expenditure, estimating that $112,806,394 additional would be required for fiscal 1917. He suggested increases in rates of taxation on individual and corporate incomes as a means of raising all or part of the additional revenues. "A nation," he said, "cannot go constantly into debt for current expenditures without eventually impairing credit."[3]

On September 8, 1916 the Emergency Revenue Act of 1914 was repealed and replaced by the Revenue Act of September 8, 1916. The new act amended the income provisions by doubling

Table 25

Chairman Kitchin's Estimate of Excess of Disbursements—1917

Estimated appropriations	$1,579,000,000
Deduct amount to be borrowed because of Mexican situation	125,000,000
Deduct sinking fund requirement	60,727,000
Deduct postal appropriation to be paid out of postal receipts	324,723,000
Total deductions	510,450,000
Balance	1,068,550,000
Deduct 5% of balance (usually expended)	53,428,000
Amount of needed revenue	$1,015,122,000
Estimated revenue under present law	748,200,000
Estimated excess of disbursements	$266,922,000

the normal tax and reclassifying the rates for additional taxes. It also levied an estate tax, a tax on munitions manufacturers, and a special excise tax on corporations for doing business measured by the fair value of the corporations' capital stock.[4]

Although there was an ordinary deficit of $29,724,865 in 1917, receipts exceeded McAdoo's estimate of $975,750,000 by some $142,424,126,[5] with large increases in both corporation and individual income taxes resulting from the increased business activity, and the resulting increased incomes.

Of the $338.5 million increase in ordinary revenue in 1917 over 1916, $234.7 million (almost 70 per cent) was due to the increase in income tax receipts. This trend toward progressivism in taxation was further reflected in the ratio of income taxes to total internal revenue, 44 per cent in 1917 compared with 24 per cent in 1916, and 19 per cent in 1915. This ratio was to get much larger during the actual war period.

The Revenue Act of September 8, 1916 emphasized progres-

Table 26
Ordinary Receipts, 1916–1917
(millions of dollars)

Source	1916	1917	Increase
Customs	$213.2	$ 226.0	$ 12.8
Internal revenue:			
Ordinary	303.5	354.4	50.9
Emergency	84.3	95.3	11.0
Corporation income	57.0	179.6	122.6
Individual income	68.0	180.1	112.1
Public lands	1.9	1.9	—
Miscellaneous	51.9	81.0	29.1
Total	$779.7	$1,118.2	$338.5

Source: U.S. Treasury Department, *Annual Report, 1916*, pp. 32–34; *ibid.,*
1917, pp. 56–58.

Note: Figures may not add to totals because of rounding.

sive taxation, not only in the total tax structure but also in the
individual income tax. Individual income tax receipts of $180.1
million in fiscal 1917 were made up of $12.3 million under the
Act of October 3, 1913 and $167.8 million under the Act of
September 8, 1916. Of the $12.3 million, $6.1 million or 49.7
per cent was paid by those whose incomes exceeded $20,000,
while of the $167.8 million collected under the 1916 Act, $160
million or 95.4 per cent was received from those with incomes
exceeding $20,000. The 1916 Act pushed the bulk of individual
income taxes onto the upper-income group, rather than onto
the middle-income group, with the low-income consumer evidently paying only a minute part of the income tax. The income
tax provisions of the 1916 Act therefore tended to transfer
savings rather than purchasing power to the government, and
contributed to rather than deterred the pressure of demand for
goods and services.

Table 27
1917 Revenue Under the Act of October 3, 1913 (Income Taxes)
(thousands of dollars)

Income Group	Surtax Rate (per cent)	Surtax	Normal Tax (1%)	Total
$ 20,000 and under	—	$ —	$6,204.9	$ 6,204.9
20,001–50,000	1	529.4	529.4	1,058.8
50,001–75,000	2	389.7	194.8	584.5
75,001–100,000	3	389.9	129.9	519.8
100,001–250,000	4	1,206.6	301.6	1,508.2
250,001–500,000	5	839.4	167.9	1,007.3
500,000 and up	6	1,034.8	172.5	1,207.3
Unassessed penalties	—	137.2	—	137.2
Offers in compromise	—	93.2	—	93.2
Total		$4,620.2	$7,701.0	$12,321.2

Source: U.S. Internal Revenue Office, *Annual Report, 1917,* pp. 228–235.

Revenue Act of March 3, 1917

Expenditures increased rapidly under the preparedness program. From a total of $344.7 million for the first six months of 1916 expenditures climbed to $506.7 million during the last six months.[6] This was an average monthly increase of $27 million in expenditures of which $24 million was in excess of receipts. During the early months of 1917 the political situation became increasingly intense and on February 1, 1917 the United States broke off diplomatic relations with Germany. Congress decided to create a special fund to be used only for naval and military preparations. This was done by the Act of March 3, 1917.[7] "An Act to provide increased revenue to defray the expenses of the increased appropriations for the army and navy and the extensions of fortifications and for other purposes." In this Act the

Table 28
1917 Revenue Under the Act of September 8, 1916 (Income Taxes)
(millions of dollars)

Income Group	Surtax Rate *(per cent)*	Surtax	Normal Tax *(2%)*	Total
$ 20,000 and under	—	$ —	$ 7.8	$ 7.8
20,001–40,000	1	7.0	14.0	21.0
40,001–60,000	2	6.5	6.5	13.0
60,001–80,000	3	6.1	4.0	10.1
80,001–100,000	4	5.7	2.8	8.5
100,001–150,000	5	11.1	4.4	15.5
150,001–200,000	6	8.2	2.7	10.9
200,001–250,000	7	6.2	1.7	7.9
250,001–300,000	8	5.2	1.3	6.5
300,001–500,000	9	13.0	2.9	15.9
500,001–1,000,000	10	14.5	2.9	17.4
1,000,001–1,500,000	11	7.5	1.4	8.9
1,500,001–2,000,000	12	4.9	.8	5.7
Over $2,000,000	13	16.1	2.5	18.6
Penalties, interest, etc.		(a)	—	*
Offers in compromise		(b)	—	+
Total		$112.1	$55.7	$167.8

Source: U.S. Internal Revenue Office, *Annual Report, 1917*, pp. 228–235.
(*) $5,654.
(+) $10,340.

trend toward progressive taxation was again in evidence for the
funds were to be raised from an addition to the estate tax and
an excess profits tax. The estate tax rates were increased from 1
to 1½ per cent on estates below $50,000 and to 15 per cent from
10 per cent on estates over $5 million. This 50 per cent increase

was imposed on each bracket. The excess profits tax was applied to all partnerships and corporations except those which were tax-exempt or derived their income from agriculture or personal services. The tax rate was 8 per cent of the amount by which the net income exceeded $5,000 plus 8 per cent of invested capital. The Act of March 3 was never put into actual use, since one month later the United States entered the war and the Treasury was faced by far greater financial problems.

McAdoo's Tax Policy

On April 4, 1917 the Senate passed the declaration of war by a vote of 82 to 6, and two days later it was passed by the House by a vote of 373 to 50. Secretary McAdoo was immediately confronted with the task of raising the necessary funds with which to carry out the war program.

McAdoo took up the financial history of the Civil War with the hope that it might provide some suggestions for the current financing procedure.[8] In his own words, he "did not get much in the way of inspiration or suggestion ... except a pretty clear idea of what not to do. The financial part of it was a hodge-podge of unrelated expedients."[9] However, he was impressed by two things — the successful methods used by Jay Cooke in his selling campaign, and the failure of Secretary Chase to appeal directly to the public for financial support during the war. This failure on the part of Chase to appeal to the public was considered by McAdoo to be a fundamental error. In his comment on Chase's failure can be found the philosophy of war finance which McAdoo was to carry throughout the war: "Any great war must necessarily be a popular movement. It is a kind of crusade; and, like all crusades, it sweeps along on a powerful stream of romanticism. Chase did not attempt to capitalize the emotion of the people, yet it was there and he might have put it to work."[10]

War Revenue Act of 1917

ESTIMATES OF WAR COSTS

On April 5, 1917 McAdoo asked Congress to provide immediately $3,502,558,629, plus $3,000,000,000 for advances to the allies, to place the United States on a wartime basis and to finance the war for one year from the date of the appropriation. Of the $3.5 billion, $3,404,932,484 was for the Army and Navy, and the remainder for the other departments as collateral war expenditures.[11] The $3.4 billion was estimated as sufficient to enable the government to raise and equip one million men during the year, but not beyond June 30, 1918. McAdoo's estimates were based for the most part on figures compiled by the Council of National Defence and took into consideration special price reductions on copper and other materials promised by manufacturers.[12] While no detailed figures were given, McAdoo made the following recommendations:[13]

1.	To provide 1,000,000 men and materials within one year	$2,932,537,933
2.	To increase the size of the Navy from 87,000 to 100,000 men, and the Marine Corps from 17,500 to 30,000 men	179,855,761
3.	Materials for Naval establishment	292,538,790
4.	Department of Justice	353,145
5.	U.S. Patent Office (military patents)	144,200
6.	For the establishment of a Coast Guard telephone system	600,000
7.	Department of Commerce (Bureau of Standards).	440,000

8. For the coast and geodetic and steamboat
   inspection   400,000

9. Civil Service   20,000

10. Additional watchmen for State, War, and
    Navy departments   28,800

MCADOO'S RECOMMENDATIONS

Both President Wilson and Secretary McAdoo favored raising as much of the war cost as possible by taxation. Wilson stated that "so far as practicable the burden of the war should be borne by taxation of the present generation rather than by loans."[14] McAdoo, in a letter to Cleveland H. Dodge of New York on April 14, wrote "as to taxation, my feeling has been that fifty per cent of the cost of the War should be financed by it . . . one of the most fatal mistakes that governments have made in all countries has been the failure to impose fearlessly and promptly upon the existing generation a fair burden of the cost of war. . . . I favor a reduction of the income tax exemption from $3,000 to $1,500 for single persons, and to $2,000 or $2,500 for married persons . . . a large surtax upon incomes in excess of one or two million dollars, with a corresponding increase all along the line."[15] These statements of Wilson and McAdoo on taxation both contain the mistaken concept that the costs of the war can be postponed by the use of loans rather than taxes to finance the war.

On April 15 McAdoo submitted to the Senate Finance Committee suggestions as to new sources of taxation by which half of the $3.5 billion could be raised. Changes were proposed in taxes on incomes, excess profits, liquors, tobacco, sugar, and many other commodities. Specific recommendations and the amounts of estimated revenue from each are as follows:[16]

	(millions of dollars)
Retroactive 50 per cent increase on corporate and individual income taxes for 1916, collectable in June 1917	$165.
Lower exemptions to $1,500 and $2,000 on present incomes and an increase in the surtax. (40% on $1 million and over)	340.
Increases in excess profits	226
Customs duties on goods admitted free	206.
Freight transportation	100.
Sugar excise	92.
Refined petroleum	75.
Stamp taxes (amusements)	75.
Distilled spirits	73.
Miscellaneous stamp taxes	51.6
Passenger transportation	35.
Fermented liquors	30.
Tobacco	25.
Autos, trucks, and motorcycles	19.8
Soft drinks	19.2
Cigarettes	17.
Rectified liquor	12.5
Musical instruments	7.
Glucose	6.
Denatured alcohol	5.
Tobacco dealers and products	8.8
Total	$1,588.9

In addition to the above specific recommendations, McAdoo also suggested the possibility of taxing state and municipal salaries and the interest on state and municipal securities.[17] Of the $1,588.9 million in taxation recommended by McAdoo $731 million, or 46 per cent, was in the form of income and profits taxes.

The Academic Controversy

Controversies arose on all levels regarding the proposed tax bill. In the academic field learned professors wrote heated tracts favoring one side or another. In Congressional hearings, special-interest groups made themselves heard in their pleas for speical consideration. Bankers and businessmen were vociferous in their pleas for tax relief. Legislators were torn between political expediency and revenue needs. Only the consumers had no voice to represent them.

In the academic field, lines were drawn sharply between those who favored financing the war mainly if not entirely from taxes and those who frowned upon this extreme point of view. Among the former were such noted economists as Professors O. M. W. Sprague of Harvard, Irving Fisher of Yale, and E. Dana Durand of Minnesota. Their argument was that government reliance on loans would lead to an inflation of credit, a general and rapid rise in prices, an increase in the money costs of the war, a reduction in real incomes and discriminatory profits. They favored conscription of incomes by high progressive income taxes.[18] These economists stressed social equitability and anti-inflation in their reasoning. Durand preferred taxation to borrowing because "tax policy is more likely than bond policy to mean the ultimate payment of war burdens in the manner which is socially equitable."[19] Sprague stated: "I am strongly of the opinion that a great modern war, enormously costly as it is, can and should be mainly, if not entirely, financed from the proceeds of taxes collected during its progress."[20] Sprague advocated taxes on nonessential goods and activities and on consumer goods, so that taxation might also serve as an anti-inflation weapon.

These views were criticized by other economists such as Professors E. R. A. Seligman and R. M. Haig of Columbia and C. J. Bullock of Harvard.[21] Their criticism was aimed at the amount of taxation rather than the idea of taxation, for the necessity for some taxes was conceded by these critics, but they considered 50 per cent of the war cost far too large an amount for taxation if incentives were to be maintained. Seligman thought in terms of a long expensive war and placed the cost of the first year at $10 billion as a conservative estimate. He considered the economic motives the important ones, minimizing the idea of an appeal to patriotism. He assailed Mc-Adoo's 50 per cent tax plan and stressed the depressing effects of high tax rates on production and consumption.[22]

The case for taxation was brought before Congress by a letter from a group of Yale University economists headed by Professor Henry W. Farnum and signed by Farnum, Irving Fisher, Fred R. Fairchild, Clive Day, Ray B. Westerfield, H. G. Hayes, George P. Comer and E. O. Fairness.[23] The plan proposed by this group suggested taxation of (a) all war profits, (b) individual incomes, with lower exemptions and increased rates, and (c) high consumption tax on luxuries. The arguments emphasized:

(a) Current income must in any case pay the war expenditures. Bonds versus taxes is a choice of whether the government will take income with or without a promise to repay. Borrowing creates no new capital.

(b) Taxation prevents inflation by preventing competition with the government for goods.

(c) Justice—if the taxation is postponed, returning soldiers will be forced to pay taxes to repay the bond indebtedness.

(d) Taxation increases war efficiency by keeping down costs, and produces teamwork through the sharing of the tax burden.

The arguments presented were concentrated mainly along the lines of inflation, equitability, and production incentives. The group which advocated a relatively larger amount of borrowing stressed the depressing effects of taxation on production incentives. The group which favored greater taxation stressed equitability, anti-inflation, and the undesirability of postponing the costs of the war to the future.[24] Only Professor Sprague suggested the diversion of resources from consumers to the government by a tax on consumption. The other tax exponents assumed an automatic drop in spending through the impact of the income tax. This was strict reliance on overall monetary policy rather than an attempt to relieve the price pressure where it was bound to occur—at the consumer level.

THE HOUSE REVENUE BILL

In April 1917 McAdoo's tax plan was taken under consideration by the House Ways and Means Committee and a subcommittee was named to formulate a tax plan. Chairman Kitchin openly advocated high taxes on incomes and profits and worked to soften the blow upon the "great silent masses" and to make the profiteers pay the monetary costs.[25] He advocated financing the war primarily through taxation, with the belief that it would be cruel and unjust to shift the burden of war costs,[26] and tried to convince others to go along with this policy, including Secretary McAdoo.[27]

The subcommittee disagreed violently over the proposed bill, with Representative Fordney arguing against radical increases of excess profits and corporation taxes, while on the other hand Representative Rainey urged that confiscatory taxes be imposed on incomes of $100,000 and over.[28] This stalemate in the subcommittee served only to delay the bill and shortly thereafter the House Ways and Means Committee rejected the work of the subcommittee and decided to raise $1,800,000,000 as McAdoo had requested.[29] Three weeks later the House passed a tax bill which was substantially the same as McAdoo's initial recommendation. It was estimated to raise $1,868,929,900 in new taxes of which about $900 million was in the form of income and profits taxes, including $108 million additional to be collected on 1916 incomes.[30]

BUSINESS VIEWS ON TAXATION

Banking and business had much to say both before and after the House tax bill was passed. Their voices were heard and their thoughts made known in print and in Congressional testimony.

In April, when McAdoo had asked J. P. Morgan for suggestions on financing the war, Morgan recommended that not more than 20 per cent of the amount to be spent be obtained by taxation. He stressed the danger of discouraging investors by a scale of taxation which they might consider unjust.[31]

The United States Chamber of Commerce, under the chairmanship of Wallace D. Simmons, a St. Louis hardware dealer, came out with the following plan for raising tax revenues:[32]

Tax Item	(millions of dollars)
Individual income taxes	$ 400
Excess profits taxes	200
50 per cent increase on first class postage	100
Stamp taxes	250
Customs duties increase	100
Excise taxes	550
Total	$1,600

Besides Mr. Simmons, members of the committee were T. S. Adams of Yale, O. M. W. Sprague of Harvard, John H. Gray of Minnesota, and Edward A. Filene, the Boston merchant.

Lucius Teeter, vice-president of the Chicago Association of

Commerce, objected to the retroactive features of the House plan, as well as to the height of the tax, the proposed increase in postage rates, and the proposed increase in the tariff (he suggested postponement of this). Teeter advocated a "reasonably moderate" taxation program, making increases later if necessary.[33]

Otto Kahn proposed that the burden of taxation on capital be divided over a number of years, and warned against the dire effects on incomes if the fund of capital were to be suddenly reduced by taxation. He suggested a Federal sales tax of $\frac{1}{2}$ to 1 per cent.[34] Mr. Kahn's statement suggested that the wages fund theory had not yet been forgotten by American businessmen.

Table 29
Government Expenditures and Wholesale Prices, 1917

Month	Expenditures[a] (millions of dollars)	Price Index[b] (1910–1914 = 100)
January	$ 73.5	149
February	68.3	153
March	74.1	157
April	97.5	167
May	124.8	176
June	202.9	178
July	227.9	180
August	396.1	182
September	432.1	180
October	494.5	178
November	622.2	179
December	698.3	180

Source: (a) U.S. Treasury Department, Annual Report, 1920, pp. 772–775. (b) G. F. Warren and F. A. Pearson, Prices, p. 13.

MCADOO CHANGES HIS ESTIMATE

While the revenue bill was being considered by the Senate, McAdoo changed his estimates on the amount of expenditures and the proportion to be raised by taxation. At the start of the war McAdoo thought that half of the cost should be raised by taxation. On further thought, influenced by the persuasive arguments of the antitax group, he concluded that financing one-third of the cost by taxation would be enough of a burden on the people—"if you take the whole of a man's surplus income through taxes, you cannot expect him to buy bonds, nor can you expect industry to expand and prosper."[35]

Expenditures for fiscal 1918, estimated in April at $3.5 billion plus $3 billion for loans to the allies, were estimated in July at $15 billion, including loans to the allies. This estimate was raised again in December 1917 to $12.3 billion exclusive of loans to the allies, which were now estimated at $6.1 billion.[36] Actual disbursements were rising from month to month under the impetus of increased expenditures and rising prices.

Senate Hearings on the Proposed Tax Bill

At the Senate hearings the special interests were outspoken in their bids for tax relief. The bankers opposed the retroactive income tax and through P. D. Cravath protested the income taxes on stock dividends.[37] Groups of business men bewailed the unfairness of the excess profits taxes.[38] C. H. K. Curtis, publisher of the *Saturday Evening Post,* and Samuel Gompers, president of the American Federation of Labor, took issue with the proposed mail rate increase.[39] The Real Estate Advisory council objected strenuously to the tax on deeds and mortgages.[40] Mr. J. Kessler protested by letter the proposed tax on grain and molasses but endorsed the tax on distilled spirits.[41]

One could, by their words, picture a steady stream of people passing into the obscurity of the poorhouse if these taxes were imposed. Each spokesman admitted the need for taxation but argued that his group would be discriminately injured by an increased tax. Representative Kitchin remarked that there was not an item in the bill that had not been protested against, with everybody willing that someone else should pay the taxes.[42]

THE DEBATE IN THE SENATE

In the Senate the debate dragged on through the summer of 1917, the chief issue being the corporation income and profits tax. On August 14 Senator La Follette of Wisconsin made public a report urging that the bulk of war taxes be laid on incomes and profits. He also charged that the proposed tax measures were inadequate for financing the war,[43] and stated a desire that taxation be increased to yield $3.5 billion. In advocating higher taxes on war profits, he was joined by Senators Johnson of California, Hollis of New Hampshire, and Jones of New Mexico.[44] Senator Simmons, chairman of the Senate Finance Committee, then admitted that the rates upon income and war profits were not fixed at the highest level consistent with the best revenue-producing results because of a desire to leave a margin for subsequent legislation.[45]

On August 23, La Follette proposed an amendment imposing new income surtaxes from 1 per cent on incomes of $5,000 up to 50 per cent on incomes of $1,000,000 and over. This amendment was fought by a group led by Senators Lodge and Weeks. Lodge insisted that 30 per cent was ample, and taxes should not be increased lest business be injured. The amendment was rejected 58–21.[46]

Senator Bankhead of Alabama entered the debate with an attack on the base years for the excess-profits tax, and progressive rates. He favored a straight income tax on profits and claimed that an average of 1911–1913 income as a base would affect inequalities on certain companies. He proposed instead that the taxpayer be allowed to select two out of three prewar years as a base for normal profits taxes, and desired that a literal translation be given to "war profits."[47] Senator Underwood fought to the last the entire war-profits tax, both rate and base, aided by Senators Bankhead and Borah, who supported the Bankhead substitute for the tax base. Underwood urged a high tax on profits in excess of 18 per cent with no graduated rates.[48] Another opponent of the war-profits tax was Senator Hardwick, who declared that the tax would "seriously affect the cotton milling industries of the South."[49]

Other Senators were equally outspoken on other tax issues. Senator McCumber took issue with the whole policy of taxation, declaring with economic naïvete that the costs of the war should be postponed by "borrowing." His argument was that as the current generation was supplying the men and supplies, the future generations should pay the greater part of the cost. Senator Phelan entered a plea for the California wine producers, and urged a reduction of the tax on sweet wines. Senator Weeks proposed to eliminate the additional tax on second-class mail in sympathy with the newspaper and publishing business which he said "were hit harder than any other business."[50]

By the beginning of September the war profits proposal was ready for a vote. On September 5 the Senate accepted the Committee's proposals on war profits. On the same day Senators La Follette, Hollis, and Johnson proposed amendments to increase the rate. All were voted down. Senator Bankhead's amendment to use actual invested capital for a base was also voted down. Two days later the income tax provisions were accepted.[51] On September 10, 1917, the Revenue Bill was passed by the Senate by a vote of 69 to 4, and then went into conference to iron out the House-Senate differences. Senators Borah, Gronna, La Follette, and Norris voted against the bill.

The Senate bill was estimated to raise $2.4 billion, $600 million more than the House bill. The Senate bill had dropped the retroactive tax on 1916 incomes and raised the war excess-profits tax by $800 million. In conference a deadlock which lasted from September 14 to September 27 grew out of a disagreement over the war-profits tax. The argument concerned the rates, the exemption, and the definition of capital stock. It was finally agreed that the term should include the cash value of patents, trade-marks, good will and tangible property paid for with stock or property.[52] The War Revenue Act was finally passed on October 3, 1917, six months after the entrance into the war. By this time the monthly deficit was more than $400 million and rising rapidly.[53]

THE CHANGES IN THE BILL

Until McAdoo's amended estimate of the war cost was made known, the Senate had attempted to cut the revenue from taxation by about one-third. The House bill was estimated to bring in additional revenue of $1.8 billion, about one-half of McAdoo's original estimate of the war cost during the first year. The Senate bill was estimated to add $2.4 billion in revenue which was only one-sixth of McAdoo's revised estimate of $15 billion. The Senate deleted the retroactive tax on 1916 incomes, the tariff increase, the increase in mail rates, and many of the excises. Lowered in the Senate were taxes on transportation, tobacco and tobacco products, automobiles, and admissions. The largest change was an increase of $800 million in taxes on war excess profits.

In the joint committee the tax on wines which the Senate had increased was again lowered; the tax on transportation was increased as was the tax on admissions. Brought back into the tax structure was the increase in postal rates deleted by the Senate, and the inheritance tax and several excise taxes.

Table 30
**Estimated Additional Revenue for 1918 Under the House Bill,
the Senate Bill, and the War Revenue Act of 1917**

Source of Taxation	House Bill	Senate Bill	War Revenue Act of 1917
	(millions of dollars)		
Individual and corporation income	$ 598.7	$ 842.2	$ 851.
Income 1916 (retroactive)	108.	—	—
War excess profits	200.	1,060.	1,000.
Distilled spirits	100.	135.	135.
Rectified spirits	7.5	5.	5.
Fermented liquors	37.5	46.	46.
Wines	6.	21.	7.
Tobacco and tobacco products	68.2	56.6	63.4
Transportation of persons and materials	172.75	130.75	157.3
Electric, gas, and local telephone service	30.	—	—
Automobiles and motorcycles	68.	40.	40.
Tires, tubes, musical instruments, jewelry, motion pictures	34.	—	—
Amusement admissions	60.	19.	50.
Inheritance	6.	—	5.
Tariff (100% increase)	200.	—	—
Mail increase	89.	—	76.
Others	83.27	61.12	99.17
Total	$1,868.90	$2,416.67	$2,534.87
Estimate under existing law	1,333.5	1,333.5	1,333.5
Total	$3,202.4	$3,750.17	$3,868.37

Source: *Commercial and Financial Chronicle*, September 15, 1917, p. 1049; *ibid.*, October 6, 1917, p. 1363.

WAR REVENUE ACT OF 1917 [54]

1. *Income Taxes.* Exemptions were reduced to $1,000 for single persons and $2,000 for married persons. A normal tax was imposed of 2 per cent on all incomes over the exemptions. In addition to the normal tax there was a 2 per cent tax on incomes over $3,000 for single persons and $4,000 for married persons. There were also additional surtaxes ranging from 1 per cent on incomes over $5,000 for single persons and $7,000 for married persons, up to 50 per cent on incomes in excess of $1,000,000.

2. *Business Taxes.* A normal tax of 4 per cent in addition to the existing 2 per cent. Exemptions of $3,000 for corporations and $6,000 for partnerships and proprietorships. The excess-profits tax exempted net income equal to 7–9 per cent of invested capital used in the business during 1911, 1912, 1913. If the firm was not in business during that period an 8 per cent deduction of net income was to be allowed. Excess-profits tax rates over and above the exemptions were:

> 20 per cent of the first 15 per cent of income
> 25 per cent of the next 5 per cent of income
> 35 per cent of the next 5 per cent of income
> 45 per cent of the next 7 per cent of income
> 60 per cent of the remaining income

In the case of excess profits chiefly from personal or professional services, the rate was to be 8 per cent on net incomes in excess of the above exemptions of $3,000 and $6,000 for single and married persons respectively.

3. *Estate Taxes.* Rates were imposed at the rate of $\frac{1}{2}$ per cent on estates valued below $50,000 up to 10 per cent on estimates valued above $10,000,000. This represented an increase of from 2 to 25 per cent.

4. *Postal Rates*. These were increased 50 per cent, and the zone system was instituted for second-class mail at increased rates.

5. *Other Taxes*. A war tax on distilled spirits which raised the rate from $2.20 to $3.20 per gallon. Tax on beer was raised from $1.50 to $3.00 per barrel. Taxes were imposed also on other beverages, tobacco and tobacco products, documents, playing cards, parcel post, stock transfers, sales of produce futures, and admissions and dues.

6. *Excise Taxes*. On automobiles, jewelry, musical instruments, sporting goods, cameras, cosmetics, toilet articles, patent medicines, moving-picture films, motor boats, and yachts.

On the whole, the revenue act was praised by those who had advised against an attempt to finance the war mainly through taxation. Professors Seligman, Bullock and Taussig praised the bill as a wise enactment. The proponents of taxation, Professors Sprague, Fisher, H. C. Adams and Ray G. Blakey, commented that it would lead to inflation, encourage waste, increase inequalities in income and wealth, and prevent wartime efficiency,[55] with Blakey adding that the inadequacy of the tax measure would shift the war burden upon the future. John Maynard Keynes, the British economist, pointed out that taxes on profits and incomes were much less severe than corresponding British taxes.[56] While Seligman generally favored the bill he disagreed completely with the excess-profits tax provision. He called it the "most serious objection to the law," and said that while he could see something in the graduated tax on income and capital, the excess-profits tax did "penalize enterprise and ingenuity."[57]

Secretary McAdoo seemed to think that the possible complexity of the law might lead to some doubt as to its meaning. Accordingly the Secretary, in order to avoid any doubt as to its meaning, and any effect on industry which "unwise interpretation or enforcement" might have, organized a group of business and professional men designated as "excess-profits tax advisers."[58] After some months, regulations were issued interpreting the principal features of the law and establishing the administrative procedure.

Table 31
Internal Revenue Receipts, 1917–1918
(millions of dollars)

Source	1917	1918	Net Increases
Income and profits	$359.7	$2,839.0	$2,479.3
Estates	6.0	47.5	41.5
Distilled spirits, fermented liquors, and alcoholic beverages	278.3	443.8	165.5
Tobacco and tobacco products	102.2	156.2	54.0
Transportation of persons and materials	—	70.7	70.7
Corporation capital stock	—	25.0	25.0
Admissions	—	28.6	28.6
Munitions manufacturers	27.7	—	(27.7)
Miscellaneous	35.5	88.2	52.7
Total	$809.4	$3,699.0	$2,889.6

Source: U.S. Treasury Department, *Annual Report, 1917*, p. 190; *ibid., 1919*, p. 497.

The War Revenue Act of 1917, combined with the increase in business activity during 1917–1918, greatly expanded Federal revenues. For the first time in the history of the United States, internal revenue receipts exceeded $1 billion. The $3,699 million was $4\frac{1}{2}$ times the amount collected in 1917 and 7 times the amount collected in 1916. While the collections from all sources increased, by far the largest increase was from income and profits. These two taxes together with the estate tax represented $2,520.8 million of the total increase of $2,889.6 million or 87 per cent. The tax system was without doubt a victory for the adherents of progressive taxation, but it did not achieve the anti-inflation results which they had predicted.

Individual income taxes in fiscal 1918 added very little to the fight against inflation. The groups with incomes under $3,000, representing 77.7 per cent of the taxpayers, contributed only 3.6 per cent of the individual income tax receipts.[59] This was undoubtedly far more than they had contributed under the Act of September 8, 1916, when only 4.6 per cent was contributed by the $20,000 and under group. The 1917 Act did shift some of the tax burden to the middle-income group ($3,000 to $20,000) and to this extent did endeavor to put a brake on the price pressure. The individual income tax, however, still remained to a large extent a tax on savings rather than a tax on excess purchasing power.

NOTES

[1] United States Congress, House Ways and Means Committee, *Report to Accompany H.R. 16763, to Increase the Revenue and for Other Purposes*, July 5, 1916, p. 1.
[2] *Ibid.*
[3] U.S. Treasury Department, *Annual Report, 1915*, pp. 51–52.
[4] *Ibid., 1916*, p. 113.
[5] *Ibid., 1917*, pp. 56–58.
[6] *Ibid., 1920*, pp. 772–775.
[7] *39 U.S. Statutes at Large*, p. 1000.
[8] William G. McAdoo, *Crowded Years*, pp. 372–374.
[9] *Ibid.*, p. 373.
[10] *Ibid.*, p. 374.
[11] *New York Times*, April 6, 1917, p. 1–2.
[12] *Ibid.*
[13] *Commercial and Financial Chronicle*, April 7, 1917, pp. 1337–1338.
[14] *New York Times*, April 6, 1917, p. 2.
[15] Mary Synon, *McAdoo*, pp. 222–223.
[16] *New York Times*, April 16, 1917, pp. 1, 3; *Commercial and Financial*

Chronicle, April 21, 1917, pp. 1553–1554.

[17] *New York Times*, April 16, 1917, p. 3.

[18] O. M. W. Sprague, "Loans and Taxes in War Finance," *American Economic Review, Supplement*, March 1917, pp. 199–223; Edward D. Durand, "Taxation vs. Bond Issues for Financing the War," in *Financial Mobilization for War*, a symposium of the Western Economic Society.

[19] Edward D. Durand, "Taxation Versus Bond Issues for Financing the War," *Journal of Political Economy*, February 1916, p. 26.

[20] O. M. W. Sprague, "The Conscription of Income," *The Economic Journal*, March 1917, p. 2.

[21] E. R. A. Seligman and R. M. Haig, "How to Finance the War," *Columbia War Papers, No. 7*; C. J. Bullock, "Financing the War," *Quarterly Journal of Economics*, May 1917, pp. 357–379.

[22] E. R. A. Seligman, "Loans versus Taxes in War Finance," *Annals of the American Academy of Political and Social Science*, January 1918, pp. 52–82.

[23] *Congressional Record, 65th Cong.*, 1st Sess., 55; 2045–2046.

[24] This viewpoint was also held by some legislators, for example, John J. Fitzgerald, Chairman of the House Committee on Appropriations. "To rely chiefly on loans would place the burden upon posterity," in "Task of Financing the War," *Annals of the American Academy of Political and Social Science*, January 1918.

[25] Alex M. Arnett, *Claude Kitchin and the Wilson War Policies*, p. 241.

[26] *Ibid.*, p. 253.

[27] *Ibid.*, p. 250.

[28] *New York Times*, April 28, 1917, p. 4.

[29] *Ibid.*, May 2, 1917, p. 1.

[30] *Commercial and Financial Chronicle*, September 15, 1917, pp. 1049–1050.

[31] McAdoo, *Crowded Years*, p. 383.

[32] *Commercial and Financial Chronicle*, April 28, 1917, p. 1656.

[33] Chicago Association of Commerce, *Taxation and Business*, pp. 106–109.

[34] *Commercial and Financial Chronicle*, August 8, 1917, p. 663.

[35] McAdoo, *Crowded Years*, p. 384.

[36] U.S. Treasury Department, *Annual Report, 1917*, pp. 56, 72.

[37] *New York Times*, May 10, 1917, p. 16; May 12, 1917, pp. 1, 13.

[38] *Ibid.*, May 12, 1917, pp. 1, 13.

[39] *Ibid.*, May 13, 1917, p. 6.

[40] *Ibid.*, May 13, 1917, IV, p. 1; May 14, 1917, p. 3.

[41] *Ibid.*, May 5, 1917, p. 15.

[42] Arnet, *Claude Kitchen and the Wilson War Policies*, p. 252.

[43] *Commercial and Financial Chronicle*, August 18, 1917, pp. 662–663.

[44] *Ibid.*, August 25, 1917, p. 763.

[45] *Ibid.*, August 18, 1917, pp. 662–663.

[46] *Ibid.*, August 25, 1917, p. 763.

[47] *Congressional Record*, August 16, 1917, p. 6067.

[48] *Ibid.*

[49] *Ibid.*

[50] *Ibid.*, pp. 662–663.

[51] *Ibid.*, September 8, 1917, p. 955.

[52] *Ibid.*, September 29, 1917, p. 1259.

[53] U.S. Treasury Department, *Annual Report, 1920*, pp. 772–775.

[54] *40 U.S. Statutes at Large*, p. 300.

[55] "Financing the War," *Annals of the American Academy of Political and Social Science*, January 1918; Irving Fisher, "How the Public Should Pay for the War," *Annals of the American Academy of Political and Social Science*, July 1918, pp. 112–117; C. J. Bullock, "Financing the War," *Quarterly Journal of Economics*, May 1917, pp. 146–157.

[56] J. M. Keynes, "New Taxation in the United States," *Economic Journal*, December 1917, pp. 561–565.

[57] E. R. A. Seligman, *Essays in Taxation*, p. 705.

[58] Ernest Bogart, *Direct and Indirect Costs of the Great World War*, p. 171.

[59] United States Treasury Department, Internal Revenue Office, *Annual Report, 1918*, pp. 104–105.

8

The War Revenue Act of 1918

The Need for Increased Revenue

By April 1918, Federal expenditures had reached more than $1 billion a month and were increasing rapidly. By July 1918 the monthly deficits were exceeding $1 billion.

Early in the year Representative Kitchin came out in favor of a new revenue measure,[1] but at the time he received no encouragement from the Administration. With estimated expenditures in fiscal 1918 of $18.4 billion, McAdoo was willing to delay tax legislation for the time being. According to his annual report for 1917, he favored giving the economy an opportunity to adjust itself to the existing revenue laws, and saw no need to consider further legislation at the time. He feared that increased taxation would have an unfavorable effect on war production and would interfere with the sale of Treasury bonds at 4 per cent.[2]

By May 1918, with expenditures increasing rapidly and Treasury bonds being issued at $4\frac{1}{4}$ per cent, McAdoo appealed

Table 32
Federal Ordinary Receipts and Disbursements, 1918
(millions of dollars)

Month	Receipts	Disbursements	Deficit
January	$ 103.1	$ 813.1	$ 710.0
February	98.5	751.1	652.6
March	155.7	894.9	739.2
April	208.7	1,094.2	885.5
May	594.4	1,252.7	658.3
June	2,446.6	1,289.4	1,157.2*
July	122.4	1,409.2	1,286.8
August	151.9	1,520.1	1,368.2
September	151.8	1,582.7	1,430.9
October	151.0	1,454.3	1,303.3
November	310.3	1,894.9	1,584.6
December	203.5	1,914.9	1,711.4
Total	$4,697.9	$15,871.5	$11,173.6

Source: U.S. Treasury Department, *Annual Report, 1920,* pp. 772–775.
* Surplus.

to Congress for additional revenue. He sent letters to both Senator Simmons and Representative Kitchin requesting increases in the income tax and the excess-profits tax,[3] but by this time neither of the Congressmen was in favor of enacting a new revenue law in the face of the forthcoming November elections.[4] The feeling in Congress was that instead of increasing taxes, they should reduce appropriations.[5]

McAdoo next took his case to President Wilson. On May 8, 1918 he wrote "As I understand it, Congress is anxious to avoid new revenue legislation at this time but it is unescapable. Unless this matter is dealt with now firmly and satisfactorily, we shall invite disaster in 1919."[6] He pleaded for a special message to Congress by President Wilson but he apparently did not have any great confidence that his request would be granted, for two weeks later he again wrote to the President.[7] "It is with the greatest reluctance that I have been forced to the conclusion that new revenue legislation must be enacted at the present session of Congress ... the Treasury will have to disburse during the fiscal year ending June 30, 1919, approximately $24,000,000,000." He wanted one-third of this amount to be assessed in taxes and made available in cash. He also desired a higher rate on war profits superimposed on the existing tax rate, a higher tax on unearned incomes, and a heavy excise tax on all luxuries.[8]

McAdoo's urgency made itself felt, and on May 27, 1918, President Wilson took up McAdoo's cause before a joint session of Congress.[9] He appealed for immediate and more adequate resources for the Treasury. "Additional revenues," he stated, "must manifestly be provided for. It would be a most unsound policy to raise too large a proportion of them by loans."[10] He went directly to the point, urging higher taxes on incomes, war profits, and luxuries. He hoped this way to tax the sources of loans to industry, which he blamed for inflation.

On June 5, 1918 McAdoo appeared before the House Ways and Means Committee and stated his case for increased taxes. His message emphasized not only the need for increased revenue to meet war expenditures, but also the need for an increase in the normal tax as a method of stabilizing the prices of government bonds both during and after the war period.[11] The increase in the normal tax, from which the current issues were exempt, would make these issues more attractive to buyers, and help to stabilize the price of government bonds which were currently selling below par. He further predicted that when the war was over two things would occur—the government bonds would be selling at a premium and at the same time the normal tax would be either reduced or abolished. He calculated that the reduction of the tax rate, reducing, as it would, the tax-exemption privilege, would again restore the price of government bonds to or near their par value.[12]

In this message McAdoo seemed to be as much perturbed by the failure of the Liberty Bonds to sell at par as he was over the expected Treasury deficits. Also, he did not foresee that the problem in the postwar government bond market would be that the bonds would sell below par, rather than at a premium.

Business Reaction to Taxes

While McAdoo and Wilson were pleading for increased tax revenues, businessmen and their representatives were loud in their cries of persecution and discrimination under the existing revenue act. A stream of witnesses appeared before the House Ways and Means Committee testifying to the injustice of the excess-profits taxes.[13] G. W. Graham requested that motor trucks be classed as public utilities so as to escape the tax on them as motor vehicles.[14] The eminent counsel for the Express-man's League complained that the existing law discriminated in favor of parcel post.[15] Several representatives of the motion picture industry along with representatives of vaudeville managers argued against a proposed increase in the tax on admissions.[16] The American Newspaper Publishers Association opposed the zone system and the increased postal rates for second-class mail.[17]

The House Ways and Means Committee Bill

A difference of opinion developed between the House Ways and Means Committee and the Secretary of the Treasury over the excess-profits tax base and the normal tax rates. In August McAdoo urged the committee to greater speed so that the new

revenue bill could be enacted before the start of the Fourth
Liberty Loan campaign on September 28, 1918. In order to
impose a greater share of the tax burden on the richer corporations he proposed a tax of 80 per cent on war profits as an
alternative to the existing excess-profits tax.[18] To bolster the
price of Treasury bonds (exempt from normal taxes), he proposed an increase in the normal tax rates to 12 per cent on earned
incomes and 15 per cent on unearned incomes over $4,000. The
committee, on the other hand, favored comparable normal tax
rates of 10 and 13 per cent.[19] The Treasury and the House
committees differed also on the excess-profits tax base. The
Treasury favored the average of 1911 to 1913 profit for the
exemption while the committee favored an exemption based on
current invested capital.[20]

Early in September 1918 the committee bill, estimated to raise
$8 billion, was reported to the House of Representatives.[21] It
represented a compromise between the desires of the House
Committee and the recommendations of the Treasury. While
the differential between earned and unearned incomes was
dropped, normal tax rates were increased to 6 per cent on
incomes below $4,000 and 12 per cent on incomes above $4,000.
The maximum surtax was now 65 per cent and the maximum
total tax rate was now 77 per cent compared to 67 per cent under
the existing law. The 80 per cent alternative war-profits tax was
included. However, the excess-profits tax rate started at 35 per
cent, although McAdoo desired a lower starting rate for excess
profits so as to give the small businessman some tax relief.[22] On
September 20 the bill passed the House and went to the Senate.

Debate in the House of Representatives

The House debate on the committee bill lasted from September 6 to September 14. Chairman Kitchin upheld the bill on
all points. Representative Caraway of Arkansas attacked a

proposed tax on cotton. Representative Longworth of Ohio attacked the high income and profits taxes as discriminatory taxes on wealth and proposed that an increase in the tariff and consumption taxes be imposed instead. Representative Merritt of Connecticut attacked the inheritance tax as confiscatory.[23] Representative Fordney advocated substituting higher customs duties for parts of the tax measure. He also pointed out that $6 billion of the $24 billion of expected expenditures were for loans to the Allies. Since these loans were to be repaid, net expenditures would therefore only amount to $18 billion, and the $8 billion tax measure would cover not $\frac{1}{3}$ but 45 per cent of the actual expenditures, a greater tax burden than that of any other country in the world.[24]

Senate Finance Committee Hearings

At the hearings before the Senate Finance Committee the business interests kept up their never-ending series of complaints and pleadings.[25] John Hinkley of the Baltimore Stock Exchange protested against the tax on dues and membership in commodity and stock exchanges.[26] Benjamin C. March representing the Farmers National Committee on Finance proposed that income taxes be raised and fewer bonds be issued.[27] William H. Martin of Petersburg, Virginia protested the tax on cigarettes for export on behalf of the tobacco industry.[28] Senator Dillingham read a letter from a constituent who manufactured pipe organs protesting a 10 per cent tax on the sale of this commodity.[29] Theater managers protested a 20 per cent tax on theater tickets. They forecast that the tax would force the closing of many theaters and that despite the higher tax rate there would be a lower net return to the government.[30] An unusual note was added when the Cut-Over Land Conference of the South in all seriousness proposed a $1 per capita tax on dogs. This figure was raised to $2 per capita by the American Association of Woolen and

Worsted Manufacturers who were eagerly joined by the National Association of Hosiery and Underwear Manufacturers, the National Association of Retail Clothiers, and the More Sheep More Wool Association of the United States.[31]

Mayors Hylan of New York and Marx of Detroit added their complaints to that of private business, protesting that the proposed tax on municipal bonds would make future financing impossible, and favor old bondholders.[32] The tax on gasoline was attacked by H. L. Doherty, who represented the oil industry.[33] Otto Kahn summarized all of the arguments of private business with his accusation that the proposed bill would penalize industry, success in business, and thrift.[34]

The Senate Finance Committee

The House bill was formally presented to the Senate on September 23, 1918, and was subjected to the usual senatorial sniping. Senator Thomas of Colorado objected to the tax on official salaries, the alternative method of computing the profits tax, and the amount of expected revenue. The alternative method of computing corporate profits taxes, he called nonuniform and discriminatory. He attacked high tax revenue as a hindrance to commerce, agriculture, and industry, aside from the fact that it was unnecessary in the first place.[35] Thomas was joined by Senator Reed Smoot of Utah who called the alternative system "a piece of bungling absurdity" designed to reach as few voters as possible, and a prohibitive tax on American industry. He advocated a 1 per cent sales tax estimated to yield $1 billion.[36]

The debate dragged on into October, and McAdoo wrote to Senator Simmons urging more speed. The Senate Finance Committee thereupon decided to meet daily at 10:00 a.m., earlier than their usual meeting time, and to cut short the luncheon period.[37]

The Senate Finance Committee made several changes in the House bill. In order to stimulate consumption and withdrawals from warehouses, the tax on distilled spirits was reduced from $8 to $6.40 a gallon. This was still double the existing tax rate. The tax on oil pipe-line transportation was increased from $6\frac{1}{2}$ to 8 per cent. A tax cut from 10 to 5 per cent was made on automobiles, motorcycles, tires, and accessories. The tax on club dues was reduced from 20 to 10 per cent, and the proposed tax on memberships in commodity exchanges and boards of trade was completely eliminated.[38]

On October 22 the Committee lowered surtax rates on incomes below $100,000 and raised the rates on incomes of $100,000 and over. The 80 per cent tax on war profits was retained, but the excess-profits tax rates were lowered on smaller profits, as McAdoo had originally requested from the House of Representatives, and were applied also to partnerships and individuals.[39] On October 24 an inheritance tax was substituted for the estate tax.[40] The inheritance tax was to be imposed not on the gross estate but on the net inheritance of the heir after State taxes were deducted. The rates ranged from 1 per cent on inheritances of $10,000 up to 25 per cent on inheritances over $2,500,000.[41]

Despite McAdoo's repeated requests for greater speed, Chairman Simmons announced late in October that the bill would not be reported to the Senate until after the November election.[42] Shortly after the election the war ended. With the war over, McAdoo revised his estimated expenditures for 1919 and recommended revisions in the proposed revenue bill. In a letter to Senator Sirnmons he revised his estimated expenditures from $24 billion to $18 billion, and suggested that the revenue bill be reduced to produce $6 billion in calendar 1919 and $4 billion in 1920. The letter further suggested that excess profits taxes be retained at no higher than the current levels, and that individual and corporation income taxes be increased. A request for quarterly payments of income and profits taxes was also included.[43]

The Senate Finance Committee resumed its deliberations on what was by this time a postwar tax bill. The tax of 20 per cent on luxuries was eliminated, as was the 2 cent tax on gasoline and the use tax on automobiles. The tax on brokers was reduced from $100 to $40, with reductions also in the taxes on tobacco products and many commodities classed as semiluxuries. The committee adopted a $4 billion revenue goal for 1920, rejecting a proposal by Senator Gore to let the $6 billion revenue goal apply also to 1920 and use the extra $2 billion to reduce the Federal debt.[44] The revised committee bill was presented to the Senate on December 6, 1918.

The Debate in the Senate

In the Senate the debate lasted two weeks. Senators Smoot and Penrose objected to the provision for 1920 revenue as being too far in advance to legislate. Penrose also took issue with the height of the tax levy and suggested that profits taxes be completely abolished and replaced with a general and uniform tax on incomes. Senator La Follette introduced a substitute bill containing tax increases, especially on large incomes and profits.[45] After twelve hours of debate during which the La Follette substitute bill was voted down and the luxury taxes were restored, the War Revenue Bill was passed by the Senate.[46]

War Revenue Act of 1918

The revenue bill came out of conference on February 8, 1919, and was passed by the House the same day, and by the Senate on February 13.[47] President Wilson was then in Europe so that the official signature had to await his return. The major provisions of the bill, which contained tax provisions for 1919 as well as 1918, are as follows:[48]

1. Personal exemptions were retained at $1,000 and $2,000.

2. The normal tax was to be 12 per cent for 1918 and 8 per cent for following years.

3. Surtaxes were graded and increased from 1 per cent on incomes between $5,000 – 6,000, up to 65 per cent on incomes over $1 million.

4. Excess-profits taxes were changed. A distinction was made between excess profits and war profits with the excess profits applicable only to corporations. Invested capital was still to form the basis of computation.

5. The deduction of losses not directly connected with trade or business was permitted, and the limitation on the deduction of interest charges was removed.

6. The base for excess-profits tax was a deduction of $3,000 and 8 per cent of invested capital. The base for war profits tax was a deduction of $3,000 plus an amount equal to 10 per cent of net income on invested capital or average prewar net income on invested capital used in the taxable year.

7. Tax rates for 1918:
    (a) 30 per cent between exemption and 20 per cent on invested capital.
    (b) 65 per cent over 20 per cent on invested capital.
    (c) 80 per cent of excess net income over the exemption less any amounts paid under (a) and (b).

8. Tax rates for 1919:
    (a) 30 per cent reduced to 20 per cent.
    (b) 65 per cent reduced to 40 per cent.

(c) Limitation — 30 per cent of amount between $3,000 and $20,000 plus 80 per cent of net income in excess of $20,000.

9. Estates valued from $50,000 up to $2 million were taxed at from 1 per cent to 12 per cent. Estates valued at more than $10 million were taxed at 25 per cent.

10. Other changes:
    (a) Tax on Pullman tickets lowered from 10 to 8 per cent.
    (b) Rates on telephone and telegraph messages were increased.
    (c) Beverage taxes were doubled.
    (d) New excise and luxury taxes were added.
    (e) Taxes on tobacco products were increased about 50 per cent.
    (f) Special taxes were imposed on brokers and merchants.

11. All taxes were made payable in four quarterly installments.

12. A special tax was imposed on firms employing children under 14 in some industries, and from 14 to 16 for more than eight hours a day, or in the nighttime. (This section was later declared unconstitutional.)

The anticipated revenue from the new tax bill was $6 billion, of which $4.7 billion, or 78 per cent, consisted of income, profits, and estate taxes. This was the same as the percentage which was received in 1918 from these sources.

Actually the full impact of the new revenue bill did not occur until fiscal 1920, when internal revenue receipts amounted to $5,407.5 million compared with $3,850.2 million in fiscal 1919. Of this $1,557.3 million difference in revenue, $1,356.1 million was in income and profits taxes which were now payable in quarterly installments. In this way part of the 1920 receipts was in payment of the 1918 tax which would otherwise have been

Table 33
Estimated Revenues from the Senate and the House Bills
and the Revenue Act of 1918
(millions of dollars)

Source	House Bill	Senate Bill	Revenue Act of 1918
Individual and corporate income	$2,376.2	$2,207.	$2,213.
War excess profits	3,200.	2,400.	2,500.
Estates and inheritances	110.	75.	100.
Transportation and insurance	192.5	229.	243.
Beverages	1,137.6	450.	450.
Tobacco products	341.2	240.6	245.
Admissions and dues	109.	54.	54.
Excise taxes	516.3	123.	175.
Special taxes	165.	73.9	—
Stamp taxes	32.	31.	31.
Miscellaneous and floor taxes	2.6	70.	75.
Total	$8,128.5	$5,953.5	$6,086.0

Source: *Commercial and Financial Chronicle,* December 14, 1918, pp. 2233–2234; *ibid.,* February 8, 1919, p. 530.

paid into the Treasury in June 1919. Because of this delayed payment process, the percentage of income, profits and estate taxes to the total dropped from 78 per cent in 1918 to 70 per cent in 1919, but increased to 75 per cent in fiscal 1920.

The increase in the normal tax rate under the Revenue Act of 1919 imposed a greater burden on the low- and middle-income groups. In 1920 the low-income group (see Table 35) paid 7.7 per cent of the total personal tax yield compared with 3.8 per cent in 1917. The middle-income group paid 32.9 per cent of the tax in 1920 compared with 20.7 per cent in 1917. The share of the upper-income group in the personal income tax decreased during the war from 75.5 per cent in 1917 to 59.4 per cent in 1920. Thus while the income tax provisions remained highly

Table 34
Internal Revenue Receipts, 1919–1920
(millions of dollars)

Source	1919	1920	Total
Income and profits	$2,600.8	$3,956.9	$6,557.7
Estates	82.0	103.6	185.6
All other	1,169.4	1,347.0	2,514.4
Total	$3,850.2	$5,407.5	$9,257.7
Percent of tax from incomes, profits and estates	70%	75%	72.8%

Source: U.S. Treasury Department, *Annual Report, 1919*, p. 497; *ibid., 1920* p. 601.

Table 35
Personal Income Tax Returns and Yields, 1917–1920
(calendar year, in percentages)

Income Group	Tax Returns			
	1917	1918	1919	1920
$1,000–$3,000	71.4	68.2	65.6	72.2
3,000–20,000	27.2	30.9	33.4	27.1
20,000 and over	1.4	.9	1.0	.7
Total	100.0	100.0	100.0	100.0

Table 35

(continued)

Income Group	Tax Yields			
	1917	*1918*	*1919*	*1920*
$1,000–$3,000	3.8	5.5	4.1	7.7
3,000–20,000	20.7	28.2	26.1	32.9
20,000 and over	75.5	66.3	69.8	59.4
Total	100.0	100.0	100.0	100.0

Source: Statistical Abstract of the United States, 1924, p. 162.

progressive during the war there was a definite shift in emphasis from the high-income group in the Act of 1916 to the middle- and low-income groups in the Acts of 1917 and 1918.

NOTES

[1] *New York Times*, January 27, 1918, p. 6.

[2] U.S. Treasury Department, *Annual Report, 1917.*

[3] *Ibid., 1918*, pp. 46–49; *New York Times*, May 10, 1918, p. 5.

[4] Roy G. Blakey and Gladys C. Blakey, "The War Revenue Act of 1918," *American Economic Review*, June 1919, p. 157; *New York Times*, May 11, 1918, p. 1.

[5] *New York Times*, May 13, 1918, p. 12.

[6] Mary Synon, *McAdoo*, pp. 231–246.

[7] *Ibid.*

[8] U.S. Treasury Department, *Annual Report, 1918*, pp. 23–24; *New York Times*, June 4, 1918, p. 1.

[9] Woodrow Wilson, *Address delivered at a Joint Session of Congress on the Finances*, May 27, 1918.

[10] *Ibid.*, p. 4.

[11] United States Congress, House Ways and Means Committee, *Hearings on the Proposed Revenue Act of 1918*, 65:2, p. 11. (*Note:* In June 1918, all government bond issues were selling below par, with prices of the 4's of 1927–42

and 1932–47 ranging from 93 to 95.20). *Commercial and Financial Chronicle*, Monthly Review, June 1918.

[12] House Ways and Means Committee, *Hearings*, 65:2.

[13] *New York Times*, June 14, 1918, p. 15.

[14] *Ibid.*, p. 9.

[15] *Ibid.*, June 18, 1918, p. 24.

[16] *Ibid.*, June 19, 1918, p. 9.

[17] *Ibid.*, June 22, 1918, p. 8.

[18] *Commercial and Financial Chronicle*, August 17, 1918, pp. 650–651. McAdoo originally wanted both but T. S. Adams, advisor to the Treasury, suggested the alternative; see Blakey, "The Revenue Act of 1918," p. 164.

[19] *Commercial and Financial Chronicle*, August 24, 1918, pp. 752–753.

[20] *Ibid.*, August 10, 1918, p. 557.

[21] *Ibid.*, September 7, 1918, pp. 942–943.

[22] *Ibid.*, September 7, 1918, p. 943.

[23] *Ibid.*, September 14, 1918, pp. 1052–1054.

[24] *Ibid.*

[25] Senate Finance Committee, *Hearings on H. R. 12863 to Provide Revenue and Other Purposes*, 65:2.

[26] *Commercial and Financial Chronicle*, September 14, 1918, pp. 1054–1055.

[27] *Ibid.*

[28] *Ibid.*

[29] *Ibid.*

[30] *Ibid.*

[31] Senate Finance Committee, *Hearings*, 65:2, pp. 471–472.

[32] *Commercial and Financial Chronicle*, September 14, 1918, p. 1055.

[33] *New York Times*, October 9, 1918, p. 24

[34] *Ibid.*, October 11, 1918, p. 10; *Commercial and Financial Chronicle*, October 12, 1918, pp. 1428–1429.

[35] *Commercial and Financial Chronicle*, September 28, 1918, pp. 1245–1248.

[36] *Ibid.*, September 7, 1918, p. 943.

[37] *Ibid.*, October 5, 1918, pp. 1325–1326.

[38] *Ibid.*, October 12, 1918, pp. 1427–1428.

[39] *Ibid.*, October 26, 1918, pp. 1618–1619; November 2, 1918, pp. 1707–1708.

[40] *Ibid.*, October 26, 1918, pp. 1619.

[41] *Ibid.*, November 2, 1918, pp. 1707–1708.

[42] *Ibid.*

[43] *Ibid.*, November 16, 1918, pp. 1877–1878.

[44] *Ibid.*, November 30, 1918, pp. 2048–2049.

[45] *Ibid.*, December 21, 1918, pp. 2330–2331.

[46] *Ibid.*, December 28, 1918, pp. 2422–2423.

[47] *Ibid.*, February 15, 1919, p. 618.

[48] *40 U.S. Statutes at Large*, pp. 1057–1152; U.S. Treasury Department, *Annual Report, 1919*, p. 497.

9

The Liberty and Victory Loans

Since tax receipts came far short of expenditures, the government was forced to borrow. McAdoo's wartime borrowing program, like his taxation policy, contained a series of conflicting measures, each of which was inconsistent with the achievement of another part of the program.

McAdoo's plan of borrowing was based on his criticism of Secretary Chase's failure to appeal directly to the public. McAdoo intended to carry his selling campaign directly to the public, appealing to patriotic rather than to commercial motives. He "did not intend to sell the bonds on a commercial basis. Purchasing government securities was to be the expression of a fundamental patriotism."[1] This fundamental patriotism, he was sure, would allow him to sell bonds at an interest rate which was lower than the current market rate. This policy of low government interest rates was pursued throughout the war, causing other problems which plagued the Treasury and were more detrimental to the economy than higher interest rates would have been.

Through the borrowing program, McAdoo evidently planned to accomplish the diversion of purchasing power from consumers to the government. There can be no doubt that he neither intended nor desired the inflation that accompanied the war borrowing. In his report of 1917, his philosophy unequivocally reflected an attitude of economy and saving rather than of business as usual:

> What is of superlative importance ... is that our people shall be impressed with the necessity of economizing in the consumption of articles of clothing, food, and fuel, and of every other thing which constitutes a drain upon the available supplies, materials, and resources of the country.[2]
>
> The great financial operations of the government cannot be carried forward successfully unless the people ... save their money and lend it to the government.[3]
>
> The man who subscribes for a government bond ... is not a patriot if he immediately sells that bond on the market when he does not imperatively need the money.[4]
>
> The lender is supposed to deny himself something which releases, in turn, a demand on the vital supplies of the country.[5]

McAdoo also suggested to Congress the raising of funds through war savings stamps so the "American people would have the opportunity and encouragement to economize and save."[6] This program, put into effect in November 1917, was intended primarily to tap the savings of people of small means.

Practices in the Borrowing Program

While McAdoo's borrowing plan was intended to tap the savings of the nation and thus divert resources to the war program without inordinately inflating prices, from the very start the plan was doomed to failure. Two reasons explain this — first, McAdoo's fear that the bond selling campaign would not be successful; and second, his insistence on selling bonds at an interest rate which would not appeal to investors.

Because the war would require an unprecedented amount of borrowing, McAdoo feared that the nonbank public would not meet the need for funds. In order to ensure the full sale of each bond issue, his intention of carrying the campaign directly to the public was changed in practice to greater reliance on bank borrowing, both direct and indirect, inadvertently causing an expansion rather than a diversion of the money supply.

The Treasury desired to divert funds from consumption and private investment to the government. This was consistent with administration anti-inflation desires, but at the same time the Treasury encouraged individuals to buy the bonds with bank credit, thus encouraging additions to the total money supply. While attempting to reduce the money cost of the war through a policy of low interest rates on government obligations, the Treasury lowered the incentive of nonbank lenders to purchase government securities. And above all, McAdoo, always fearful that the bond issues might not be successful, relied far too greatly on short-term certificates and on bank borrowing.

The low interest rate of government bonds as compared to railroad and industrial bonds caused the governments to sell below par throughout most of the war period, and by June 1920 most governments were selling in the 80's,[7] rather than at a premium as McAdoo had forecast. This depression in government bond prices brought on efforts by the Treasury to maintain the bonds at or near par by special tax favors to bondholders, which partly nullified the saving of the low interest rate claimed by McAdoo, and by the establishment of a bond purchase fund, with which the Treasury could support the bonds in the open market. Neither of these measures was successful in maintaining the governments at par.

The Liberty and Victory Loan campaigns were quantitatively successful inasmuch as each offering was oversubscribed. Unfortunately, the distribution of bond holdings and the effect of McAdoo's choice of interest rates on the market prices of the issues were not equally successful.

The First Liberty Loan

McAdoo originally estimated that $2 billion could be raised at once and without difficulty through a bond issue by a popular subscription. The plan then contemplated was to decide on a permanent rate of interest, giving the first issue the same rate as subsequent issues.[8] The next day, with an increased demand for tax-exempt bonds, and with New York State 4's being offered and sold at $105\frac{5}{8}$ for a yield of $3\frac{3}{8}$ per cent,[9] Charles E. Mitchell, president of the National City Company, suggested that the Treasury sell thirty-year, $3\frac{1}{2}$ per cent bonds, convertible into higher rate bonds if any such should be issued later. He thought that $2 billion could be floated.[10] McAdoo agreed with this suggestion.

Other bankers also offered their advice to the Treasury. White-Weld and Company suggested an issue of $1 or $2 billion at 4 per cent. Guy Emerson, vice-president of the National City Bank, suggested a maximum of $1 billion, as did J. P. Morgan. Paul M. Warburg was the only banker who believed that $2.5 billion of long-term bonds could be sold.[11] Frank A. Vanderlip, president of the National City Bank, who was later to take a large part in the selling campaign, said that "at least $500 million of $3\frac{1}{2}$ per cent bonds with a convertible feature can be disposed of immediately."[12]

Disregarding the advice offered by the bankers and all others whom he consulted,[13] McAdoo decided on a $2 billion issue with a $3\frac{1}{2}$ per cent coupon. The $3\frac{1}{2}$ per cent interest rate decision was made because it "was a little lower than the rates usually paid by savings banks. They were afraid that large withdrawals of their deposits would be made if the rate was higher."[14] The deciding influence on the amount of the loan was a "hunch."[15] McAdoo later defended his low interest rate policy as a saving of an immense sum to the people of the United States.[16]

McAdoo made known to Congress his decision regarding the interest rate on the first bond issue. While many disagreed with his reasoning that a low rate would lower the cost of the war and prevent depreciation of other forms of securities,[17] there were many who stood fast for the $3\frac{1}{2}$ per cent rate. Senator Kenyon agreed with McAdoo that $3\frac{1}{2}$ per cent bonds could be sold by an appeal to patriotic motives.[18] Representative Fitzgerald would have resorted to compulsion, whatever that may have meant, to keep the interest rate as low as possible.[19] There were also those who believed that the $3\frac{1}{2}$ per cent rate would put the bonds on a business basis, that they could compete on a yield basis with comparable securities in the money market.

Suggestions as to the denominations of the bonds were offered both before and after the passage of the Liberty Bond Act. In the House, Representative Howard favored a $25 denomination bond so as to widen the market for the issue.[20] The Federal Reserve Bank of New York moved for the issuance of $10 certificates convertible into $50 bonds.[21] Billy Sunday, the evangelist, suggested a denomination as low as $1.[22]

The first Liberty Loan Act authorizing the issue of $5 billion of bonds at $3\frac{1}{2}$ per cent was passed on April 24, 1917,[23] and on May 2 McAdoo announced that the first issue would be $2 billion and appealed to all citizens to subscribe. On May 9 the terms, denominations, and maturities were agreed upon and made public after a conference in the office of Secretary McAdoo attended by John S. Williams, Comptroller of the Currency; W. P. G. Harding, governor of the Federal Reserve Board; Paul M. Warburg, vice-governor of the Federal Reserve Board; Oscar T. Crosby and Robert W. Wooley, assistant secretaries of the Treasury; William Woodward, president of the Hanover National Bank of New York; William B. Franklin, president of the American Investment Bankers Association; and George R. Cooksey, assistant to the Secretary of the Treasury.[24]

The bonds of the first issue were offered on May 14, 1917. The amount was $2 billion and the interest rate was $3\frac{1}{2}$ per cent. They were to mature in thirty years but were callable by the Treasury after fifteen years. The lowest denomination was $50. All sales were to be at par and the bonds were not to carry the circulation privilege, that is, they could not be used as security by the national banks against national bank note issues.

In June 1917 the rate on four- to six-month prime commercial paper was $5\frac{1}{8}$ per cent; U.S. 3's (1914–1946) were selling at 87 on the New York Stock Exchange for a yield to maturity of 3.43 per cent. U.S. 4's of 1925 were selling at 105 for a yield to maturity of 3.37 per cent; and the yield on high-grade railroad bonds was 4.28 per cent.[25] On the basis of the current market prices for other governments and other triple A bonds, therefore, the $3\frac{1}{2}$ per cent rate on the First Liberty Loan was not too low. Yet the bonds were made exempt from all taxes but estate and inheritance taxes; thus, the interest on the bonds was not taxable under the income tax. To a person paying the maximum income tax rate of 67 per cent, the $3\frac{1}{2}$ per cent tax-free income from the Liberty Bonds was equivalent to a 10.6 per cent interest rate on a taxable bond. As a further inducement to purchase, the bonds were convertible at the option of the holder into any future issue bearing a higher interest rate.

Purchasers could buy the bonds on the installment plan with payment terms as follows:[26]

> 2 per cent upon subscription
> 18 per cent on June 28, 1917
> 20 per cent on July 30, 1917
> 30 per cent on August 15, 1917
> 30 per cent on August 30, 1917

At first the bonds sold poorly. One week before the subscription books were closed, New York appeared to be the only district meeting its quota, but thereafter sales picked up. During the last two weeks of the loan drive many banks and other corporations declared extra dividends, called "Liberty Loan dividends," to enable the recipients to subscribe to the loan. When the subscriptions were totaled, all districts but three had exceeded their quotas, and $3,035,226,850 had been subscribed, an oversubscription of 52 per cent, which was quite astonishing to some observers.[27]

More than 4 million subscriptions were received with about 99 per cent in amounts from $50 to $10,000.[28] The 99 per cent of subscriptions accounted for $1,296,684,850 out of total subscriptions of $3,035,226,850, or 42 per cent of the total. Because only $2 billion of bonds were allotted, the 99 per cent of subscriptions were 65 per cent of total allotments. This was regarded by McAdoo as a sign that the lower-income groups were subscribing, but this was a doubtful concept, since subscriptions of $10,000 or even $1,000 could be by no means considered as emanating from low-income groups.

The administration considered the First Liberty Loan a great success from every point of view. The oversubscription of

Table 36
Subscriptions and Allotments, First Liberty Loan

Amount	Subscriptions	Allotments
$50–$10,000	$1,296,684,850	$1,296,684,850
10,050–100,000	560,103,050	336,061,850
100,050–250,000	220,455,600	99,205,000
Over $250,000	957,983,350	268,048,300
Total	$3,035,226,850	$2,000,000,000

Source: U.S. Treasury Department, *Annual Report, 1917*, p. 7.

$1,035 million and the number of subscribers created special enthusiasm. The Treasury announced that "the bonds were bought in the calm exercise of patriotism and sound business judgment after a campaign of education and information."[29]

The Treasury's enthusiasm was not shared by all. E. R. A. Seligman did not agree that the loan was either successful or good policy. He criticized the failure of the $3\frac{1}{2}$ per cent interest rate to appeal to business motives, the tax-exemption feature, which he declared would set up a special class of nontax-paying people, the failure to borrow more and tax less, and the campaign organization.[30]

The Second Liberty Loan

Repayment of short-term indebtedness, loans to the Allies, and the steadily increasing war expenditures soon depleted the Treasury of the proceeds from the First Liberty Loan. The Treasury balance in the Federal Reserve banks fell from $301 million on June 29 1917 to $143 million one month later, and to $71 million by September 28, 1917.[31] Secretary McAdoo, in conference with Chairman Kitchin of the House Ways and Means Committee on August 14, declared that it would be necessary for Congress to authorize an additional $9 billion for war expenses, of which $4 billion would be used for further loans to the Allies. Within an hour plans were begun for raising the required sum, and a meeting of the committee was called for August 25.[32]

On August 17 McAdoo submitted recommendations to the House Ways and Means Committee asking for authority to float a $7.5 billion, 4 per cent bond issue of which $3 billion would replace the $3 billion of the first issue which had not been offered for subscription, and $4 billion would provide for additional loans for the Allies. He proposed that the bond issue be subject only to income surtaxes, war-profits taxes, and excess-profits taxes. In addition, McAdoo requested additional certificates of indebtedness up to $2 billion, and an equal amount of war savings certificates in a form available for small investors.[33]

The committee was not inclined to argument. Representative Moore of Pennsylvania, the ranking Republican committee member in the absence of Representative Fordney, issued a statement indicating that the Republicans would support authorization of the bonds. "The disposition of Congress for the present is to let the President have what he wants for the purposes of the war."[34] Some members of the Committee favored dividing the issue into $3\frac{1}{2}$ per cent nontaxable and 4 per cent taxable bonds, but McAdoo held out for the 4 per cent taxable bonds.[35]

On September 1 McAdoo announced that the Second Liberty Loan Campaign would begin on October 1 and close one month later. The details of the issue could not be given until Congress acted on the pending bill.[36] Loan bills were passed by the House on September 6 and by the Senate on September 16. After several minor changes in conference regarding the expense allowance, the bill was returned to Congress on September 19. Two days later the Second Liberty Bond Act had passed both Houses and on September 24 it was signed by President Wilson.

Under this Act the Treasury was authorized to issue a total of $7,538,945,460 of bonds including the $3 billion unissued under the first loan. The interest rate was to be 4 per cent, reflecting both the rise in market interest rates and also the fact that the second issue had none of the tax exemptions of the first except the exemption from the normal income tax, and a surtax exemption on the income from $5,000 face value of the bonds.[37] The second issue was convertible into later issues, but only if converted within six months after each issue. Any bonds of the first issue which were converted into the 4's of the second issue were to carry the rights of the second issue only. Thus if converted there would be a loss of the tax-exemption privilege and the unlimited conversion privilege attached to the first issue. This issue was to be redeemable starting in 1927 and was to mature in 1942. Like the first issue the bonds were to be sold at par and would not carry the circulation privilege.

In testimony before the Senate on September 28[38] McAdoo explained the changes in the second bond issue. According to McAdoo, the first issue did not make the widest appeal since the low interest rates did not offer any advantage to the masses of people. The tax exemption privilege appealed to large investors and created a special class of nontaxpayers. He pointed out that under the pending tax bill, the tax-exemption privilege could mean that the $3\frac{1}{2}$ per cent tax-free return could be equal to a taxable return of $9\frac{1}{2}$ per cent.[39] "We cannot sell bonds," he said, "in billions on the basis of what they may be worth to the very rich. They must be offered to all people alike at one price and should appeal to all alike and on equal terms."[40] Thus McAdoo continued to stress his interest in the broadest possible bond market.

McAdoo kept the normal tax exemption so as to keep from offering a higher rate of interest with a resulting drop in other bond prices.[41] While asserting that the 4 per cent issue would sell on its investment merits, he reiterated that patriotism was the primary motivating force, and urged all Americans to economize, save, and buy bonds.

The amount of the Second Liberty Loan was $3 billion, but McAdoo announced that he would allot additional bonds up to half of the oversubscription. The offering was made on October 1, 1917 with the subscription books closing on October 27.[42] The installment plan for the second issue was:

2 per cent upon subscription
18 per cent by November 15, 1917

40 per cent by December 15, 1917
40 per cent by January 15, 1918

While the final subscription amounted to $4.6 billion, a 54
per cent oversubscription, it was not too easily attained. From
October 1 to October 13 only 19 per cent of its total $1.5 billion
allotment and only 39 per cent of its daily allotment was subscribed in the New York district.[43] In a speech in San Diego,
McAdoo intimated that if the Liberty Loan should fail there
would be a possibility of the conscription of wealth.[44] The
Federal Reserve Bank of Richmond drew up and circulated a
yield chart showing that the net yield after taxes on the 4 per
cent issue did not fall below $3\frac{1}{2}$ per cent until the $80,000 income
bracket was reached.[45] James R. Curtis, Secretary and General
Counsel of the New York Federal Reserve Bank, urged corporations to take advantage of the provision in the War Revenue
Act of 1917 that the 10 per cent tax on undistributed profits
would not apply to those profits invested in obligations of the
United States issued after September 1, 1917.[46]

A heated argument grew out of a speech made by Representative Clark in which he accused a "ring" of financiers of

Table 37
Subscriptions and Allotments, Second Liberty Loan

Amount	Subscriptions	Allotments
$50–$10,000	$1,866,926,100	$1,866,926,100
10,050–50,000	621,543,250	621,543,250
50,050–100,000	359,865,900	323,879,600
100,050–200,000	242,220,800	181,665,800
Over $200,000	1,526,976,250	814,751,400
Total	$4,617,532,300	$3,808,766,150

Source: U.S. Treasury Department, Annual Report, 1917, p. 10–11.

plotting to make the second loan a partial failure so as to boost the interest rate. Benjamin Strong questioned the veracity of the accusation and J. P. Morgan pointed out that even though New York was behind on its quota it was still ahead of all other districts both in the amount and the percentage of its quota subscribed. Clark, unable to prove his charge, withdrew it two days later.[47] By this time McAdoo had announced that the loan had been oversubscribed.

Of the 9,400,000 subscribers, 9,306,000 or 99 per cent subscribed to amounts of $50 to $50,000. Total allotments allowed by the Treasury amounted to $3,808,766,150 of which $1,866,926,100 went to those subscribing in amounts between $50 and $10,000.[48] Thus in the second loan, subscriptions in amounts up to $10,000 amounted to 40 per cent of total subscriptions and 49 per cent of the alloted bonds, compared with the comparable percentages of 42 per cent and 65 per cent in the first loan. The second loan therefore drew a smaller percentage of the savings of the low-income groups than did the first loan.

The second loan brought out somewhat more sharply the plan of the war loan program. It fixed the plan of par sales for war bonds and denied them the circulation privilege. The limited privilege of conversion was a step in the direction of making each issue stand on its own merits as McAdoo desired.[49] The policy of complete tax exemptions on government bond interest was reversed. While McAdoo still spoke confidently of patriotic bond purchases, the second issue was a recognition of the fact that bonds could be sold on a large scale only to those persons of more than average means. The raising of the interest rate to 4 per cent combined with the partial tax exemptions was designed to appeal to the middle-income group rather than to either the high or low-income groups. McAdoo did not entirely give up the attempt to borrow from the low-income group, but instead emphasized the sale of war savings stamps and certificates to this segment of the population.

The Third Liberty Loan

In the spring of 1918 the need of the Treasury for cash and the approaching maturities of outstanding debts made a third loan necessary.[50] Outstanding certificates of indebtedness on March 20 amounted to $2,760.6 million, besides which the 3 per cent loan of 1908–1918 amounting to $64 million was to fall due shortly.[51] Treasury deficits between September 1917 and April 1918 ranged between $322 million and $886 million monthly.[52] The bonds of the previous loans were selling below par, and the general banking opinion was that the interest rate should be raised to $4\frac{1}{2}$ per cent.[53] In March 1918, the bonds of the second loan were selling at an average price of 96.44 and yielded 4.4 per cent to the earliest call date and 4.15 per cent to maturity.[54] The Treasury stood firm in its policy that the "interest rate would not of itself maintain the bonds at par."[55] McAdoo was confident that the market price of the old issues would in no way deter the sale of a new issue at par, and he stated that the "patriotism of the American people was not measured by interest rates, nor determined by the fluctuations

Table 38
Subscriptions to the Third Liberty Loan

Amount	Number of Subscribers	Amounts
$50–$10,000	18,354,315	$2,770,933,150
10,050–50,000	17,236	443,587,950
50,050–100,000	3,538	226,865,400
100,050–200,000	905	151,956,700
Over $200,000	821	583,155,400
Total	18,376,815	$4,176,516,850

Source: U.S. Treasury Department, *Annual Report, 1918*, p. 9.

in the market price of government bonds on the Stock Exchange."[56]

At a conference attended by McAdoo, the members of the Federal Reserve System, and the Chairman of the Liberty Loan committees there was a further discussion of interest rates. While there was not complete agreement on a $4\frac{1}{4}$ per cent rate, they did agree that this rate would have a lesser disturbance on the money market than would a $4\frac{1}{2}$ per cent rate.[57] McAdoo decided to recommend that Congress authorize a $4\frac{1}{4}$ per cent nonconvertible bond issue. He believed that the result would be a stabilization of the interest rate as far as possible, and the elimination of the conversion feature which both he and Kitchin thought brought on a demand for higher interest rates by the holders of the convertible bonds.[58]

The fall in the market price of the previous loans was of great concern to both Congress and the Treasury. Representative Wood introduced a resolution in the House making it unlawful to trade in Liberty Bonds below par, and McAdoo strongly urged its support.[59] Cordell Hull introduced a bill to provide for a fund not in excess of $60 million, which the Treasury could employ to support the market price of the bonds by open market purchases when the bonds sold below par.[60] Neither resolution became a law but the Third Liberty Loan did provide an authorization for the Treasury to purchase annually 5 per cent of each outstanding Liberty Bond issue except the first issue of $3\frac{1}{2}$'s.[61]

In addition to the price-support clause, the Third Liberty Loan Act provided for an increase in the total authorization to $12 billion and of loans to the Allies to $5.5 billion. As $5.8 billion had been allotted in the two previous bond campaigns, the maximum allowable in the third was $6.2 billion. The total amount of certificates of indebtedness allowable to be outstanding was increased to $8 billion. The interest rate was increased to $4\frac{1}{4}$ per cent but the bonds were not convertible into any future issue bearing a higher interest rate as were the first two issues.

Several other features were contained in the third issue which were designed to make it more attractive to certain types of investors. Any bonds bearing interest at higher than 4 per cent and owned by any person six months prior to his death would be received by the United States at par plus interest in payment of estate or inheritance taxes. This was clearly intended to encourage the third issue to be bought and held. Another provision arranged for the acceptance of Liberty Bonds as security for bidders and government contractors for guaranteeing proposals on contracts, and as security at face value for payments of excise taxes.[62]

On April 6, 1918 the Treasury offered $3 billion of the new $4\frac{1}{4}$ per cent nonconvertible bonds, maturing in ten years, dated May 9, 1918. Any prior issues converted into the third issue would lose their convertibility.

Lewis B. Clarke, president of the American Exchange Bank

Table 39
Number of Bonds of Third Liberty Loan Delivered

Denomination	Number of Pieces	Amounts
$50	14,192,244	$ 709,612,200
100	7,649,218	764,921,800
500	863,005	431,502,500
1,000	1,464,444	1,464,444,000
5,000	47,534	237,670,000
10,000	45,700	457,000,000
50,000	596	29,800,000
100,000	707	70,700,000
Total	24,263,448	$4,165,650,500

Source: U.S. Treasury Department, *Annual Report, 1918*, p. 12.

of New York, commented that it was gratifying that only $3 billion was required, and declared the $4\frac{1}{4}$ per cent interest rate to be satisfactory. Francis L. Hine, president of the First National Bank of New York, commented favorably on the sinking-fund provisions, the amount of the loan, and their acceptability for payment of inheritance taxes. These sentiments were echoed by other bankers, including O. E. Pomeroy of the Bankers Trust Company, Herbert K. Twitchell of the Chemical National Bank, G. C. Van Tuyl, Jr., of the Metropolitan Trust Company, and Edwin T. Merrill of the Union Trust Company, all of New York.[63]

Subscriptions for $4,176,516,850 were received from 18,376,815 subscribers. Of this amount $2,770,933,150 of subscriptions was received from 18,354,315 subscribers in amounts between $50 and $10,000. Since all subscriptions were accepted, 99.8 per cent of the subscribers received 66.5 per cent of the issue while the remaining .2 per cent of the subscribers received 33.5 per cent of the bonds.[64]

The main features of the Third Liberty Loan were the abandonment of the conversion feature, the increase in the interest rate, the price support provision, and the receivability of the bonds in payment of estate and inheritance taxes. The increase in the interest rate and the receivability provisions, which offset the abandonment of the conversion feature, were designed to make the issue more attractive. The sinking fund provision was tacit acknowledgment that the Liberty Bonds would most likely continue to sell below par.

The Fourth Liberty Loan

Starting in July 1918, monthly deficits exceeded $1 billion and showed no sign of declining.[65] This made necessary further issues of short-term certificates, and during June and July 1918 $2.2

billion of the certificates were sold. By October 1, 1918 outstanding certificate indebtedness due on or before January 30, 1919 amounted to $4.7 billion.[66]

The chief problem confronting the Treasury in its contemplation of the terms for the Fourth Liberty Loan was the maintenance of market prices at par. In a letter to Chairman Kitchin on September 5, 1918 McAdoo admitted that the bond-purchase fund was not very effective in sustaining the market price, and suggested that a government agency replace the stock exchanges as a market for government bond dealings. The bonds presumably would be repurchased at par by the government. While this plan was not adopted during World War I, it did eventually become an integral part of the loan program during World War II. McAdoo's idea, remarkably like the policy adopted in the 1939–1945 conflict, was clearly stated in the letter.

> I feel that we all owe a duty to the millions of subscribers of small means, not merely to pay them a fair rate of interest ... but to take such measures as may be necessary to insure to them a market for the bonds at approximately par in case their necessities are such as to force them to realize upon the investment which they have made in the Government's obligations.
>
> To make such a plan effective, it would be necessary to put an end to dealings in bonds on the exchanges, and accordingly to substitute an active and adequate market through the banking houses of the United States acting in close cooperation with an instrumentality of the Government, probably the War Finance Corporation.[67]

It was clear that whatever strength existed in the bond issues was due to the tax exemption rather than to the interest rate, for although all Liberty Bonds were selling below their face value, the $3\frac{1}{2}$'s were higher than any of the others.[68] A tax exemption on the new issue equal to that of the first would undoubtedly stimulate sales to upper income groups and cause conversion of the old $3\frac{1}{2}$'s into the new issues. This did not exactly fit McAdoo's plans. He pointed out that while the interest rate had gone up $\frac{1}{4}$ per cent, surtaxes had increased by as much as 150 per cent. In order to achieve a par market for the new issue it would be necessary to either raise the interest rate or extend the tax exemption privilege. McAdoo chose the latter method.

> In order to give the numerous small holders of Liberty Bonds the advantage of a market upon which they may sell their bonds in case of necessity, and also to attract subscriptions from the great number of investors of ample means, but not of great wealth, it will be necessary immediately either to increase the interest rate or to neutralize the increased surtaxes by freeing the bonds to a limited extent from such taxes.
>
> I recommend that a portion of the income of these bonds should be free from surtaxes for the period of the war and for a brief period thereafter ... rather than to increase the intérest rate.[69]

McAdoo also was influenced by the fact that Liberty Bonds were in competition with billions of dollars of tax-exempt bonds of states and municipalities.[70]

The Fourth Liberty Loan contained all the provisions Mc-Adoo desired. Five billion dollars worth of bonds were authorized and the amount of War Savings Certificates was increased by $2 billion. On September 28 McAdoo offered for subscription $6 billion of $4\frac{1}{2}$ per cent nonconvertible fifteen- to thirty-year bonds, to be dated October 24, 1918.[71] The Treasury retained the right to allot bonds up to the full amount of the subscription. The important provision in this issue was the contingent tax-exemption feature, which was used to promote the sale of the current issue, and at the same time to promote the support of the older issues which were selling below par. The new bonds, like the old ones, were exempt from the normal tax. In addition, for a period extending to two years after the war, they were exempt from surtaxes, excess profits taxes, and war profits taxes on the income from $30,000 principal. A further exemption from the above taxes was granted to the holders of the new issue on the income from all previous issues except the first $3\frac{1}{2}$'s (which were already tax-exempt) up to $45,000 principal or one and one-half the holdings of the new Fourth Loan, whichever amount was smaller. [72] The combined tax exemption privilege to each holder now included the income from $75,000 principal of the "taxable" issues, all income from the first nontaxable issue, and a surtax exemption on the income from $5,000 principal of the second issue. This situation could clearly exempt all bondholders except the very large ones from any tax payments on bond interest, and according to one student of the bondholdings during the period, this situation did exist to a large extent with "the bonds ordinarily held in such proportions as to result in complete exemption." [73]

Subscriptions to the Fourth Loan totaled $6,959,187,700, an oversubscription of 15 per cent. [74] While about 85 per cent of the subscriptions were for $50 and $100 bonds, these represented only 9.8 per cent of the bonds. [75] A total of 22,777,680 subscriptions was received, which was equal to 21.9 per cent of the population. [76]

The results of the Fourth Liberty Loan campaign showed a great participation by the low-income group in a numerical

Table 40
Subscriptions to the Fourth Liberty Loan

Amount	Number of Subscribers	Per Cent	Subscription	Per Cent
$50	13,468,440	59.13	$ 673,422,000	9.8
100	5,850,147	25.69	585,014,700	8.4
150–950	2,558,513	11.23	862,566,900	12.4
1,000–4,950	723,823	3.18	999,253,950	14.3
5,000–9,950	89,634	.39	481,794,700	6.9
10,000 and over	87,123	.38	3,357,135,450	48.2
Total	22,777,680	100.00	$6,959,187,700	100.0

Source: U.S. Treasury Department, *Annual Report, 1919*, p. 225.

sense, but not in the amount of bonds purchased. The bonds were still being sold primarily to the large subscribers who represented less than .4 per cent of the total subscribers and an infinitesimal part of the population.

The Victory Loan

By November 27, 1918 the proceeds from the Fourth Loan had been exhausted and the Treasury thought it wise to plan one last great popular loan campaign in the Spring.[77] The Treasury was told that there could be no further successful appeals to patriotism and that the problem must be approached in a "distinctly cold-blooded mood."[78] The Treasury did not agree that it was possible to float a large loan on a strictly commercial basis so soon after the others. The plan was to postpone the offering until the latest possible time in order to give the country time to recover from the "tremendous transactions" involved in the Fourth Liberty Loan, to permit the progress of readjustment to the utmost limit, and to afford the largest measure of preparation for the issue to be floated under such "unusual and untried conditions." Accordingly, Carter Glass, the new Secretary of the Treasury, wrote to Chairman Kitchin of the House Ways and Means Committee asking for greater leeway in matters of rates, maturities, and the timing of the loan. He asked for—[79]

1. An increase in the authorization of bonds from $20 billion to $25 billion.

2. The removal of the interest rate limit on bonds maturing in less than ten years.

3. Authorization of an issue not to exceed $10 billion of interest-bearing, noncirculating notes with maturities from one to five years.

4. Authorization of the payment of a premium at maturity on bonds and notes.

5. Exemption of the War Savings Certificates from income surtaxes.

6. Authority to determine the exemptions from taxation in respect to future issues of bonds and notes, and to enlarge the exemption of existing Liberty Bonds in the hands of new subscribers.

7. Extension of the conversion period of the 4 per cent bonds of the Second Liberty Loan.

8. Creation of the $2\frac{1}{2}$ per cent cumulative sinking fund for retirement of the war debt.

Glass based his need for a new bond issue on the fact that the floating debt on February 13, 1919 was almost $5 billion and increasing at the rate of $1.4 billion a month. He also estimated that expenditures for fiscal 1919 would exceed McAdoo's estimate of $18 billion. While the total authorization he asked for amounted to some $22 billion he desired a maximum authorization for all types of $10 billion, using any or all of the authorized types of debts.[80]

The House Ways and Means Committee was uncooperative in granting Glass the power to fix the interest rate on the new issue,[81] and the authority to determine the tax exemption on the new issue was also denied the new Secretary.[82] In the Senate, a Republican filibuster caused grave doubt that the Victory Loan would ever be passed. On March 2 the bill finally passed the Senate after the collapse of the filibuster which was marked by more than twenty hours of debate. Republican amendments which failed to pass were one by Senator Penrose to reduce the funds of the War Finance Corporation from $1 billion to $500 million, an amendment by Senator Sherman to reduce the short-term note authorization from $7 billion to $5 billion, and one by

Senator Kenyon proposing that a vignette of Theodore Roosevelt appear on the new securities.[83] The bill as finally passed by Congress gave Glass most of his demands. It provided for (a) an issue of one- to five-year notes up to $7 billion; (b) the terms and the interest rates were to be decided by the Treasury; (c) additional tax exemptions; (d) the conversion privilege granted to holders of the second issue 4's to convert into $4\frac{1}{4}$'s, which had expired on November 9, 1918, was revived, and a cumulative sinking fund was authorized equal to $2\frac{1}{2}$ per cent of the aggregate of Liberty and Victory Bonds outstanding on July 1, 1920 less the amount of foreign obligations held by the United States.[84] There were also additional provisions, one for further loans to foreign governments for a period of eighteen months after the war, another for conversion of short-term foreign obligations into long-term debt which was to mature not later than 1938.

On April 21, 1919 Glass offered $4.5 billion of three- to four-year $4\frac{3}{4}$ per cent notes, exempt from all taxes except estate, inheritance and normal income taxes. They were convertible into $3\frac{3}{4}$ per cent notes, which were exempt from the normal income tax as well as the surtax. At the time the government issues were all selling below par with the $3\frac{1}{2}$'s at about 99, and with the other issues between 93.10 and 96.10.[85] The reason for the short maturities was given by Glass in a public statement, "I believe that a short-term issue will maintain a price at about par after the campaign far more readily than would a longer term issue."[86] However, there was a far more serious reason for the short maturities of the Victory Bonds. There remained outstanding nearly $1.5 billion of $3\frac{1}{2}$'s which still retained the conversion privilege, while the 4's and $4\frac{1}{4}$'s could not be converted. By limiting the maturities of the Victory Loan to five years, the term "notes" could be used instead of "bonds" and the new issue would therefore become ineligible for conversion purposes for the $3\frac{1}{2}$'s. Thus the great obstacle to a higher interest rate and tax exemptions was done away with.

To further bolster the market price of the older issues, the same expedient was used as in the Fourth Loan. A tax exemption was allowed on the income from the old bonds of three times the amount of Victory notes purchased, but not to exceed $20,000.

The Victory Loan drive brought $5,249,908,300 in subscriptions from 11,803,095 subscribers. The oversubscription was 16.41 per cent, about the same as that of the Fourth Loan, but only 11.3 per cent of the population took part compared with 21.9 per cent in the Fourth Loan.[87] Sixty per cent of the subscriptions were for amounts of less than $10,000 and were allotted in full, while the remaining subscriptions were pro-rated.

Summary

Total authorizations of the five bond issues amounted to $27 billion, of which only $18.5 billion was officially offered for subscription. Subscriptions amounted to $24.1 billion, of which $21.4 billion was allotted.

Table 41
Summary of Liberty and Victory Loans
(millions of dollars)

Loan	Authorized	Offered	Subscribed	Allotted
First	$ 5,000.	$ 2,000.	$ 3,035.2	$ 2,000.
Second	4,500.	3,000.	4,617.5	3,808.8
Third	2,500.	3,000.*	4,176.5	4,176.5
Fourth	8,000.	6,000.	6,992.9	6,964.5
Fifth	7,000.	4,500.	5,249.9	4,498.3
Total	$27,000.	$18,500.	$24,072.1	$21,448.1

Note: Totals may not add up because of rounding.
*$500,000,000 represented unused portions of first two authorizations.

Table 42
Subscriptions Not Allotted from Each Loan

First	$1,035,226,850.
Second	808,766,150.
Third	– – – – –
Fourth	28,402,450.
Fifth	751,595,650.
Total	$2,623,991,100.

The Liberty and Victory Loans were issued at increasingly higher interest rates, combined in each case with some type of tax exemptions. Neither McAdoo's desire for a permanent interest rate nor his desire for an almost completely taxable issue was accomplished. The Treasury, in its eagerness to keep the interest rate low, was forced to grant tax concessions, instigate credit buying of bonds, and resort to the banking system for bond sales.

The average subscription to the five war issues was $445. This

Table 43
Subscribers and Subscriptions to the Five War Loans

Loan	Subscribers	Subscriptions	Average Subscription
First	4,000,000	$ 3,035,226,850	$759
Second	9,400,000	4,617,532,300	491
Third	18,376,815	4,176,516,850	227
Fourth	22,777,680	6,959,187,700	305
Fifth	11,803,895	5,249,908,300	445
Total	66,358,390	$24,038,372,000	$445

figure in itself leads to no conclusion as to the income groups participating in the bond purchases. However, an examination of the denominations of the outstanding war bonds shows that of the $19.4 billion outstanding on June 30, 1920, only $3.9 billion, or 20 per cent, was in the denomination of $50 and $100 representing the low-income bracket. There is also the probability that many of the larger purchases were in the smaller denominations. Many corporations, such as the U.S. Steel Corporation, American Woolen Company, E. W. Bliss Corporation, and Union Bag and Paper Company, purchased large quantities of bonds which were later used for dividend payments to shareholders.[88] U.S. Steel Corporation took $128 million of the four Liberty Loans,[89] with the total corporate subscriptions probably extending to many times that amount. This tended to adjust the percentage of the smaller denomination bonds purchased and held by the low-income group to somewhat less than 20 per cent.

Table 44
Liberty Bonds and Victory Notes Outstanding, June 30, 1920

Denomination	Number of Pieces	Amount
$ 50	30,456,794	$ 1,522,839,700
100	23,436,472	2,343,647,200
500	3,611,476	1,805,738,000
1,000	8,028,471	8,028,471,000
5,000	279,972	1,399,860,000
10,000	311,531	3,115,310,000
50,000	5,117	255,850,000
100,000	8,793	879,300,000
Total	66,138,626	$19,351,015,900

Source: U.S. Treasury Department, Annual Report, 1920, pp. 428–429.

This does not mean that the Treasury was defeated in its aim of selling to the low-income groups. On the contrary, the 54 million $50 and $100 bonds, even after being subjected to an adjustment for larger purchases in small denominations, represented a notable achievement in bond selling to a population unversed in the techniques of finance, and not particularly noted for saving propensities.

However, the fact remains that the bond sales making up the bulk of the Treasury loan receipts were in amounts of $1,000 and higher, with the $1,000 bond being the most popular. This represents the purchases of the middle-income groups, the upper-income group, and banking and other institutions.

NOTES

[1] William G. McAdoo *Crowded Years*, pp. 380–381.
[2] U.S. Treasury Department, *Annual Report, 1917*, p. 1.
[3] *Ibid.*, p. 3.
[4] *Ibid.*
[5] *Ibid.*, p. 4.
[6] *Ibid.*, p. 2.
[7] *Commercial and Financial Chronicle*, Monthly Reviews, 1917–1920.
[8] *New York Times*, April 6, 1917, p. 2.
[9] *Ibid.*, April 7, 1917, p. 14.
[10] *Commercial and Financial Chronicle*, April 7, 1917, p. 1339.
[11] McAdoo, *Crowded Years*, pp. 383–384.
[12] *Commercial and Financial Chronicle*, April 7, 1917, p. 1333.
[13] McAdoo, *Crowded Years*, p. 382.
[14] *Ibid.*, p. 382.
[15] *Ibid.*
[16] *Ibid.*, p. 381.
[17] U.S. Treasury Department, *Annual Report, 1917*, p. 4.
[18] *Congressional Record*, 65:1, p. 759.
[19] *Ibid.*, p. 628.
[20] *Ibid.*, p. 679.
[21] *New York Times*, May 23, 1917, p. 3.
[22] *Ibid.*, p. 22.
[23] *40 U.S. Statutes at Large.*
[24] *Commercial and Financial Chronicle*, June 1917, p. 14. *New York Times*, May 3, 1917, p. 1; May 10, 1917, p. 1.
[25] *Commercial and Financial Chronicle*, Monthly Review, June 1917;

Frederick R. Macaulay, *Movements of Interest Rates, Bond Yields and Stock Prices.*

[26] U.S. Treasury Department, *Annual Report, 1917*, p. 8.

[27] *Commercial and Financial Chronicle*, July 1917, pp. 13–14.

[28] U.S. Treasury Department, *Annual Report, 1917*, p. 7.

[29] *Commercial and Financial Chronicle*, July 14, 1917, p. 129.

[30] E. R. A. Seligman, "On Fiscal Policy," in *Financial Mobilization for War*, Western Economic Society, pp. 1–12.

[31] Federal Reserve Board, *Annual Report, 1917*, p. 15.

[32] *Commercial and Financial Chronicle*, August 18, 1917, p. 657.

[33] *Ibid.*, August 25, 1917, p. 764.

[34] *Ibid.*

[35] *Ibid.*, September 1, 1917, p. 863.

[36] *Ibid.*, September 8, 1917, p. 946.

[37] Act of September 24, 1917, *40 U.S. Statutes at Large.*

[38] Senate Finance Committee, *Hearings and Brief on H. R. 4280, an Act to Provide Revenue to Defray War Expenses and for Other Purposes*, 65:1.

[39] *Ibid.*

[40] *Ibid.*, p. 10–11.

[41] *Ibid.*

[42] *Commercial and Financial Chronicle*, September 29, 1917, pp. 1254–1255.

[43] *Ibid.*, October 20, 1917, p. 1577.

[44] *Ibid.*, p. 1576.

[45] *Ibid.*, p. 1575.

[46] *Ibid.*, p. 1580.

[47] *Ibid.*, October 26, 1917, p. 1; October 27, 1917, p. 1; October 28, 1917, p. 1.

[48] U.S. Treasury Department, *Annual Report, 1917*, pp. 10–11.

[49] *Senate Finance Committee*, Hearings 65: 1, pp. 7, 12.

[50] U.S. Treasury Department, *Annual Report, 1918*, p. 5.

[51] *Ibid.*, *1917*, p. 61; *1920*, pp. 284–287.

[52] *Ibid.*, *1920*, pp. 772–775.

[53] *Ibid.*, *1918*, p. 5.

[54] *Commercial and Financial Chronicle*, Monthly Review, April 1917.

[55] U.S. Treasury Department, *Annual Report, 1918*, p. 6.

[56] *Ibid.*

[57] *Commercial and Financial Chronicle*, March 30, 1918, p. 1292.

[58] U.S. Treasury Department, *Annual Report, 1918*, p. 6; *Congressional Record*, Vol. 56, pp. 4315, 4322–4323.

[59] *New York Times*, December 18, 1917, pp. 10, 13.

[60] *Ibid.*, February 9, 1918, p. 2.

[61] U.S. Treasury Department, *Annual Report, 1918*, p. 7.

[62] *Ibid.*, pp. 73–74.

[63] *Commercial and Financial Chronicle*, March 30, 1918, pp. 1294–1295.

[64] U.S. Treasury Department, *Annual Report, 1918*, pp. 5–7.

[65] *Ibid.*, *1920*, pp. 772–775.

[66] *Ibid.*, pp. 284–287.

[67] *Ibid.*, *1918*, pp. 14–17.

[68] *Commercial and Financial Chronicle*, July–December 1918.

[69] U.S. Treasury Department, *Annual Report, 1918*, pp. 15–16.

[70] *Ibid.*, p. 16.

[71] *Ibid.*, pp. 17, 19.

[72] *Ibid.*, pp. 175–177.

[73] Robert A. Love, *Federal Financing*, p. 180.

[74] U.S. Treasury Department, *Annual Report, 1919*, p. 225.

[75] *Ibid.*, p. 31, p. 225.

[76] *Ibid.*, p. 225.

[77] *Ibid.*, pp. 56–57.

[78] *Ibid.*, p. 33.

[79] *Ibid.*, pp. 34–35.

[80] *Ibid.*, pp. 35–44.

[81] *New York Times*, February 14, 1919, p. 13.

[82] *Ibid.*, February 19, 1919, p. 1.

[83] *Commercial and Financial Chronicle*, March 8, 1919, p. 919.

[84] U.S. Treasury Department, *Annual Report, 1919*, pp. 44, 235–240.

[85] *Commercial and Financial Chronicle*, May 1919.

[86] U.S. Treasury Department, *Annual Report, 1919*, pp. 45–46.

[87] *Ibid.*, p. 52.

[88] Alexander D. Noyes, *The War Period of American Finance, 1908–1925*, p. 189; *New York Times*, September 28, 1916, p. 16.

[89] U.S. Steel Corporation, *Annual Report, 1918*, p. 34.

10

Treasury Certificates of Indebtedness

The funds for war purposes were to only a limited extent obtained in advance of disbursements. When war was declared in April 1917 the Treasury was without a sufficiently adequate source of income to meet the rapidly increasing monthly disbursements, and quickly turned to short-term borrowing. This policy continued throughout the war period and was of such magnitude that the major achievement of the Liberty and Victory Loans was the funding of the short-term debt.

The use of short-term debt certificates during periods of war was not unknown in American finance. Certificates of indebtedness had been used during the War of 1812, the Mexican War, and the Civil War, and a provision for their issue had been enacted by the Spanish War Revenue Act. They had also been used during the crises of 1837, 1857 and 1907. The Payne-Aldrich Tariff Act had re-enacted the certificate of indebtedness provision of the Spanish War Revenue Act and imposed a limitation of $200 million as the maximum amount allowable to be outstanding at any one time. The Revenue Act of March 3, 1917 empowered the Secretary of the Treasury to borrow from time to time "such sum or sums as, in his judgment, may be necessary to meet public expenditures, and to issue therefore certificates of indebtedness in such form and in such denominations as he may describe."[1] The rate of interest to be paid was not to exceed

Table 45
Treasury Certificates of Indebtedness, March 1917-July 1919
(thousands of dollars)

Series	Date of Issue	Interest Rate (per cent)	Maturity	Amount (000)
1	1917, March 31	2	1917, June 29 $	50,000.
2	April 25	3	June 30	268,205.
3	May 10	3	July 17	200,000.
4	May 25	$3\frac{1}{4}$	July 30	200,000.
5	June 8	$3\frac{1}{4}$	July 30	200,000.
6	August 9	$3\frac{1}{2}$	November 15	300.000.
7	August 28	$3\frac{1}{2}$	November 30	250,000.
8	September 17	$3\frac{1}{2}$	December 15	300,000.
9	September 26	4	December 15	400,000.
10	October 18	4	November 22	385,197.
11	October 24	4	December 15	685,296.
12	November 30	4	1918, June 25	691,872.
13	1918, January 2	4	June 25	491,822.5
14	January 22	4	April 22	400,000.
15	February 8	4	May 9	500,000.
16	February 15	4	June 25	74,100.
17	February 27	$4\frac{1}{2}$	May 28	500,000.
18	March 15	4	June 25	110,962.
19	March 20	$4\frac{1}{2}$	June 18	543,032.5
20	April 10	$4\frac{1}{2}$	July 9	551,226.5
21	April 15	4	June 25	71,880.

Table 45

(continued)

Series	Date of Issue	Interest Rate (per cent)	Maturity	Amount (000)
22	April 22	$4\frac{1}{2}$	July 18	517,826.5
23	May 15	4	June 25	183,767.
24	June 25	$4\frac{1}{2}$	October 24	839,646.5
25	July 9	$4\frac{1}{2}$	November 17	759,938.
26	July 23	$4\frac{1}{2}$	November 21	584,750.5
27	August 6	$4\frac{1}{2}$	December 5	575,706.5
28	August 20	4	1919, July 5	157,552.5
29	September 3	$4\frac{1}{2}$	January 2	639,493.
30	September 17	$4\frac{1}{2}$	January 16	625,216.5
31	October 1	$4\frac{1}{2}$	January 30	641,069.
32	November 7	$4\frac{1}{2}$	March 15	794,172.5
33	December 5	$4\frac{1}{2}$	May 6	613,438.
34	December 19	$4\frac{1}{2}$	May 20	572,494.
35	1919, January 2	$4\frac{1}{2}$	June 3	751,684.5
36	January 16	$4\frac{1}{2}$	June 17	392,381.
37	January 16	$4\frac{1}{2}$	June 17	600,101.5
38	January 30	$4\frac{1}{2}$	July 1	687,381.5
39	February 13	$4\frac{1}{2}$	July 15	620,578.5
40	February 27	$4\frac{1}{2}$	July 29	532,381.5
41	March 13	$4\frac{1}{2}$	August 12	542,197.
42	March 15	$4\frac{1}{2}$	June 16	407,918.5
43	April 10	$4\frac{1}{2}$	September 9	646,025.
44	May 1	$4\frac{1}{2}$	October 7	591,308.
45	June 3	$4\frac{1}{2}$	September 15	526,918.5
46	June 3	$4\frac{1}{2}$	December 15	238,711.5
47	July 1	$4\frac{1}{2}$	September 15	326,468.
48	July 1	$4\frac{1}{2}$	December 15	511,444.
Total				$21,954,163.

Source: U.S. Treasury Department, *Annual Report, 1920*, pp. 284–287.

3 per cent, the maturity was not to exceed one year, and the sum outstanding at any one time was extended to $300 million, an increase of $100 million in allowable outstanding certificates. Between March 31, 1917 and July 1, 1919 the Treasury issued 48 series of certificates totaling $21,954,163.

The Treasury announced at an early date its intention of making use of this method of financing. In anticipation of the income taxes due in June 1917, the Treasury on March 27, 1917 borrowed $50 million directly from the twelve Federal Reserve banks by an issue of 2 per cent, 90-day certificates. The total amount subscribed was $66.6 million, of which $50 million was actually allotted.[2] These certificates were held as investments by the Reserve banks until maturity, so that the certificates effectively increased the money supply by $50 million. McAdoo called this inflationary move "an additional demonstration of the usefulness of the new Reserve System to the country."[3]

The report of the Ways and Means Committee on the First Liberty Loan Bill set forth that "in view of the fact that a very large portion of the taxes now levied and proposed to be levied at a future date will be payable yearly, and therefore will not be capable of yielding a continuing flow of revenue into the Treasury, your committee deems it advisable to recommend the authorization of the issuance of $2 billion worth of certificates of indebtedness, payable within one year, to the end that the Treasury may at all times have ample means of securing funds to meet the immediate needs of the Government." On April 20, 1917 McAdoo announced his intention of using this authorization as soon as the bill became a law.[4]

First Liberty Loan Anticipation Certificates

Under the provisions of the First Liberty Loan Act, the Secretary of the Treasury was empowered to borrow up to $2 billion by the issuance of certificates of indebtedness bearing not more than $3\frac{1}{2}$ per cent interest, and maturing in one year or less. The certificates were exempt from all taxation except estate and inheritance taxes. Unlike the issue of March 27, the Federal Reserve banks were not to absorb these certificates directly but were to act as distributors in placing the certificates among member banks and trust companies in their districts. The banks were urged to use the certificates in payment of Liberty Loan subscriptions for themselves and their customers.[5]

Between April 25 and June 8, the Treasury issued four series of certificates in anticipation of the First Loan proceeds. The first issue was for $268 million and the remaining three for $200 million each, for a total of $868 million. The issue of April 25 was originally intended to carry a $2\frac{1}{2}$ per cent rate but was raised to 3 per cent in order to achieve a wider market.[6] The interest rate was increased to $3\frac{1}{4}$ per cent with the third issue (May 25), and was further increased in later issues up to $4\frac{1}{2}$ per cent. The certificates were offered to financial institutions through the facilities of the Federal Reserve banks. Of the $268 million raised by the April 25 issue, $200 million was lent to Great Britain in exchange for a 3 per cent note. This lowered the borrowing rate for that country which had been borrowing at $4\frac{1}{2}$ to 5 per cent. The maturities for the four issues were sixty days each with the exception of the fourth (June 8) issue which had an even shorter maturity. With such short maturities, the certificates were more like the current Treasury bills.

The Treasury considered the cash payments for the certificates an excellent method of meeting the requirements for a steady flow of funds to cover government obligations. When the certificates were used to pay for bond subscriptions the result was the equivalent of steady payment and application of funds without the heavy impact on the money market that would have been caused by the drawing off of large amounts of funds at unexpected periodic intervals.[7]

The total amount of the first four issues in anticipation of the

First Liberty Loan was $868,205,000. equal to 43.4 per cent of the receipts from the loan. This amount remained outstanding until June 30 when the issue of April 25 matured, leaving $600 million outstanding. By July 30 the receipts from the First Liberty Loan enabled the Treasury to pay off the outstanding certificates and free itself from certificate indebtedness. However, this situation lasted only a few days and was never repeated during the war period.

Second Liberty Loan Anticipation Certificates

On July 31 McAdoo again authorized the Federal Reserve banks to receive subscriptions for certificates. A total of $300 million was offered at $3\frac{1}{2}$ per cent, $\frac{1}{4}$ per cent higher than the rate of the last three issues, $\frac{1}{2}$ per cent higher than the issue of April 25th, and the same rate as that of the First Liberty Loan. Subscriptions closed on August 7, with the certificates to mature on November 15. McAdoo, in announcing the new issue of certificates, described them as convertible into any bonds "offered for subscription by the United States hereafter and before the maturity of the certificates."[8]

On August 18 McAdoo announced a new offering of $250 million, with subscriptions to be received until August 25. The interest rate was continued at $3\frac{1}{2}$ per cent. The intention of the Treasury regarding future issues of certificates was contained in a statement accompanying the announcement: "It is expected that certificates of indebtedness will be issued from time to time somewhat in advance of the immediate requirements of the United States. The primary object of this is to avoid the financial stress which would result from the concentration of the payments for a great bond issue upon a single day (which cannot be avoided wholly by provision for payment by installments as a great proportion of subscribers prefer to make payment in full on one day as a matter of convenience)."[9]

Although this was the stated purpose of the certificate borrowing, it is probable that the provision for funds could not have been delayed much longer. The last two installments of the First Liberty Loan were not due until August 15 and 30 respectively. Assuming the last two Liberty Loan installments unpaid, and 43.4 per cent of the loan paid for by certificates, Treasury cash receipts up to August 15 from the First Loan were completely nonexistent. With an ordinary deficit of $466 million in July and August, 1917, it is evident that the Treasury was hardpressed for cash.

The Second Liberty Loan Act contained three provisions pertaining to the certificates of indebtedness:[10]

(a) The maximum limit on the interest rate was removed.

(b) The total amount allowable to be outstanding at any one time was increased from $2 billion to $4 billion.

(c) The tax exemption provisions of new certificates were to be the same as those of the Second Liberty Bonds.

In the period prior to the receipt of the Second Liberty Loan proceeds, the Treasury sold a total of six issues of certificates, three under the authority of the First Loan Act and three under the authority of the Second Loan Act. The latter three issues bore a 4 per cent interest rate, $\frac{1}{2}$ per cent higher than the rate on the first three issues, so as to conform with the interest rate on the second bond issue. Total proceeds of the Second Loan anticipation certificates amounted to $2,320.5 million, equal to 61 per cent of the proceeds of the loan. They were all acceptable at par and interest if tendered in payment of the first installment on the Second Loan, and each issue was subject to redemption as a whole upon ten days notice on or after the date set for payment of the first installment of the loan. Payment for subscriptions to the August 9 issue was made by the subscribing banks to the Federal Reserve banks in cash and the proceeds were redeposited with those subscribing banks duly qualified to act as government depositories. After the August 9 issue the Treasury adopted the device of permissive payment by credit, whereby the subscribing depository banks made payment by merely crediting the account of the Treasurer of the United States. Since the reserve requirements did not apply to government deposits, the transaction was no different in its effects from that of printing paper money except that the Treasury had to pay interest. This device was put into effect by the Treasury without Congressional discussion or public notification. The Treasury announcement on the issue of August 28, 1917, made no mention of payment by credit nor did the Federal Reserve Board.[11] The proceeds of the certificates were used to meet immediate needs, to anticipate receipts, and to extend credit to foreign nations.[12]

Certificates in Anticipation of 1918 Tax Receipts

In November 1917 the Treasury resumed the sale of certificates, this time in anticipation of the proceeds of the war income and excess profits taxes payable in June 1918. The authorization for this was contained in Section 1010 of the War Revenue Act of October 3, 1917, which gave collectors the authority to receive certificates of indebtedness in payment of income and excess profits taxes.

The purpose of this tax-exemption issue was "to relieve any possible congestion or disturbance of the money market such as might be caused by the payment of taxes due between June 15 and June 25, estimated to amount to over $2 billion."[13] On November 20 the Treasury gave notice that subscriptions would be received through the Federal Reserve banks for a limited amount of 4 per cent Treasury certificates of indebtedness dated November 30, 1917, and to mature June 25, 1918. The certificates were receivable at par and accrued interest at or before maturity in payment of income or excess profits taxes, but were not receivable in payment of Liberty bonds or for bond subscriptions. The tax exemptions were the same as those of the outstanding issues. A further advantage was a ruling by the Commissioner of Internal Revenue which permitted certificates of indebtedness to be included in "invested capital" in the calculation of the excess profits tax.[14] On November 30, when the books were closed, subscriptions amounted to $691,872,000.

Maturing certificates on December 15, 1917 amounted to $1,385,296,000, but the Treasury did not have the funds to meet these payments. Between January 2 and May 15, 1918, five series of tax-anticipation certificates were sold for a total of $1,624,403,500. All series carried an interest rate of 4 per cent and were to mature on June 25, 1918. The sale of these issues was not too successful with the exception of the issue of January 2. The proceeds of the 1918 tax anticipation issues amounted to only 57 per cent of the $2,839 million yield of the 1918 income and excess profits taxes in fiscal 1918.

Third Liberty Loan Anticipation Certificates

In January 1918 further certificates were sold in anticipation of a Third Liberty Loan which was not yet formally authorized. On January 17 the Treasury authorized a $400 million issue dated January 22, maturing on April 22, and bearing a 4 per cent interest rate. Three weeks later the Treasury announced a formal plan for borrowing in anticipation of the Third Liberty Loan, the actual sale of which it was deemed best to postpone "until conditions will insure a wide distribution of the bonds throughout the country."[15]

The new plan called for changes in the method of issuing certificates, and in the method of selling. Instead of issues at irregular intervals and different amounts, it was proposed to offer regularly every two weeks, beginning February 8, 1918, six issues of $500 million each of not more than 90-day maturities. The certificates would still be distributed through the Federal Reserve banks to the banking system for their own behalf and for their customers. Instead of optional subscriptions, the Treasury urged uniform proportionate subscriptions from every national bank, state bank, and trust company at 1 per cent of its gross resources weekly. The total resources of the 25,180 commercial banks and trust companies on June 20, 1917, was $30.8 billion so that about $600 million would be subscribed every two weeks for the certificates.[16]

The first issue under this plan was offered on February 6, 1918, $500 million of 4 per cent, three-month certificates. The Treasury also appealed to each bank individually, stressing the patriotic duty of the banks to subscribe to the certificates. "If each bank will do its share... approximately $3 billion will be raised between now and the next Liberty Loan."[17] While the number of subscriptions greatly exceeded the number subscribing to the January 22 issue, the subscriptions were only $100 million larger. Only two districts, New York and Kansas City, exceeded their allotments.[18]

With the next issue the Treasury increased its efforts. The quotas were modified; the minimum denomination was lowered from $1,000 to $500; and upon the advice of the Federal Advisory Committee the interest rate was increased to $4\frac{1}{2}$ per cent.[19] The banks were assured that there would be no further increases in the interest rate in connection with the Third Liberty Loan anticipation certificates, and patriotism was again emphasized in the Treasury announcements.[20] Three more issues were offered, dated March 20, April 10, and April 22. The April 22 issue was partly a refunding of the January 22 issue due on that date.

Total sales of the six issues amounted to $3,012,085,500,

which was equal to 72.1 per cent of the proceeds from the Third Liberty Loan. This compared to a 60.9 per cent ratio in connection with the Second Loan and 43.4 per cent in connection with the First Loan.

Fourth Liberty Loan Anticipation Certificates

The Act of April 4, 1918 increased the allowable outstanding certificates from $4 billion to $8 billion. There was also an attempt to obtain foreign lenders by the provision that certificates might be issued payable in foreign exchange and that foreign depositories could be used for the receipt of the proceeds.

The Treasury resumed its sale of certificates almost immediately after the sale of the Third Liberty Loan. An announcement was made that the Treasury needs would require the sale of about $6 billion of certificates up to November 1, 1918. It was anticipated that $750 million of certificates would be issued every two weeks, of different maturities not exceeding four months. A change was also made from the policy of moral suasion characteristic of the Third Loan certificates to a policy of almost compulsion. The Federal Reserve banks were to advise all banks and trust companies in each district of the amount of certificates they were expected to subscribe to, estimated at about 5 per cent of banks' resources per month.[21]

In its operation, the program underwent some changes. A total of seven issues were sold with the last one offered on October 1 instead of November 30 as originally contemplated. Only the first two issues were in the amounts of $750 million. The fifth and sixth issues were in the amount of $600 million, and the other three issues were for $500 million.

Total allotments for the seven issues were $4,665,820,000 equal to 67 per cent of the Fourth Liberty Loan proceeds. All the issues carried a $4\frac{1}{2}$ per cent interest rate, which was $\frac{1}{4}$ per cent larger than the rate on the Fourth Liberty Loan.

1919 Tax-Anticipation Certificates

On August 16, 1918 the Treasury offered the first of the eight issues in the "tax series of 1919" certificates. The issue was dated August 20, carried an interest rate of 4 per cent, and was to mature on July 5, 1919. Up to August 30, Fourth Liberty Loan anticipation certificates were made acceptable for payment for the tax certificates. To the extent that the loan certificates were tendered in payment for the tax certificates it was a refunding operation.

Sales of this issue were lower than those of any other since the issue of April 15. Between August 16 and November 6 only $157,552,500 was sold. With loan-anticipation certificates at $4\frac{1}{2}$ per cent and 60- to 90-day paper at 6 per cent,[22] a 4 per cent issue was pushing patriotism to the wall. On November 7 a $4\frac{1}{2}$ per cent issue was offered to mature on March 15, 1919. This issue sold $794,172,500. Six more issues were sold between January 16, 1919 and July 1, 1919, all bearing a $4\frac{1}{2}$ per cent interest rate and maturing at different intervals between June 17, 1919, and December 15, 1919.

The eight tax-anticipation issues brought $3,116,855,000 to the Treasury. Of this amount $2,278,943,000 was received during fiscal 1919 and the remainder in fiscal 1920. The 1919 tax certificates were equal to 87.6 per cent of the 1919 receipts of $2,601 million from income and profits taxes.

Victory Loan Anticipation Certificates

On November 27, 1918 the proceeds of the Fourth Liberty Loan were exhausted.[23] A new series of $4\frac{1}{2}$ per cent certificates was planned, the first of which was to be dated December 5, 1918, with similar issues to be offered every two weeks. Each issue would be between $500 and $750 million and the Federal

Reserve banks were to notify each bank in the district of the amount of certificates they were expected to take. The allotment to each bank was estimated at approximately 5 per cent a month of the gross resources of the bank.[24]

Between December 5, 1918 and May 1, 1919, ten series of certificates were issued in anticipation of the Victory Loan. Each issue bore a $4\frac{1}{2}$ per cent interest rate and a five-month maturity. Each issue brought in proceeds of well over $500 million with the ten issues totaling $6,157,589,500. Since outstanding anticipation certificates exceeded the proceeds of the Victory Loan by $1,659.3 million or 36.8 per cent, the loan proceeds were not sufficient to retire the certificates when they matured, and some issues had to be refunded.[25]

Summary

Early in the war McAdoo stated that he favored the liberal use of certificates to ease the strain on the banking system.[26] This policy was not only carried out to the letter, but was viewed by the Treasury as a major accomplishment in the financial program. Commenting on the certificate issues, the Treasury, in 1919, gave its opinion:

> This means of temporary financing has provided the government with funds in advance of receipts from the sales of bonds or notes or in anticipation of revenue from income and profits taxes, and has served the additional helpful purpose of distributing the payments of bond and note subscriptions and of taxes gradually over extended periods of time, avoiding tremendous transfers of funds on any one date and consequent money stringency.[27]

Nowhere in this statement is any sign of regret that the Treasury was forced to resort to short-term borrowing. There is neither an indication of the size of the certificate issues, nor an indication of the fact that they were largely bought by the banking system, adding still more fuel to the inflationary fire.

From March 31, 1917 until July 1, 1919 the Treasury borrowed $21,815,451,500 through the issue of tax and loan certificates. Of this amount, $17 billion was in anticipation of loan proceeds of $21.4 billion, so that 79.4 per cent of the loan proceeds were used to refund the certificates.

As summarized in Tables 46 and 47, the sales of anticipation certificates increased both in amount and in the ratio of certificates to bond sales. From $868 million in anticipation of the First Loan the amount increased to $6,158 million in anticipation of the Victory Loan. The percentage of certificate sales to loan sales increased from 43.4 per cent for the First Loan to 136.8 per cent for the Victory Loan.

The interest rate went from 3 per cent on the April 25, 1917

Table 46
Treasury Certificates Sold in Anticipation of Loan and Tax
Receipts, 1917–1919
(thousands of dollars)

In Anticipation of	Series*	Amount (000)
First Liberty Loan	2,3,4,5	$ 868,205.
Second Liberty Loan	6,7,8,9,10,11	2,320,493.
Third Liberty Loan	14,15,17,19,20,22	3,012,085.5
Fourth Liberty Loan	24,25,26,27,29,30,31	4,665,820.
Victory Loan	33,34,35,37,38,39,40, 41,43,44	6,157,589.5
1917 Tax receipts	1	50,000.
1918 Tax receipts	12,13,16,18,21,23	1,624,403.5
1919 Tax receipts	28,32,36,42,45,46,47,48	3,116,855.
Total		$21,815,451.5

Source: U.S. Treasury Department, *Annual Report, 1920*, p. 287.
* See Table 45.

Table 47
Ratio of Anticipation Certificates to Liberty
and Victory Loan Receipts
(millions of dollars)

Source	(a) Receipts	(b) Certificates	Ratio (b) to (a)
First Liberty Loan	$ 2,000.	$ 868.2	.434
Second Liberty Loan	3,808.8	2,320.5	.609
Third Liberty Loan	4,176.5	3,012.1	.721
Fourth Liberty Loan	6,964.5	4,665.8	.670
Victory Loan	4,498.3	6,157.6	1.368
Total Loans	$21,448.1	$17,024.2	.794

Source: Tables 41 and 46.

issue to $4\frac{1}{2}$ per cent starting on February 27, 1918. The interest rate was increased for two reasons: (a) to have the certificates carry the same rate of interest as the loans they anticipated, and (b) to secure a wider distribution of the certificates. Even the $4\frac{1}{2}$ per cent rate was lower than market rates on prime four- to six-month commercial paper which ranged between $5\frac{1}{8}$ and 6 per cent from June 1917 to July 1919.[28]

Of the two types of certificates offered by the Treasury, there was less difficulty in selling the loan certificates compared with the difficulty in selling the tax certificates. Some definite comparisons will illustrate this difference. On February 8, 1918 the Treasury sold $500 million of loan certificates at 4 per cent while one week later a 4 per cent tax certificate issue brought in only $74 million. On January 16, 1919 both loan and tax certificates were offered at the same interest rate. The tax certificate sales amounted to $392 million while the loan certificate sales brought in $600 million. On March 13, 1919 the proceeds of a loan certificate issue was $542 million while the proceeds of a tax-certificate issue two days later were $408 million. The reason for the comparative ease of selling the loan certificates was two-fold. First was the moral suasion instituted by the Treasury upon member banks through the Federal Reserve banks. Second was the obvious fact that the purchase of government obligations required no sacrifice of reserves on the part of the member bank. The result was that the certificates of indebtedness were mostly in the hands of the banking system.

Of the forty-eight issues of certificates, the first was the only one sold directly to the Reserve banks. The subsequent issues were sold through the Reserve banks to member and nonmember banks, trust companies, individuals and other nonbank investors. Although the Treasury endeavored through patriotic appeals to sell the certificates to nonbank investors, it was not successful. Neither increased interest rates nor patriotic exhortations could bring about this desired result so long as the certificate interest rate still remained below the market rate for similar investments.

A breakdown of subscriptions to the certificates issued in anticipation of the Third and Fourth Liberty Loans in terms of the type of subscribers shows that of a total of $7.6 billion of subscriptions, only $1.3 billion or 17 per cent came from non-bank subscribers,[29] these of course being large individual and corporate investors. $2.9 billion or 38 per cent was subscribed in the New York district, $957 million or 12.6 per cent in the Chicago district, with the remaining 49.4 per cent subscribed in the other ten districts. National banks subscribed for $4.3 billion representing 56 per cent of total subscriptions, while all other banks and trust companies subscribed for 27 per cent.[30]

This situation did not change materially during the postwar period. In December 1919 the Federal Reserve Board reported that the Treasury certificates of indebtedness were "held largely by banks."[31] In 1920 the Treasury found it necessary to again increase interest rates on certificates in an attempt to secure their distribution among nonbank investors.

Table 48

Certificate Issues Sold and Maturing on the Same Day,
November 30, 1917–July 1, 1919

(thousands of dollars)

Date	Amount of Issue	Amount Maturing	Amount Refunding
November 30, 1917	$691,872.	$ 250,000.	$ 250,000.
April 22, 1918	517,826.5	400,000.	400,000.
June 25, 1918	839,646.5	1,624,403.5	839,646.5
July 9, 1918	759,938.	551,226.5	551,226.5
December 5, 1918	613,438.	575,706.5	575,706.5
January 2, 1919	751,684.5	639,493.	639,493.
January 16, 1919	992,482.5	625,216.5	625,216.5
January 30, 1919	687,381.5	641,069.	641,069.
March 15, 1919	407,918.5	794,172.5	407,918.5
June 3, 1919	765,630.	751,684.5	751,684.5
July 1, 1919	837,912.	687,381.5	687,381.5
Total			$6,369,342.5

Source: Table 45.

The great number of the issues and their short maturities were also of considerable financial embarrassment to the Treasury. Of the $21.9 billion of the certificates issued, $6.4 billion or 29 per cent was borrowed on the same day as a like amount matured. This amount was therefore merely an exchange of securities, which gave the Treasury no additional cash.

The short-term loan program, even more than the Liberty Bond program, caused an increase in the money supply. By all available indications the certificates were purchased for the most part by the banking system and were not redistributed to any large extent to nonbank investors.

NOTES

[1] *39 U.S. Statutes at Large*, p. 1000.
[2] *Commercial and Financial Chronicle*, March 31, 1917, p. 1209.
[3] *Federal Reserve Bulletin*, April 1917, p. 240.
[4] *Ibid.*, May 1917, p. 342.
[5] J. H. Hollander, *War Borrowing*, pp. 28–34.
[6] *Commercial and Financial Chronicle*, May 1917, pp. 14, 15.
[7] *Federal Reserve Bulletin*, June 1917, p. 424.
[8] *Commercial and Financial Chronicle*, August 4, 1917, p. 438.
[9] *Federal Reserve Bulletin*, September 1917, p. 664.
[10] U.S. Treasury Department, *Annual Report, 1917*, p. 13.
[11] *Federal Reserve Bulletin*, September 1917, pp. 651–652, 664.
[12] U.S. Treasury Department, *Annual Report, 1917*, p. 14.
[13] *Federal Reserve Bulletin*, December 1917, p. 918.
[14] *Commercial and Financial Chronicle*, December 22, 1917, 2405; December 29, 1917, p. 2497.
[15] *Federal Reserve Bulletin*, March 1918, p. 161.
[16] U.S. Treasury Department, Comptroller of the Currency, *Annual Report, 1917*, p. 108.
[17] *Federal Reserve Bulletin*, March 1918, p. 161.
[18] *Ibid.*; pp. 153–154, 162.
[19] Federal Reserve Board, *Annual Report, 1918*, p. 851.
[20] *Federal Reserve Bulletin*, March 1918, p. 162.
[21] *Commercial and Financial Chronicle*, June 22, 1918, p. 2607.
[22] *Ibid.*, November 1918.
[23] U.S. Treasury Department, *Annual Report, 1919*, p. 56.
[24] *Ibid.*, pp. 56–57.
[25] *Ibid.*, pp. 57–58.
[26] *New York Times*, April 27, 1917, p. 1.
[27] U.S. Treasury Department, *Annual Report, 1919*, p. 54.
[28] *Commercial and Financial Chronicle*, Monthly Reviews.
[29] Federal Reserve Board, *Annual Report, 1918*, pp. 207–208.
[30] *Ibid.*
[31] *Ibid., 1919*, p. 4.

I I

War Savings Certificates

Because certificate sales were scarcely noticed by the lower-income groups, and because the Liberty and Victory Loans were comparatively unsuccessful in separating them from their newly found purchasing power, the Treasury devised a third method of borrowing to accomplish this purpose.

In his recommendations to the House Ways and Means Committee concerning the Second Liberty Loan, McAdoo included a recommendation that $2 billion of War Savings Certificates be issued in a form available to small investors.[1] The original plan involved the sale of five-year bonds through the post offices and other agencies in denominations as low as $5. A bond could be purchased on the partial payment plan and would be worth $6 at maturity. To keep the bonds out of the hands of the large investors, it was proposed that individual holdings be limited to $1,000.[2]

The stated purposes of the War Savings Certificates were to "greatly encourage thrift and economy," and to provide that "every man, woman, and child, however small their means, may be given an opportunity to assist the Government in the financing of the War."[3] In a speech before the American Bankers Association in Atlantic City, New Jersey on September 28, 1917, McAdoo gave the outline of the plan as contained in the Second Liberty Bond Act.

The Treasury proposed to issue and sell War Savings Certificates in denominations as small as $5, maturing in five years "and upon such a reasonable plan that the humblest person in the land may be encouraged to save all that he can and to invest in an absolutely safe security bearing interest."[4] The value of the campaign for War Savings Certificates," said McAdoo, "is not alone in the amount of money that may be saved, but in teaching the people of the United States on a nationwide scale and through an intelligent presentation of the facts, the value of thrift and saving. Its beneficial effects ought to survive the war and have a permanent influence upon the future economy of the country."[5]

A War Savings Committee was set up under the chairmanship of Frank A. Vanderlip to organize a selling campaign for the war savings stamps. Other members of the committee were Frederic A. Delano of the Federal Reserve Board, Henry Ford of Detroit, Eugene Meyer, Jr. of New York, Mrs. George Bass of the Women's Liberty Loan Committee, and Charles L. Paine, Secretary and Treasurer of the Boot and Shoeworkers International Union. After consulting with Secretary McAdoo it was decided to delay the offering of the savings certificates so as not to compete with the Second Liberty Loan drive.[6] The plan was inaugurated on Monday, December 3, 1917, and the first issue of certificates was dated January 2, 1918, and was to mature on January 1, 1923.[7]

These obligations were evidenced by a war savings stamp costing from $4.12 to $4.23, depending on the month during which it was purchased. During December 1917 and January 1918 the savings stamps were sold at $4.12 each. At the beginning of each succeeding month the cost of a stamp increased one cent. With the first war stamp the purchaser received a War Savings Certificate containing spaces for twenty stamps. The interest rate on the stamps, if held to maturity, was 4 per cent per annum, compounded quarterly on the average price of stamps during 1918. A provision was made for those persons having certificates and needing cash which allowed them to turn in the stamps upon ten days written notice. After the required ten-day waiting period, they would receive the cost of each stamp plus one cent for each month the stamp was held.[8]

A further effort was made to tap the savings of those who could not afford even the $4.12 stamp. It was arranged that thrift stamps could be purchased for as little as 25 cents at any time at post offices, banks, trust companies, and at many other places where accredited persons acted as selling agents. The thrift stamps were affixed to cards which were supplied without cost to the buyer. When the card contained $4 in thrift stamps it could be turned in, together with the price difference, for a war savings stamp.[9] In this manner, the Treasury tapped the savings of school children and low-income groups.

The following year one important change took place in the war savings program. The amount of allowable individual holdings was changed from $1,000 in total to $1,000 of each year's issue.[10]

Under the direction of Frank A. Vanderlip and the National War Savings Committee, the gospel of thrift was slowly but steadily disseminated throughout the country. With the co-operation of the postal service and thousands of volunteers, the war savings program successfully accomplished what the Liberty Loans and certificate issues could not do — tap the savings of the low-income group directly into the Treasury. Up to October 31, 1918 there were 233,287 volunteer agents receiving no pay, and 151,361 war savings societies all working to make the savings program a success.[11]

In order to meet the demand for savings certificates in single

denominations larger than $5, the Treasury, in July 1919 an-
nounced the issue of two additional denominations. There was
a $100 maturity certificate selling for from $82.40 to $84.60,
and a $1,000 maturity certificate selling for from $824 to $846,
depending upon the month during which the certificates were
purchased. These were called Treasury Savings Certificates but
were still part of the 1919 series of War Savings Certificates and
subject to the provision that it was unlawful for any individual
to hold more than $1,000 in maturity value of any one series.
The Treasury Savings Certificates were registered in the Treasury, and it was provided that redemption was to be made by the
Treasury rather than through the post offices as were the $5
certificates. The new certificates could also be redeemed prior
to maturity if the holder needed cash, but not before the second
month following the purchase. The interest if held to maturity
equaled 4 per cent of the average issue price. If the certificate

Table 49
Issue Price of Treasury Savings Certificates per $100 Maturity

Month Purchased	Issue Price
January	$82.40
February	82.60
March	82.80
April	83.00
May	83.20
June	83.40
July	83.60
August	83.80
September	84.00
October	84.20
November	84.40
December	84.60

Source: U.S. Treasury Department, *Annual Report, 1919*, p. 296.

was turned in prior to maturity the holder received the purchase price plus twenty cents per $100 maturity for each month the certificate was held after the purchase was made.[12]

Monthly sales of War Savings Certificates increased rapidly, and from March 1918 to January 1919 were well over $50 million a month. The peak monthly sales occurred in July 1918, when $211.4 million was sold. After July 1918 sales declined somewhat and from February 1919 on they declined rapidly.

Unfortunately, redemptions of the savings certificates were heavy. Of the issue of 1918, 35 per cent were redeemed by September 30, 1920, and while redemptions of the other issues were not as large, total redemptions to September 30, 1920 amounted to $372.3 million or 31.7 per cent of total sales. Redemptions increased from year to year and were so great in

Table 50
Redemption Value per $100 Maturity Treasury
Savings Certificate Issued January 1919

Month	1919	1920	1921	1922	1923
January	$82.40	$84.80	$87.20	$89.60	S 92.00
February	82.60	85.00	87.40	89.80	92.20
March	82.80	85.20	87.60	90.00	92.40
April	83.00	85.40	87.80	90.20	92.60
May	83.20	85.60	88.00	90.40	92.80
June	83.40	85.80	88.20	90.60	93.00
July	83.60	86.00	88.40	90.80	93.20
August	83.80	86.20	88.60	91.00	93.40
September	84.00	86.40	88.80	91.20	93.60
October	84.20	86.60	89.00	91.40	93.80
November	84.40	86.80	89.20	91.60	94.00
December	84.60	87.00	89.40	91.80	94.20
January 1, 1924	—	—	—	—	100.00

Source: U.S. Treasury Department, *Annual Report, 1919*, p. 297.

Table 51
Cash Receipts from War Savings Certificates
(thousands of dollars)

Month	1917	1918	1919	1920
January		$ 24,559.7	$70,996.0	$ 8,987.5
February		41,148.2	15,816.5	5,221.2
March		53.967.9	10,143.1	6,063.4
April		60,973.0	9,572.7	4,815.4
May		57,956.6	6,558.2	3,553.0
June		58,250.5	5,269.5	3,107.9
July		211,417.9	5,176.9	2,359.3
August		129,044.2	6,201.2	2,231.5
September		97,614.6	6,111.9	1,814.7
October		89,084.1	7,316.5	1,889.8
November		73,689.8	8,020.4	—
December	$10,236.5	63,970.8	9,124.3	—
Total				$1,172,264.7

Source: U.S. Treasury Department, *Annual Report, 1920*, pp. 144–145.

Table 52
Sales and Redemptions of War Savings
Certificates to September 30, 1920
(thousands of dollars)

Series	(a) Sales	(b) Redemptions	Ratio of (b) to (a)
1918	$ 971,913.8	$340,333.6	.35
1919	160,307.2	27,602.4	.17
1920	40,043.7	4,351.3	.10
Total	$1,172,264.7	$372,287.3	.317

Source: (a) Table 50. (b) U.S. Treasury Department, *Annual Report, 1920*, p. 145.

Table 53

Sales and Redemptions of War Savings Bonds,

1918-1920

(millions of dollars)

Fiscal Year	*(a) Sales*	*(b) Certificates*	*Ratio of (b) to (a)*
1918	$ 352.8	$ 3.0	.008
1919	738.2	134.0	.18
1920	73.2	199.8	2.73
Total	$1,164.2	$336.8	.29

Source: U.S. Treasury Department, *Annual Reports, 1918–1920.*

fiscal 1920 that they exceeded sales by $126.6 million, being 2.73 times the amount of sales in that year.

Summary

The War Savings Certificates program was more successful than any of the other borrowing methods in diverting purchasing power from spenders to the government. The inability of the program to be fully effective was due to a case of "too little and too late."

The largest sales of savings certificates was made during the actual period of belligerency. The drop in sales was not a slow monthly process, but a sudden, sharp drop in February 1919. Had the program been inaugurated in April 1917 instead of December, there is ample reason to assume that at least $500 million more of the certificates could have been sold. This assumes an average monthly sale of about $60 million from April to December 1917, $21 million less per month than in 1918. The change in the maturities in July 1919 seems an indication that savings were finding their way into the war savings program, and that the very small investor had virtually left the field.

The case of redeeming the bonds before maturity also weakened the effectiveness of the program. The seriousness of debt redemption was greater with the savings certificates than with the other types of debt, since the repayment was made to the low-income group and was immediately transferred into demand for goods. This ease of redemption, combined with the late start of the program, reduced the deflationary effects obtained through the sale of War Savings Certificates.

NOTES

[1] *Commercial and Financial Chronicle,* August 25, 1917, p. 764.
[2] *Ibid.,* September 1, 1917, p. 863.
[3] U.S. Treasury Department, *Annual Report, 1917,* p. 19.
[4] William G. McAdoo, *The Second Liberty Loan,* p. 14.
[5] *Ibid.*
[6] *Commercial and Financial Chronicle,* September 29, 1917, pp. 1255–1256.
[7] U.S. Treasury Department, *Annual Report, 1917,* p. 19.
[8] *Ibid.,* pp. 19–20.
[9] *Ibid.,* p. 20.
[10] *Ibid., 1918,* p. 16.
[11] *Ibid.,* p. 32.
[12] *Treasury Department Circular,* Nos. 143, 149; U.S. Treasury Department, *Annual Report, 1919,* pp. 295–296, 302.

I 2

Conversions, Redemptions, and Retirements of the Liberty and Victory Loans

During the war period several changes took place which affected the amount of the debt and the structure of the interest rate. These changes were largely due to conversions and to retirements of part of the debt. Bonds of the First and Second Liberty Loans were both convertible into issues bearing a higher interest rate. The first issue had a perpetual conversion privilege, while the second had a limited conversion privilege which was later extended by a provision of the Victory Loan Bill.

Redemption and retirements of bonds were achieved through many methods, the most important of which was the 5 per cent bond purchase fund provided for in the Third Liberty Loan Bill. But in addition to the purchase fund, there were sinking-fund retirements, repayments of foreign loans, gifts, forfeitures, earnings of the Federal Reserve banks, and bonds accepted in payment of estate and inheritance taxes. Up to November 15, 1920 almost $2 billion was retired through these means.[1]

Conversions

Although the First Liberty Loan was convertible, its tax-exemption privilege was so attractive to most of the bondholders that there was a relatively small number of conversions into higher interest bonds in comparison with conversions of the Second Liberty Loan.

Total conversions of the First Loan, including reconversions of the 4's of 1932–1947, amounted to $579.4 million, equal to 29 per cent of the allotments of the First Loan. Conversions of the Second Loan amounted to $3.0 billion, which was equal to 79 per cent of allotments. The difference in the ratio of conversions to allotments of the respective bond issues evidenced the value of the tax exemption to the wealthier holders of the first bond issue.

The conversions changed 79 per cent of the Second Liberty Loan 4's into $4\frac{1}{4}$ per cent bonds, and 29 per cent of the first

Table 54

Conversions of First and Second Liberty Loans to June 30, 1919

First Liberty Loan	
Converted into 4's of 1932–1947	$ 170,449,300
Converted into $4\frac{1}{4}$'s of 1932–1947 *	408,935,200
Total First Liberty Loan converted	$ 579,384,500
Second Liberty Loan converted into $4\frac{1}{4}$'s of 1927–1942	$3,034,609,850
Total Conversions	$3,613,994,350

Source: U.S. Treasury Department, *Annual Report, 1919*, pp. 79–80.

*Includes $397,869,700 originally converted into 4's of 1932–1947 and later reconverted into $4\frac{1}{4}$'s of 1932–1947.

$3\frac{1}{2}$'s into 4's and $4\frac{1}{4}$'s. This increased the annual interest charge on the first issue by $4 million, and on the second issue by $9 million, for a total increase of $13 million in annual interest charges to the Treasury. The conversion of the bonds therefore nullified in part the supposed saving to the Treasury of the low interest rate.

Retirements

By the authority conferred upon it by Section 6 of the Act of April 4, 1918, the Treasury was empowered to purchase bonds in the open market in order to stabilize the open-market price. As a matter of practical convenience the services of the War Finance Corporation were utilized to carry out the bond purchase plan. Bonds were purchased by the corporation at the market price for its own account and were subsequently taken over by the Treasury at average cost and accrued interest.[2]

While the bond purchase plan did not succeed in maintaining a par market for the war bonds, it did enable the Treasury to

Table 55
Bonds Purchased under the Bond Purchase Plan to June 30, 1920
(thousands of dollars)

Issue	Par Value	Price Paid	Accrued Interest
First 4's and $4\frac{1}{4}$'s	$ 36,912.	$ 34,722.	$ 532.
Second 4's and $4\frac{1}{4}$'s	478,688.	452,359.	6,896.
Third $4\frac{1}{4}$'s	433,308.	414,068.	3,680.
Fourth $4\frac{1}{4}$'s	566,987.	530,548.	6,524.
Victory $3\frac{3}{4}$'s and $4\frac{3}{4}$'s	249,001.	245,869.	3,500.
Total	$1,764,896.	$1,677,566.	$21,132.

Source: U.S. Treasury Department, *Annual Report, 1920,* p. 109.

repurchase $1,765 million of bonds at a 5 per cent discount. The difference between the par value and the price paid for the bonds appeared as a miscellaneous receipt of the Treasury.[3]

As a result of repayments of foreign loans, the Treasury was able to repurchase $89 million of Third $4\frac{1}{4}$'s and $30 million of Fourth $4\frac{1}{4}$'s for which the Treasury paid $114.5 million. The $114.5 million was equal to 96 per cent of the par value of the bonds purchased.

Section 7 of the Federal Reserve Act as amended by the Act of March 3, 1919[4] provided that the Secretary of the Treasury could apply the earnings from the franchise tax on the Federal Reserve banks to the reduction of the outstanding bonded indebtedness. Under this authority the Treasury used the 1919 franchise tax receipts to repurchase $2.9 million par value of Second $4\frac{1}{4}$'s at a cost of $2.7 million. Since these transactions occurred in 1920 when the bond market was lower than it had been in the years 1917–1919, the Treasury was able to make these purchases at an average discount of 7 per cent.

The Third Liberty Loan provided that any bonds bearing an

Table 56
Liberty and Victory Issues Used in Payment of Estate
and Inheritance Taxes to November 15, 1920

Issue	Par Value
First $4\frac{1}{4}$'s	$ 163,200.
Second $4\frac{1}{4}$'s	2,577,650.
Third $4\frac{1}{4}$'s	4,091,250.
Fourth $4\frac{1}{4}$'s	2,931,550.
Victory $4\frac{3}{4}$'s	18,100.
Total	$9,781,750.

Source: U.S. Treasury Department, *Annual Report, 1920*, p. 113.

interest rate higher than 4 per cent and owned by a person six months prior to his death would be received by the United States at par plus accrued interest in payment of estate or inheritance taxes.[5] Under this provision, the Treasury received and retired $9,781,750 of bonds up to November 15, 1920.

In addition to the purchases and tenders in payment of taxes, small amounts were received by the Treasury as the result of gifts and on account of forfeitures of subscriptions. Gifts were in the par value of $12,850 and forfeitures amounted to $3,550.

The provision in the Victory Loan Act for a sinking fund caused the Treasury to repurchase $15 million par value of bonds between July and November, 1920.

The total retirements up to November 15, 1920 amounted to $1,912 million, equal to 8.9 per cent of the $21,448 million allotted. In addition to the $1,912 million, $40.3 million of bonds were owned by the War Finance Corporation on that

Table 57
**Bonds Retired on Account of Gifts and Forfeitures
to November 15, 1920**

Issue	Gifts	Forfeitures
First $3\frac{1}{2}$'s		$ 50.
First $4\frac{1}{4}$'s	$ 350.	50.
Second 4's	7,700.	—
Second $4\frac{1}{4}$'s	2,150.	—
Third $4\frac{1}{4}$'s	1,350.	700.
Fourth $4\frac{1}{4}$'s	1,350.	2,650.
Victory $4\frac{3}{4}$'s	—	100.
Total	$12,850.	$3,550.

Source: U.S. Treasury Department, *Annual Report, 1920*, p. 112.

date.[6] If these were considered as retirements, it would bring the total percentage of retirement up to 9 per cent.

Whether the Treasury retirements had any effect at all on the government bond market remains a moot point. Certainly the Treasury purchases did not succeed in maintaining the bonds at par, but there is the possibility that bond prices might have dropped lower without the purchase plan. However, up to 1920 the open-market purchases acted merely as a refunding operation, so long as the Treasury was running a deficit, for each bond purchase was made by the sale of another bond with the entire transaction being a negation of one act by the commission of another. Only in 1920 when there was a surplus did the purchase plan lower the amount of outstanding bonds. Since government bond prices were at their lowest points in 1920, it is doubtful that the government purchases were large enough to create an effective support for the market price of the bonds.

NOTES

[1] U.S. Treasury Department, *Annual Report, 1920*, p. 113.
[2] *Ibid., 1919*, p. 82.
[3] *Ibid.*, p. 83.
[4] *40 U.S. Statutes at Large*, p. 1314, Chapter 101.
[5] U.S. Treasury Department, *Annual Report, 1918*, pp. 73–74.
[6] *Ibid., 1920*, p. 153.

13

The Effects of the War Loan Program on the Banking System

The Treasury's borrowing program, resting heavily as it did on bank credit, required many changes in the practices and policies of the banking system in order to expand the money supply sufficiently to meet the constant needs of the Treasury. The Federal Reserve System, committed to the support of the Treasury, continued its easy-money policy, and with the aid of several amendments to the Federal Reserve Act created the credit expansion potential by means of which the banking system played a major role in financing both the Treasury's operations and the business expansion which took place at the same time.

The availability of money to meet the constant needs of the Treasury was perhaps the most important single element in the smooth functioning of the war finance program. The availability of money depends primarily on the availability of reserves to the banking system, and because of this relationship reserves become the focal point of monetary policy. The effect of any transaction

177

on the reserve position of a bank must be carefully considered by a banker and steps taken to adjust it if necessary.

During World War I approximately 70 per cent of the nation's commercial deposits were in member banks, and their reserve situation fairly well determined the monetary ease or stringency in the nation. Attention may be focused, therefore, on the member banks in considering the manner in which sufficient reserves were made available to the banking system in order to meet the needs of the Treasury.

For the nation as a whole, there are five principle factors which affect and determine changes in member bank reserves:

 (a) Changes in legal reserve requirements.
 (b) Changes in Federal Reserve Bank reserves.
 (c) Changes in Federal Reserve credit outstanding.
 (d) Treasury transactions.
 (e) Changes in the amount of currency in circulation.

Legal reserve requirements determine the proportion of demand deposits which must be retained in cash. If the legal reserve ratio is 15 per cent, a reserve of $150 can support $1,000 of demand deposits. When this requirement is either raised or lowered, the volume of demand deposits which can be supported by the $150 of reserves either rises or falls. A change in the required ratio from 15 to 10 per cent, for example, creates an increase of 50 per cent in the potential volume of deposits which may be carried. This method of monetary expansion does not increase the volume of reserves, but does expand the potential volume of deposits by increasing excess reserves. Soon after the United States entered the war, this method was put into effect.

Changes in the bank reserves required by the District banks affect member bank reserves because they change the lending power of the Reserve banks which can be used by the member banks to bolster their own reserves. Under the Federal Reserve Act the Reserve banks were required to keep a 35 per cent legal reserve against deposits and a 40 per cent cash reserve against Federal Reserve notes. An increase of $1,000 in cash in the District bank could be used as a reserve against an increase of $2,857 in loans to member banks, an increase of $2,500 of Federal Reserve notes, or some combination of the two. If loans to member banks are increased, the transactions are reflected in their reserve accounts and a still further expansion becomes possible.

Federal Reserve credit affects member bank reserves in the same manner as commercial bank credit affects bank deposits. When a Reserve bank makes a loan to a member bank, the member bank's reserve account is credited with the proceeds of the loan. This additional reserve can then be used by the member bank to expand its own deposits by some multiple of the new reserve based on the legal reserve requirement.

Treasury transactions provide another source or loss of reserve funds. Assuming that Treasury transactions are cleared through its "general account" at the Reserve banks, an expenditure by the Treasury is made by check on the Reserve bank to a private individual. The check is then deposited by the individual in his own bank. When presented to the Reserve bank by a member bank, the member bank's reserve account is credited with the amount of the check. The reverse happens when a payment is made to the Treasury. Treasury transactions from an account in a member bank would merely shift the deposit from or to the Treasury but would not affect the bank's reserves unless, as was done in 1917, the legal reserve requirements were changed with respect to government deposits. With no legal reserve requirement for government deposits, a Treasury check on a member bank redeposited in the same bank would require the bank to increase its volume of reserves by an amount equal to the legal ratio of reserves. A transfer of deposits from a private account to the Treasury would give the bank an amount of free reserves equal to the legal reserve ratio of the transferred deposits. On the other hand, a purchase of a government bond by a customer would transfer the deposit to the government and expand the member bank's reserves by the amount required to maintain the transferred deposit.

An increase in currency in circulation will decrease member bank reserves unless total currency is increased by the same amount. A member bank can receive currency from its Reserve bank only by giving up part of its reserve balance. If the customers of the bank wish additional currency for whatever reason, bank reserves will fall, while a deposit of currency will increase bank reserves. Currency in circulation, unlike the other money supply determinants, depends on the desires of the people rather than the willingness or ability of the banking system to make the money available.

Federal Reserve bank operations expanded rapidly after the United States entered the war. Loans, investments, note issues and reserves all increased far beyond any prewar imaginable point. From December 1916 to December 1919, total assets of the System increased 425 per cent, from $1.2 billion to $6.3 billion. From June 1916 to June 1920 District bank reserves increased by $1,555.2 million, bills on hand increased by $2,738.7 million, and note issues increased by $3,148.4 million. The huge increase in District bank reserves enabled the District banks to expand their operations at an unprecedented rate and, at the same time, to maintain excess reserves throughout the period (see Table 58).

Commercial banks took full advantage of the easy money policy of the Treasury and the Reserve System to expand their loans and investments. Between June 1916 and June 1920, commercial banks increased their deposits by $14 billion. Total loans and investments increased by $15,883 million of which $2,996 million or 19 per cent represented an increase in government investments.

The story of the banking system during World War I is

Table 58

Federal Reserve Operations, June 1916–June 1920

(millions of dollars)

	1916	1917	1918	1919	1920
Bills discounted:					
secured by					
governments	—	—	$ 434.5	$1,573.5	$1,278.0
other	$ 21.2	$ 197.2	434.7	244.6	1,153.8
Bills purchased	71.1	202.3	216.8	304.6	399.2
Government					
obligations	57.1	70.7	259.1	231.6	352.3
Government deposits	101.2	301.0	84.5	73.6	14.2
Member bank					
reserves	457.5	1,033.5	1,557.6	1,713.0	1,831.9
Federal Reserve					
notes in circulation	152.2	508.8	1,722.2	2,499.2	3,116.7
Federal Reserve					
Bank notes in					
circulation	1.7	.9	10.4	177.1	185.6
Cash reserves[a]	553.4	1,334.3	2,006.2	2,216.2	2,108.6
Required reserves[a]	241.1	645.1	1,224.3	1,612.4	1,849.5
Excess reserves[a]	312.3	689.2	781.9	603.8	259.1
Reserve ratio[a]	83.0	75.3	61.7	52.1	43.6

Source: Federal Reserve Board, *Annual Reports, 1916–1920.* (a) *Banking and Monetary Statistics,* p. 346 (for 1916 only).

largely a story of the ways in which reserves were made available to the banking system by (a) lowering reserve requirements, (b) economizing and regulating Federal Reserve bank reserves, (c) making Federal Reserve credit available, (d) easing the possible dislocations due to Treasury transactions, and (e) providing a background of legislation and permissiveness which resulted in inflationary finance.

Table 59
Commercial Banking Operations, June 1916–June 1920
(millions of dollars)

	1916	1917	1918	1919	1920
Deposits	$22,079	$25,885	$28,011	$32,739	$36,114
Loans	15,768	18,185	20,073	22,363	28,103
Nongovernment investments	3,891	4,133	4,096	4,250	4,443
Government investments	752	1,545	3,211	5,147	3,748

Source: Federal Reserve Board, *Banking and Monetary Statistics*, p. 19.

Changes in Legal Reserve Requirements

The legal reserve requirement is the proportion of its deposits that a member bank is required to maintain in cash. Under the original Federal Reserve Act, the reserve requirements against demand deposits of member banks were 18, 15, and 12 per cent for central reserve city banks, reserve city banks, and country banks respectively, of which less than half had to be deposited in the District banks, while the remainder might be carried in the banks' own vaults. The reserve requirement against time deposits was 5 per cent for all member banks of which less than half had to be deposited in the District banks.

Under the Act of June 21, 1917, Section 19 of the Federal Reserve Act was amended so as to reduce the required reserves to 13, 10 and 7 per cent, and to require all reserves to be deposited in the District banks.[1] This amendment had a twofold effect on the banking system without an actual increase in the amount of reserves.

To the member banks, the lower reserve requirements created

excess reserves equal to the difference between the old and new amounts of legal reserves. These excess reserves formed the basis for further expansion of bank deposits. For example, a reserve city bank with $10 million of deposits and $1.5 million of reserves before the amendment would have no free reserves. After the amendment was passed, required reserves were reduced to $1 million, leaving $.5 million of free reserves which could act as a reserve base for about $5 million of additional deposits for the banking system. If all free reserves were fully utilized, central reserve city banks could expand deposits by 38.4 per cent, reserve city banks by 50 per cent, and country banks by 71.4 per cent with no increase in the volume of reserves.

As can be seen in Table 60, an enormous expansion in deposits, loans, and investments took place in the six months following the changed reserve requirements. Loans and investments of member banks increased by $4.4 billion, a 35.7

Table 60
Reserves, Loans, Investments and Deposits of Member Banks,
June 20, 1917 and December 31, 1917
(millions of dollars)

	June 20, 1917	*December 31, 1917*	*Increase (per cent)*
Reserves with Federal Reserve Banks	$ 862	$ 1,497	73.6
Loans and investments	12,453	16,896	35.7
Loans	9,370	12,316	31.4
Investments (government)	1,065	1,759	65.1
Investments (other)	2,018	2,820	39.7
Total deposits	13,397	18,668	39.3

Source: Federal Reserve Board, *Banking and Monetary Statistics*, pp. 72–73.

per cent increase, and total deposits increased by $5.3 billion or 39.3 per cent. By far the largest percentage increase was shown by government investments, which increased by 65.1 per cent over the six-month period, and accounted for 15.6 per cent of the $4.4 billion total increase in loans and investments combined.

Federal Reserve Expansion

THE BASE FOR EXPANSION

The requirement that all member bank reserves be deposited in the District banks paved the way for a greater expansion by the Federal Reserve banks, an expansion which was accomplished with no large increase in the rediscount rates and without a fall in the reserve ratio below the legal minimum. The transfer of reserves to the District banks tended to economize the gold reserves so that more credit could be extended on the basis of the same volume of reserves. The total possible expansion under the Act of June 21, 1917, can be illustrated by tracing the use of a $150,000 cash reserve of a reserve city bank assuming full utilization of the cash reserve and no increase in circulating currency.

1. June 1917—A reserve city bank possesses $150,000 in cash reserves for deposits of $1,000,000.

Member bank deposits	$1,000,000
Member bank reserves	150,000
Member cash in vault (9/15)	90,000
Member bank deposit in District banks (6/15)	60,000
District bank required reserves (35%)	21,000
District bank excess reserves	39,000
Possible District bank expansion	111,428

2. August 1917—The reserve city bank expands deposits by $500,000 based on lower reserve requirements.

Member bank deposits	$1,500,000
Member bank reserves	150,000
Member bank cash in vault (9/15)	90,000
Member bank deposit in District bank (6/15)	60,000
District bank required reserves (35%)	21,000
District bank excess reserves	39,000
Possible District bank expansion	111,428

3. August 1917—Reserves are transferred to the District bank.

Member bank deposits	$1,500,000
Member bank reserves	150,000
Member bank deposit in District bank	150,000
District bank required reserves (35%)	52,500
District bank excess reserves	97,500
Possible District bank expansion	278,571

4. Changes in possible District bank expansion:

August 1917	$278,571
June 1917	111,428
Potential increase	$167,143
Percentage potential increase	150%

5. Changes in possible member bank expansion:

Potential increase in rediscounts	$167,143
Potential increase in member bank deposits	$1,671,430

It is evident from the above illustration that the reserve transfer requirement created a far greater expansion potential than did the lowering of the legal reserve requirements. The transfer of gold from member banks to the District banks more than offset the $96.3 million of net gold exports[2] from July to

Table 61

Federal Reserve Bank Expansion, March 1917–December 1919

(millions of dollars)

Date	Total Reserves	Total Deposits	Federal Reserve Notes	Bills on Hand	Reserve Ratio
1917, March 30	$ 947	$ 842	$ 358	$ 105	.890
June 22	1,248	1,441	500	435	.716
November 30	1,676	1,969	1,057	962	.632
December 28	1,721	1,771	1,246	956	.618
1918, May 10	1,943	2,107	1,570	1,225	.603
November 8	2,101	2,349	2,558	2,172	.498
December 27	2,146	2,313	2,685	2,007	.506
1919, March 28	2,211	2,401	2,522	2,134	.519
June 27	2,216	2,437	2,499	2,123	.521
September 26	2,188	2,542	2,655	2,225	.510
December 26	2,136	2,780	3,058	2,780	.448

Source: Federal Reserve Board, *Annual Report, 1918,* pp. 15–16; *ibid., 1919,* pp. 112–113, 121–123.

September 1917, and raised the reserve ratio of the Federal Reserve banks from 70.9 per cent in June 1917 to 78.0 per cent in August 1917.[3]

Other methods were also used to accumulate and centralize the nation's gold supply. Wherever possible, Federal Reserve notes were substituted for gold and gold certificates as circulating currency. From April 1917 to June 1920 these currency media in circulation declined from $1,673 million to $447 million, a decline of 73 per cent.[4] The Reserve banks were reluctant to pay out gold coins. The Chicago branch announced that as the Federal Reserve notes were redeemable in gold only at the Treasury in Washington, and in gold or lawful money at the Reserve bank, they would not pay out a single gold coin.[5]

By the fall of 1917 the New York State banking law permitted

State banks and trust companies to count Federal Reserve notes as part of their cash reserves,[6] and the American Bankers Association recommended that all State banking laws be amended so that state banking and trust companies be permitted to carry their gold reserves with the Federal Reserve banks.[7] This meant that the gold reserves of the nonmember banks could be added to the Federal Reserve bank gold reserves, providing a still wider base for deposit and note expansion with no loss in the expansion potential of the nonmember banks.

The problem involving the loss of gold through export came up soon after the United States entered the war. From July to September 1917 net exports of gold amounted to $96.3 million,[8] and if this continued, would have resulted in a serious depletion of gold reserves. Accordingly steps were taken to halt this adverse movement. The Espionage Act of June 15, 1917 authorized the President to prohibit the export of any commodity, and in September an embargo was placed on the export of gold coin, bullion, or currency. The Trading with the Enemy Act of October 6, 1917 authorized the President to restrict foreign exchange and gold transactions. These powers were delegated to the Secretary of the Treasury, and redelegated by him to the Federal Reserve Board.[9] From September 7, 1917 to December 31, 1918, licences were granted for the export of gold in the amount of only $128,688,515,[10] and for the period from October 1917 through December 1918 there was a net gold inflow of $22.3 million.[11]

The Act of June 21, 1917, in addition to providing for the transfer of reserves to the District banks, also freed part of the gold reserves for Federal Reserve notes. Prior to this amendment gold deposited with the Federal Reserve agent by member banks as security for the note issues could not be counted as part of the reserve for deposits. The amendment allowed this security to be counted as part of the District bank's general gold reserve for either deposits or notes. This further increased the excess reserves of the Reserve banks. By June 22, 1917 District bank reserves were 32 per cent higher than they were on March 30, and by November 30, the increase had grown to 77 per cent.

With the increase in cash reserves, the Reserve banks increased their discounts and outstanding notes to an even greater degree. Between April 1, 1917 and December 26, 1919, cash reserves increased by $1,189 million or 125 per cent. On the basis of this increase in reserves, the Reserve banks increased their discounts by $2,675 million or 2,548 per cent, and Federal Reserve note issues by $2,700 million or 754 per cent. The increase in Federal Reserve currency was also due to the Act of October 5, 1917,[12] which gave each national bank the power to issue national bank notes not exceeding $25,000 each in $1 and $2 bills, and to the policy of the Treasury of converting large-denomination greenbacks into notes of small denominations.[13] This partially halted the redemption of Federal Reserve notes when money in small denominations was needed, since Federal

Table 62
Currency in Circulation, June 1916–June 1920
(millions of dollars)

Date	(a) Amount	(b) Federal Reserve Notes	Ratio (b) to (a)
June 1916	$3,362	$ 149	.044
December 1916	3,679	272	.074
June 1917	3,779	507	.134
December 1917	4,086	1,223	.300
June 1918	4,195	1,698	.404
December 1918	4,951	2,624	.530
June 1919	4,590	2,450	.534
December 1919	5,091	2,916	.573
June 1920	5,181	3,065	.591

Source: Federal Reserve Board, *Banking and Monetary Statistics*, p. 410.

Reserve notes could be issued only in denominations of $5 and higher and could now be exchanged for the new lower-denomination currency.

By the Act of June 21, 1917 and the added administrative policies the Reserve banks increased their gold holdings and provided an unprecedented base for member bank expansion.

REDISCOUNT RATES

As a further inducement for member banks to expand their loans and investments, rediscount rates at the Reserve banks were kept low throughout the war period, and in addition, a preferential rate (lower than other rates) was put into effect on discounted commercial bank paper secured by United States war obligations.

The rediscount rate per se, as a tool of monetary expansion, will influence member bank expansion only when the customers of the member banks wish to expand their deposits and when member bank reserves are fully utilized. When both of these things occur at the same time member banks must find new reserves or they will be unable to expand their deposits. While the ability of the Reserve banks to extend additional reserves are limited by their own reserves, the desire of the member banks to borrow these reserves is determined by the differential between the rediscount rate of the District banks and the rate of interest charged by the member banks. If a penalty rate (a rate higher than the interest rate) is charged by the District banks, member banks will be extremely reluctant to rediscount customer paper unless they in turn can increase their own interest rate charges. If this occurs, customers may become more reluctant to borrow unless the rate of return on the borrowed funds to the borrower is expected to exceed the bank interest rate. Therefore, if the rediscount rate policy of the Reserve banks is such that member banks are forced to raise their own rates or suffer a loss, there will be no inducement for monetary expansion by the member banks.

When the reserves are available and the rediscount rate is kept both low and at the same time lower than bank interest rates, member banks are willing to rediscount their customers' paper when additional reserves are needed. The combination of low rediscount rates and ample reserves for District bank expansion provided the necessary reserves for the member banks. The rediscount rate on eligible paper was kept at 3 per cent in New York until December 1917 when it was increased to $3\frac{1}{2}$ per cent. Other District banks held to a 4 per cent rate until April 1918 when they were increased slightly in three districts.[14] The open market rate on sixty-day paper in New York was 4 per cent in April 1917 and fluctuated between $5\frac{1}{4}$ and 6 per cent from June 1917 to the end of the war.[15] The easy money policy of the Federal Reserve therefore provided ample motivation for member bank rediscounting.

Of far greater importance in inducing member banks to borrow from the Reserve banks was the preferential rates set on member bank loans secured by government obligations. Under Section 13 of the Reserve Act District banks could extend credit to member banks, on the basis of government bonds, for ninety days on a rediscount basis,[16] and for fifteen days on member bank notes backed by government debt.[17] Under Section 14 of the Reserve Act the District banks were also given the authority to buy or sell government bonds. On June 1, 1917 the Federal Reserve banks adopted a 3 per cent rate on 15 day notes secured by government bonds.[18] From May to September 25, 1917 a $3\frac{1}{2}$ per cent rate was charged on ninety-day paper secured by the war obligations, while 4 to $4\frac{1}{2}$ per cent was charged on commercial paper.[19] While the preferential rate increased as the Liberty Loan interest increased, the differential continued between rates on government and commercial paper.

The Federal Reserve Board stated that "the Board has felt it to be its duty to adjust its discount rates in such manner as to assist the distribution of the various Treasury issues. The Board has therefore continued the policy... of giving a preferential rate of discount on notes... secured by the Government's war obligations."[20] The preferential rate made lending to customers by commercial banks on the security of government bonds highly profitable. Nonmember banks could also take advantage of the preferential rates by using member banks as intermediaries.[21] Customers could buy government bonds using bank notes for payment, and the bonds used as security for rediscounts at the Federal Reserve banks. This was a roundabout method of inflation, and the result was no different from that which would have occurred from the direct purchase of government obligations by the Reserve banks.

As a result of the preferential rate, member banks could rediscount paper secured not only by governments purchased by customers but also by their own government bond holdings. The Reserve banks therefore gave member banks a motive for using government bonds rather than commercial paper as security for rediscounts. As the member banks' discounts were predominantly secured by government obligations, the effective rediscount rate was the preferential rate rather than the rate on commercial paper. If the banks held sufficient amounts of governments (which they did) they could expand their commercial loans and rediscount their own paper secured by their own government bond holdings.

The extent to which the preferential rate was eagerly grasped by the member banks is well illustrated by the increase of Federal Reserve rediscounts and their changed composition during 1918 and 1919. Reserve holdings of paper secured by government obligations increased out of all proportion to their rediscounts of commercial paper, which not only declined

Table 63

Federal Reserve Bank Discounts, 1918–1919, Selected Dates

(millions of dollars)

| | | Secured by | | |
| | (a) Total | (b) Government | | Ratio |
Date	Discounts	Debentures	Other	(b) to (a)
1918, January 4	$ 897.2	$ 285.9	$ 611.3	31.9
February 1	896.6	305.7	590.9	34.1
March 8	838.3	264.5	573.8	31.6
April 12	1,031.7	465.6	566.1	45.1
May 3	1,170.5	606.6	563.9	51.8
June 14	1,259.0	653.9	605.1	51.9
July 12	1,378.3	606.6	771.7	44.0
August 16	1,497.6	752.1	745.5	50.2
September 13	1,853.0	1,071.3	781.7	57.8
October 10	2,093.1	1,304.4	788.7	62.3
November 15	2,109.8	1,358.4	751.4	62.4
December 27	2,006.6	1,400.4	606.2	69.8
1919, January 31	1,882.4	1,357.6	524.8	72.1
February 28	2,156.7	1,668.0	488.7	77.3
March 28	2,134.3	1,691.0	443.3	79.2
April 25	2,136.2	1,760.7	375.5	82.4
May 16	2,223.7	1,863.5	360.2	83.8
June 27	2,122.6	1,573.5	549.1	74.4
July 25	2,243.2	1,616.2	627.0	72.0
August 29	2,178.3	1,609.3	569.0	73.8
September 26	2,224.8	1,572.5	652.3	70.7
October 31	2,522.9	1,681.1	841.8	66.6
November 28	2,709.8	1,736.0	973.8	64.1
December 26	2,780.1	1,510.4	1,269.7	54.3

Source: Federal Reserve Board, *Annual Report, 1918*, pp. 9–10; *ibid., 1919*, pp. 15–16.

proportionally as a proportion of total discounts, but also declined absolutely during the first six months of both years. Commercial paper rediscounts, which stood at $611.3 million on January 4, 1918, had declined to $360.2 million or 41 per cent by May 16, 1919. During this period rediscounts secured by governments rose to a peak of $1,863.5 million. Of total bills bought and discounted, on January 4, 1918 paper secured by government war obligations amounted to $286 million out of a total of $897 million or 31.9 per cent. This percentage increased steadily throughout 1918 and 1919. By May 3, 1918 discounts secured by government debt amounted to more than 50 per cent of total discounts and by the end of the year were almost 70 per cent. There was a further increase during the early part of 1919, reaching a peak of 83.8 per cent on May 16, 1919, when $1,863.5 million of paper secured by government debt was held by the Federal Reserve system.

War Loans and the Banking System

GOVERNMENT DEPOSITS

At the time the United States entered the war there were two regulations in effect regarding government deposits in private banks. First, only Federal Reserve banks, the independent treasury and member banks could act as government depositories; second, the reserve requirements applied to government deposits as well as private deposits. The Liberty Bond Act of April 24, 1917 changed both of these stipulations.[22]

The depository regulation, if kept as it was, could have two possible effects. In the first place, it could have caused some reluctance on the part of nonmember banks to purchase government obligations. In the second place, if nonmember banks did buy governments, there would have been large transfers of funds from nonmember banks to member depository banks with a corresponding disturbance in the money market. In order to avoid these possibilities, Section 7 of the Liberty Bond Act permitted the Secretary of the Treasury to deposit the proceeds from bond and certificate sales in "such banks and trust companies as he may designate." This increased the number of possible private bank depositories from the 7,653 member banks to the 26,831 total commercial banks and permitted the Treasury to designate nonmember banks as government depositories.

RESERVE REQUIREMENTS

The nondiscriminating reserve requirements meant that if the banks bought government obligations they would have to cut down on private loans and investments.[23] If the Treasury desired to compete with the private economy for bank funds, it could not do so with the low interest rate policy it intended to pursue. The Treasury had to choose between almost complete dependence on nonbank investors in its bond selling plan or it had to create a situation which would induce the banks to increase their government security holdings. The Treasury chose the latter. Section 7 further stipulated that the legal reserve requirements of member banks were not to apply against deposits of government funds. A switch in deposits from private to government hands, therefore, increased free reserves by the amount of reserves required to maintain the private deposit, and allowed the banking system to relend or reinvest privately the amount of shifted deposits. If a bank customer purchased a $1,000 bond the $1,000 deposit would be shifted from the customer to the Treasury, and at the same time the volume of free reserves would be increased by the amount required to maintain the $1,000 deposit. This change in the reserve requirements for government deposits paved the way for the banking system to absorb a government bond or certificate

issue of any size, and still maintain private loans and investments on a large scale.

SECURITY AGAINST GOVERNMENT DEPOSITS

One additional inducement for depository banks to hold
government bonds was supplied by the Treasury. Under the
National Bank Act, the security which depository banks were
required to maintain against government deposits could be
either United States bonds or any others which were acceptable
to the Treasury. In 1917 the Treasury changed this requirement
to one which was actually a tool designed to encourage the use
of United States bonds rather than other acceptable bonds as
security for government deposits. This was done by setting up
a specific schedule of acceptable paper in predetermined ratios
of acceptability. At least 25 per cent of the securities deposited
for this purpose were to be made up of obligations of the
government. Other eligible securities were divided into four
groups. United States bonds together with those of Puerto Rico,

Table 64
Commercial Bank-Held United States Government Obligations,
June 1917–June 1920
(millions of dollars)

| | Member Banks | | | Nonmember |
Year	National	State	Total	Banks
1917	$1,043.	$ 23.	$1,066.	$ 480.
1918	2,025.	439.	2,464.	747.
1919	2,941.	862.	3,803.	1,344.
1920	2,137.	674.	2,811.	937.

Source: Federal Reserve Board, *Banking and Monetary Statistics*, pp. 20–23.

the Philippines, Washington, D.C., and Farm Loan bonds were acceptable at par value. Bonds of any state in the union were acceptable at market value. Other state paper, municipal bonds, Hawaii bonds, and Federal Reserve eligible paper were acceptable at 90 per cent of market value. Certain railroad and allied bonds were acceptable at 75 per cent of market value.[24] This change tended to encourage bank investments in governments, since lower investments would be required to secure the same amount of government deposits.

The inducements for banks, both member and nonmember, to increase their holdings of governments were a huge success. Total bank-held governments increased from $1,546 million in June 1917 to $5,147 million in June 1919, an increase of 233 per cent. During the same peiod bank investments other than governments increased from $4,133 million to $4,250 million, an increase of only 2.8 per cent. Because of the changed reserve requirements, $3,601 million increase in bank-held government debt was an addition to bank credit rather than a transfer of private to government credit, thus adding to the inflationary pressures.

LOAN RESTRICTIONS

Under the National Bank Act, a national bank could not lend to any one borrower an amount greater than 10 per cent of its capital and unimpaired surplus. This restriction was amended by the Act of September 24, 1918. Under the new amendment a national bank could until July 1, 1919 lend a single borrower an extra 10 per cent of its capital and unimpaired surplus if the loan was secured by Liberty Bonds or certificates of indebtedness, and a further amount without limit if secured by the government war obligations.[25] This meant that a national bank could lend up to 20 per cent of its capital surplus on the security of government obligations at par, and any further amount on government debt security at a small discount.

Summary

McAdoo's original plan to divert the surplus funds remaining after taxes through the sale of bonds gave way almost at once to a policy of expediency. His fear of failure, his shortsightedness regarding long-run effects of wartime fiscal policy, and his concern with the immediate costs of the war led him to sponsor and foster measures which were in complete contradiction to his stated goals. The Treasury's easy-money policy led to a vast expansion of the money supply. Between June 1916 and June 1920 the total money supply increased from $21,978 million to $37,621 million, an increase of $15,643 million.

The extent to which the increase in the money supply was represented by Federal debt can be determined by a comparison of the increases of both figures. From June 1916 to June 1919, the money supply increased by $11.4 billion while total bank-held government debt (including rediscounts) increased by $6.1

Table 65
Money Supply, June 1916 – June 1920
(millions of dollars)

	Demand Deposits	Currency in Circulation	Total	Annual Increase (per cent)
1916	$18,616	$3,362	$21,978	
1917	21,968	3,779	25,747	17.1
1918	24,435	4,195	28,630	11.2
1919	28,837	4.590	33,427	16.7
1920	32,440	5,181	37,621	12.5

Source: Federal Reserve Board, *Banking and Monetary Statistics,* pp. 19, 409.

billion or 53.5 per cent of the total. One year later, after the 1920 budget surplus had been used to contract part of the bank-held debt, the ratio of the increase stood at 30.0 per cent.[26] Since it is quite possible that some part of the bank-financed consumer bond purchases were not rediscounted the ratios are to some degree understated.

In order to facilitate Treasury borrowing through the path of least resistance, the entire banking system was reconstructed to fit the Treasury's needs. All possible impediments to purchasing government debt either directly by the banks or by private investors through bank borrowing were removed. That the Treasury loan program could have been carried out without some aid from the banks is doubtful, but the large part played by the banking system was at least partially unnecessary. Although Treasury policy might not have been wholly responsible for the monetary expansion and price inflation that took place during the war, it was an important contributing factor.

NOTES

[1] *40 U.S. Statutes at Large*, p. 232; Chapter 32.
[2] Federal Reserve Board, *Banking and Monetary Statistics*, p. 536.
[3] *Ibid.*, p. 346.
[4] *Ibid.*, p. 410.
[5] Harold L. Reed, *Development of Federal Reserve Policy*, pp. 236–237.
[6] *Commercial and Financial Chronicle*, August 25, 1917, pp. 760–761.
[7] *Federal Reserve Bulletin*, May 1, 1917, p. 335.
[8] Federal Reserve Board, *Banking and Monetary Statistics*, p. 536.
[9] Executive orders of September 7, 1917, October 12, 1917, and January 26, 1918, Federal Reserve Board, *Annual Report, 1918*, p. 36.
[10] *Ibid.*, p. 37.
[11] Federal Reserve Board, *Banking and Monetary Statistics*, p. 536.
[12] *40 U.S. Statutes at Large*, pt. 1, p. 342; Chap. 74.
[13] *Federal Reserve Bulletin*, November 1, 1917, pp. 833–834.
[14] Federal Reserve Board, *Banking and Monetary Statistics*, p. 439.
[15] *Commercial and Financial Chronicle*, Monthly Reviews.
[16] *Federal Reserve Act*, Section 13.
[17] Act of September 7, 1916, *39 Statutes at Large*, pt. 1, p. 752; Chap. 461.
[18] *Federal Reserve Bulletin*, June 1, 1917, p. 425.

[19] U.S. Treasury Department, *Annual Report, 1917*, p. 38.

[20] Federal Reserve Board, *Annual Report, 1918*, p. 5.

[21] *Federal Reserve Bulletin*, June 1, 1917, p. 426.

[22] *40 U.S. Statutes at Large*, sec. 7.

[23] Assuming that banks were using their entire expansion potential based on existing reserves and reserve requirements.

[24] U.S. Treasury Department, *Annual Report, 1917*, pp. 126, 133.

[25] *40 U.S. Statutes at Large*, pt. 1, p. 965; chap. 176; *Commercial and Financial Chronicle*, October 12, 1918, p. 1429.

[26] Table 64; Federal Reserve Board, *Banking and Monetary Statistics*, p. 19; Federal Reserve Board, *Annual Reports, 1916–1920*.

14

Economic Effects of
War Finance

The impact of war finance on a nation extends beyond the
boundaries of the banking system and permeates every walk of
economic life. The term "war finance" contains two words each
of which is meaningful and has its separate and unique implications. The economic effects of war finance therefore combine
the effects of the war and the effects of its financing. These
effects are determined to a large degree by the magnitude of the
war effort, the ability of the economy to expand production, and,
finally, the types of government receipts and expenditures.

The magnitude of the war effort, measured by government
expenditures for war purposes, represents the resources of the
nation taken from the civilian economy and thus reducing the
quantity of resources available for the production of civilian
goods. The greater the war effort the greater will be the economic
sacrifices of the civilian population, since the shift of resources
represents a shift from want-satisfying uses to nonwant-satisfy-
ing uses.[1] The total of war expenditures may therefore be considered the total sacrifice of the nation.

The total national sacrifice as described above may be either a sacrifice of effort, a sacrifice of consumption, or some combination of the two.[2] The division of the total sacrifice between effort and consumption is determined by the ability of the economy to expand its production. If production can be expanded by the amount of the war effort, civilian consumption will remain at its prewar level but the amount of effort put forth by the civilian population to retain this consumption will be increased by an amount necessary to support the war effort. This is a sacrifice of effort rather than of consumption. On the other hand, if the economy is fully utilizing its productive resources at the start of the war period and cannot expand, part of the resources previously used for civilian production will be shifted to war production, so that total effort expended in production will remain the same while consumption will be sacrificed.[3] While the extent of the war effort determines the total national sacrifice, the type of sacrifice is determined by the ability of the economy to expand its production and/or to use its productive factors more efficiently.

Moreover, although the national sacrifice of consumption and effort is directly affected by production, the way in which this sacrifice is shared by the individuals and groups within the economy depends on the methods of financing the war and the types of war expenditures. Government war expenditures are payments of money incomes to persons engaged in war production. Since this production is not used to satisfy consumer wants, money incomes are received by persons not engaged in the production of civilian goods, but this money can be used for the purchase of these goods. Government receipts from taxes and nonbank bond sales represent rights to consumer goods given up by the payers and then transferred to the producers of war goods. The payers in this case are the sacrificers, whereas the recipients are the beneficiaries of the transfer.[4] The creation of new money by government bank-borrowing and its transfer to war-goods producers increases the demand potential of this group with no corresponding decrease in the demand potential of other groups. The sacrifice in this case is borne by all demanders for as demand is increased, rising prices will force the sacrifice. This tendency for prices to rise as new and increased demand makes itself felt in the market can be mitigated to some extent if consumers save a greater part of their incomes. On the other hand, the price rise will be accentuated if government receipts come out of savings and are transferred to spenders.

A somewhat debatable and unmeasurable concept mentioned earlier is the effect of heavy taxation policies on the production incentives. Observers of American economic life are particularly impressed with the fact that "the American institutional framework frowned upon leisure and made work a fetish and production a religion."[5] It would therefore seem to require an extraordinarily high rate of taxation to create a drop in production.

Changes in National Production

Changes in the money value of the national product can be attributed to any or all of three causes. First is an increase in production brought about by the productive use of idle factors.

Table 66
Gross National Product, 1916–1920 (Fiscal Years)
(billions of dollars)

Year	Current Prices	1914 Prices
1916	$43.6	$41.3
1917	49.9	42.1
1918	61.6	42.9
1919	65.7	41.0
1920	82.8	41.1

Source: Simon Kuznets, *National Product in Wartime*, p. 138.

Second is an increase in production due to an increase in productivity of the factors. The third cause is an increase in the market prices of the goods produced. The increase in the national product during World War I was due primarily to the third cause—price increases. Gains in physical production were minor ones, and productivity declined rather than increased.

While the value of national production in current prices increased throughout the war period, the volume of physical production as measured in constant dollars of purchasing power increased but little from 1916 to 1918, and decreased thereafter. The increase in the gross national product was therefore due to increased market prices rather than to increased production. This is demonstrated by the available data on

Table 67
Employment in Industry, Employers
and Entrepreneurs, 1915–1919
(millions of dollars)

Industry	1915	1916	1917	1918	1919
Agriculture	8.6	8.5	8.6	8.6	8.7
Mining	1.1	1.2	1.2	1.2	1.2
Manufacturing	7.7	9.0	9.7	10.2	10.1
Construction	1.2	1.2	1.1	.9	1.2
Transportation and public utilities	2.7	2.8	3.0	3.1	3.3
Trade	4.1	4.3	4.3	4.2	4.4
Government	2.0	2.1	2.7	5.2	3.8
Unclassified	10.1	10.2	9.4	7.2	7.2
Total	37.5	39.3	40.0	40.6	39.8
Nongovernment employment	35.5	37.2	37.3	35.4	36.0

Source: Simon Kuznets, *National Product in Wartime*, p. 145.

productivity, employment, and production during the period.

From 1914 to 1919, the index of production per wage earner in manufacturing declined from 127 (1899 = 100) to 116.[6] Agricultural productivity showed a similar decline with the index of gross farm production per man-hour falling from 89 in 1915 (1935–1939 = 100) to 84 in 1918.[7] An increase in employment might have counteracted the decline in productivity but unfortunately this did not occur.

Industrial employment, including government, increased but little during the war. The largest expansions took place in government and manufacturing, while decreased employment occurred in construction and the unclassified sectors. Non-government employment decreased during the period so that an increase in private employment was not present to counteract the decrease in productivity. Under the circumstances total production remained fairly stable throughout the actual war period.

Production changes in specific industries showed gains in those industries where employment increased, such as mining and manufacturing, while production decreased in agriculture and construction where employment decreased.

From the data in Table 68 it seems evident that the 14 per cent expansion in production which took place between 1914 and 1916 resulted in almost full utilization of the nation's productive resources. A further 5 per cent increase occurred in 1917, but the decrease in private employment in 1918 brought production back almost to its 1916 level. The Federal Reserve Board index shows the same tendency, although on a wider scale. The increase from 1914 to 1916 in this index was 63 per cent, from 46 (1935–1939 = 100) to 75, reaching its peak of 81 in May 1917. In 1918, the index stood at 73, a decrease of 2.5 per cent from the 1916 figure.[8] The Federal Reserve Board index pertains only to mining and manufacturing.

An examination of increases and decreases in production of

Table 68

Physical Production Indexes, 1914-1918

(1914 = 100)

Industry	1914	1915	1916	1917	1918
Agriculture	100	100	92	96	101
Mining	100	109	126	133	134
Manufacturing	100	117	139	138	137
Construction	100	89	91	93	94.5
Railroad transportation	100	107	124	136	142
Gross national product	100	108	114	120	115

Source: Simon Kuznets, *National Product in Wartime*, p. 148.

specific commodities shows further evidence of the same trend. Of the seventeen commodities listed in Table 69, only six showed a better production record for the 1916–1918 period than for the 1914–1916 period, and five of the six were agricultural products. Of the thirteen commodities showing increased production during the 1914–1916 period, only five were able to expand still further during the war period. Averaging the percentage changes in the table results in an average gain of 26.1 per cent for the prewar period against an average gain of only 6.8 per cent for the war period which was due mostly to the large increases in the production of wheat, oats, rye, and coal.

The available data indicates that America's ability to produce reached its peak at about the time the actual war period started in 1917. Further expansion took place only on a minor scale and in only a few commodities.

Changes in Factor Payments

Payments to the factors of production increased along with the increase in the national income, but not at the same rate.

Table 69
Production in the United States,
1914–1918, Individual Commodities

Commodity	1914	1916	Per Cent Change 1914–1916	1918	Per Cent Change 1916–1918
Corn (billions of bushels)	2.7	2.6	− 3.7	2.5	− 3.9
Wheat (millions of bushels)	891	636	−39.8	921	+44.8
Rice (millions of bushels)	657	1,135	+72.7	1,072	− 5.5
Beet sugar (millions of pounds)	1,467	1,748	+19.4	1,530	−12.4
Cotton, 500-lb. bales (millions of bales)	16.1	11.5	−28.5	12.0	+ 4.3
Wool (millions of pounds)	290.2	288.5	− .5	298.9	+ 3.6
Oats (millions of bushels)	1,141	1,252	+ 9.7	1,538	+22.8
Rye (millions of bushels)	43	49	+14.0	91	+85.7
Lumber (billions of board feed)	37.3	39.8	+ 6.7	31.9	−20.0
Copper smelter output (millions of pounds)	1,150	1,928	+67.6	1,908	− 1.0
Lead (thousands of tons)	542	571	+ 5.3	640	+12.0
Iron ore (millions of long tons)	41.4	75.2	+81.4	69.7	− 7.3
Pig iron (millions of long tons)	23.3	39.4	+69.1	39.1	− .7
Rolled iron and steel (millions of long tons)	18.4	32.4	+76.0	31.2	− 3.7
Coal (millions of tons)	513.5	590.1	+14.9	678.2	+14.9
Coke (millions of tons)	34.5	54.5	+57.9	56.5	+ 3.7
Cement (millions of barrels)	89	92	+ 3.3	72	−21.7

Source: Statistical Abstract of the United States, 1924.

Table 70
National Income Payments, 1915-1920
(millions of dollars)

Type of Payment	1915	1916	1917	1918	1919	1920
Employee compensation	$19,052	$22,046	$25,259	$31,627	$34,604	$40,027
Entrepreneural income	9,606	11,727	16,653	15,829	20,270	16,141
Rental incomes	3,104	3,322	3,592	3,819	4,122	4,738
Corporation profits	3,445	6,384	7,350	4,714	6,806	4,471
Interest	1,575	1,631	1,760	1,967	2,585	2,702
Total	$36,782	$45,110	$54,614	$57,956	$68,387	$68,079

National Income Index (1915 = 100)

	1915	1916	1917	1918	1919	1920
Employee compensation	100	116	132	166	181	210
Entrepreneural income	100	122	173	164	211	168
Interest	100	105	112	125	164	171
Rental incomes	100	107	116	123	133	154
Corporation profits	100	185	213	137	198	130
Total	100	122	148	157	185	185

Source: Simon Kuznets, *National Product in Wartime*, p. 141.

The largest percentage increases in 1916 were entrepreneural incomes and corporation profits, the latter increasing 85 per cent over the preceding year. Wages and salaries increased steadily throughout the war period with a slight lag compared with the increase in the national income until 1917, when employee compensation increases forged ahead only to drop behind again in 1919. In 1920 wages and salary increases were again higher than the increase in national income.

Entrepreneural incomes and corporation profits fluctuated the most, with entrepreneural incomes showing a somewhat smaller fluctuation. The entrepreneural group index was consistently greater than the total index until 1920, when it fell below. The index of corporation profits showed both wide gains and declines from year to year, and, except for 1918 and 1920, were far greater than the total index.

Interest payments and rental incomes showed consistent gains throughout the period, but neither showed as great a gain in any year as did the total. The indexes of these two groups were lower than any of the others except in 1920 when the index of rental incomes exceeded that of corporation profits and the index of interest income exceeded both corporation profits and entrepreneural incomes.

Still another way of tracing the shares of distributive income is by the percentage of the total income going to each group.

During the war, employees and noncorporate entrepreneurs

Table 71

National Income, Percentage Shares, 1915–1920

(per cent)

Type of Income	1915	1916	1917	1918	1919	1920
Employee compensation	51.8	48.8	46.2	54.6	50.6	58.8
Entrepreneural income	26.1	26.0	30.5	27.3	29.6	23.9
Interest	4.4	3.6	3.2	3.4	3.8	4.0
Rental incomes	8.4	7.4	6.6	6.6	6.0	7.0
Corporation profits	9.3	14.2	13.5	8.1	10.0	6.5
Total	100.0	100.0	100.0	100.0	100.0	100.0

Source: Table 70.

increased their relative shares of income distribution at the expense of the other groups. Interest and rental incomes took a smaller share, heading steadily downward from 1915 on, while the share going to corporation profits increased during the neutrality period but decreased after 1916.

Productive Income by Industries

The transfer of purchasing power from potential consumers to the government and the addition of purchasing power by government bank-borrowing caused some changes in the relative positions of various industries within the economy. These changes need by no means be drastic ones, since most industries take some part in war production so that the relative position might be fairly well maintained even though the type of goods produced in the industry was changed.

Changes in the share of the total productive income realized by an industry may be due to an interindustry shift in purchasing, changes in the price structure, or both. With no change in prices a shift in purchasing from one industry to another will increase the share of the income going to the recipient industry and decrease the share of the other. A change in the interindustry price structure with no change in the volume of purchasing from each industry will increase the share going to the industry whose product prices have increased to a greater extent than those of the other industries.

Agriculture, mining, and manufacturing industries showed the greatest relative gains in sales during the war. These industries were the ones which received the benefit of government war spending so that the civilian sales (if any) which were lost by the transfer of purchasing power from the private to the public economy was more than made up by government purchases. Other industries which suffered by the transfer of spending included construction, trade, finance, and the service industries.

Table 72

Realized Private Production Income by Industry,
1914-1920

(percentage distribution)

Industry	1914	1916	1918	1920
Agriculture	19.7	20.2	23.4	17.3
Mining	3.6	4.1	4.1	4.3
Electric light, power, and gas	.9	.9	.8	.8
Manufacturing	21.5	25.0	26.4	27.6
Construction	3.5	3.1	2.3	3.6
Transportation and communication	11.6	10.6	10.9	12.3
Trade	19.7	17.8	15.8	16.5
Service	10.1	8.7	7.7	8.9
Finance	2.4	2.3	1.9	2.4
Other	6.9	7.4	6.6	6.3
Total	100.0	100.0	100.0	100.0

Source: Richard F. Martin, *National Income in the U.S.,* pp. 60–61.

Note: Figures may not total 100 because of rounding.

Effect of the War on Consumption

The current value of the national product expanded rapidly under the impetus of war spending but so did government war expenditures. Since production failed to keep pace, the resources needed for war production came mostly out of the civilian sector.

War expenditures averaged 14.6 per cent of the gross national product for the years 1917–1920 and reached 27.7 per cent in fiscal 1919. The nonwar economy after 1917 received not only a much smaller percentage of the national product but also a smaller absolute amount even as measured in the current inflated price level. In addition, net exports of merchandise

Table 73
Gross National Product and War Expenditures,
Current Dollars, 1916-1920
(millions of dollars)

Fiscal Year	(a) G.N.P.	(b) War Expenditures	Consumer Production	Ratio of (b) to (a)
1916	$43.6		$43.60	
1917	49.9	$ 1.34	48.56	.027
1918	61.6	13.05	48.55	.212
1919	65.7	18.21	47.49	.277
1920	82.8	5.40	77.40	.065
Total, 1917–1920	$260.0	$38.00	$222.00	.146

Source: Tables 19 and 66.

during the period 1916–1919 amounted to some $13 billion,[9] further depleting the volume of goods available for the civilian population.

Reducing both production and war expenditures to constant dollar terms creates a more realistic picture of the consumption sacrifice during the period.

Up to and including 1919, civilian production suffered a drastic decline, recovering somewhat as war expenditures declined in 1920. Taking 1916 as the base year, there was an average annual decline in real civilian production of $5.6 billion. For the four years real civilian production declined by $22.4 billion so that measured in real terms, of the $24.3 billion of goods used to prosecute the war, $1.9 billion came out of increased production and $22.4 billion resulted from a sacrifice of consumption.

Table 74
Gross National Product and War Expenditures,
1914 Dollars, 1916-1920
(billions of dollars)

Fiscal Year	G.N.P.	War Expenditures*	Civilian Production
1916	$ 41.3		$ 41.30
1917	42.1	$ 1.13	40.97
1918	42.9	9.09	33.81
1919	41.0	11.37	29.63
1920	41.1	2.70	38.40
Total, 1917–1920	$167.1	$24.29	$142.81

Source: Tables 19 and 66.
*War expenditures are deflated by the same divisor as the G.N.P. Thus for 1916, $43.6 ÷ $41.3 equals 1.056. Divisors are 1916—1.056; 1917—1.185; 1918—1.436; 1919—1.602; 1920—2.014.

Wartime Price Changes

The failure of production to keep up with the vast increase in the money supply created by government deficit financing and credit extension by the banking system was bound to be reflected in a rising price structure.

While the production increase took place primarily during the neutrality period and leveled off during the actual war period, the price structure acted conversely. Both wholesale and retail prices increased more rapidly during the war period than during the prewar period.

Wholesale prices increased 78 per cent between 1916 and 1920 as against 29.6 per cent during the prewar period and 126 per cent for the entire period. Not all commodity groups, however, followed this trend. Metal product and chemical prices increased

Table 75
Wholesale Prices, Major Commodity Groups,
1914–1920
(1913 = 100)

	1914	1916	Per Cent Change 1914–1916	1920	Per Cent Change 1916–1920
All commodities	98	127	+29.6	226	+78.0
Farm products	103	123	+19.4	218	+77.2
Foods	102	121	+18.6	220	+81.8
Clothing	98	127	+29.6	295	+132.3
Fuel and lighting	93	126	+35.5	241	+91.2
Metals and metal products	85	162	+90.6	192	+18.5
Building materials	92	120	+30.4	264	+120.0
Chemicals and drugs	101	181	+79.2	200	+10.5
House furnishings	100	106	+ 6.0	254	+139.6

Source: Statistical Abstract of the United States, 1924, p. 300.

greatly during the prewar period, having the largest increases of all groups. During the war metal and chemical prices showed the lowest increases, the greatest price increases going to other groups such as clothing and house furnishings. While the crude price controls put into effect by the wartime price-control agencies may not have been too successful from an over-all point of view, they evidently did influence certain specific price areas.[10] Nevertheless, from 1916 to 1918 the price index of controlled commodities rose somewhat higher than did the price index for uncontrolled commodities.[11]

Retail prices also had their greatest increases during the war period. The cost of living in the United States increased by 20 per cent from December 1914 to December 1916, and 73.8 per cent between December 1916 and June 1920. The largest increases occurred in furniture and clothing, both items whose raw materials were in demand for war purposes. The smallest increases took place in rent and fuel and light. Unlike wholesale prices, the cost of living during the war followed its prewar pattern, the largest wartime price increases taking place in those areas which had the largest prewar increases, while all groups maintained their relative positions with the exception of clothing and furniture.

Wartime savings failed to keep pace with the prewar level of 1916 both absolutely and in relation to the national product. Total savings for the war period amounted to $24.6 billion, averaging $6.2 billion annually, compared with $7 billion of savings in 1916. This was due to the sharp drop in corporate

Table 76
Cost of Living in the United States,
1914-1920
(1913 = 100)

	December 1914	December 1916	Per Cent Change 1914–1916	June 1920	Per Cent Change 1916–1920
Food	105.0	126.0	+20.0	219.0	+ 73.8
Clothing	101.0	120.0	+18.8	287.5	+139.6
Housing	100.0	102.3	+ 2.3	134.9	+ 31.8
Fuel and light	101.0	108.4	+ 7.3	171.9	+ 58.6
Furniture and furnishings	104.0	127.8	+22.9	292.7	+129.0
Miscellaneous	103.0	113.3	+10.0	201.4	+ 77.8
All Items	103.0	118.3	+14.8	216.5	+ 83.0

Source: Statistical Abstract of the United States, 1924, p. 310.

Table 77
Annual Savings in the United States,
1916–1920
(billions of dollars)

Year	Corporations	Unincorporated Enterprise	Individuals	Total	Savings G.N.P.
1916	$4.4	$1.1	$1.5	$7.0	.16
1917	4.7	2.1	1.2	7.0	.14
1918	1.5	1.5	1.4	4.4	.07
1919	3.5	1.4	2.7	7.6	.12
1920	1.5	1.5	2.6	5.6	.07

Source: Economic Almanac,*1941–1942*, p. 339; *ibid., 1945–1946*, p. 55.

business savings after 1917 which was greater than the increased savings of individuals and unincorporated business, both of which exceeded their prewar level of savings.

The distribution of wartime savings reflects the changes in the incomes of the groups involved, and follows these changes rather closely. Increased savings by individuals and unincorporated enterprises reflects the increased incomes received by those groups (see Table 70). The fluctuation in the annual savings of corporations illustrates both the fluctuations in corporation profits during the period and the tendency of dividends to lag behind net corporate earnings.

Since savings represent income diverted from current consumption, the trend of wartime savings offers one more explanation of the rising price level during the war period. From 1916 to 1920 the ratio of total savings to the gross national product decreased from 16 per cent to 7 per cent. This meant that demand for goods was accelerated not only by the increased money incomes but also by the failure of savings to maintain their prewar rate.

Summary

So far as production, productivity, and prices were concerned, the economic impact of World War I was experienced in two stages. Starting from a period when resources were unemployed and were available for utilization in July 1914, these resources were almost fully utilized by the middle of 1917 so that when the United States became an active participant in the conflict it became necessary to shift resource utilization from civilian into war-goods production. With no increase in productivity and total production, and with an increasing ratio of war expenditures to real gross national product, the war burden was borne almost completely by a sacrifice of consumption on the part of the civilian population.

Interindustry sharing of productive income for the most part consisted of minor changes with increases going to those industries producing war goods such as agriculture and manufacturing, and decreases in those industries catering primarily to civilian needs such as the trade and service industries. In most cases the change in the relative position of each industry within the economy was much greater from 1914 to 1916 than the change which occurred from 1916 to 1918. This suggests that the pattern of relative productive importance for the war period was determined in the prewar period.

While the relative increase in production occurred in the prewar period this was not true of price increases. Prices rose during both periods, but the increase during the war period was far greater than that which took place during the period of neutrality. Price controls had little effect on the general price level, although they did succeed in holding down prices on some specific commodities which were chiefly purchased by the government for war purposes.

In addition to the measurable effects of the war and its

financial aspects there were other factors which, while not given to measurement, had an important effect in shaping future American policies and practices. First was the position of the United States in world affairs; second was the impetus given to a broadening of government activity in the national economy; third was the influence of the Treasury on the national banking system; and fourth was the increased emphasis given to government fiscal policy as an economic variable.

When the war broke out in 1914 the United States was a debtor nation. Between the outbreak of the war and its completion the United States had become a creditor nation both in the private and government sectors. Because the war was fought entirely on foreign soil, physical reconstruction was unnecessary in the United States so that American industry needed only to transfer from war production to nonwar production. By no means an uncomplicated task, it was a simple one compared to that of war-ravaged Europe. By December 1919, 37 per cent of gold reserves of central banks and governments was in the United States.[12] America had become the most powerful nation in the world both productively and financially. In addition, there was an increased interest in world affairs which took place from that time. America learned that it could not live peacefully in blissful isolation. Although this feeling was not carried through during the 1920's, this world consciousness flared anew during the 1930's and culminated, after a second global conflict, in the United States being the prime moving spirit in the organizing of the United Nations Organization.

Equally as important as the changed international position of the United States was the extension of Federal influence over domestic economic life. Many policies adopted much later on by other administrations in both war and nonwar situations can be found in their embryonic stages during World War I. Price control, only slightly applied during World War I, reached maturity during World War II and the Korean "police action."

Federal influence in the field of labor culminating in the National Labor Relations Act of 1935 saw the light of day with the War Labor Board during World War I. The Food Administration Grain Corporation set a pattern for later agricultural assistance policies with its buying price for wheat. Thus World War I was the breeding ground for the extension of government power in economic life later put into effect by the administration of Herbert Hoover and brought into the flower of maturity by the New Deal and Fair Deal administrations of Franklin D. Roosevelt and Harry S. Truman.

The importance of the Federal Reserve System to the Treasury in the financing of the war changed the System almost immediately from an independent institution to what became almost a branch of the Treasury. The war not only sped the development of the Reserve System, but made all of its functions secondary to the Treasury's war finance program. This influence continued in modified form until World War II when the Federal Reserve System became once again partly if not wholly, subservient to the Treasury. Thus what was to have been a decentralized reserve banking system gave way to strong centralization, and became more of a government bank than a bankers' bank.

The growth of the Federal debt during the war led to the postwar development of economic thought along the lines of fiscal policy as a method of influencing economic life. The growth of the national income and the part played in this growth by government deficit finance found its way into the thoughts and writings of a new group of economists.[13] Federal debt was conceived of as a tool of government economic management instead of merely a method of meeting an excess of expenditures.

World War I finance can therefore be held responsible for the start of many important and far-reaching policy changes and the extension of many other policies which radically changed the concept of government and increased its importance as a determining and influencing factor in the economic welfare of the nation. While these trends were present in prewar days, the wartime emergency gave this movement its impetus, and with but a few brief intermissions it has remained a potent force in our national economy.

NOTES

[1] At some later date part of the resources may be returned to want-satisfying uses through the sale of army surplus to the civilian population, or by the use of war facilities for nonwar purposes.

[2] Consumption equals the quantity of goods available for nonwar purposes. Effort may be defined as the utilization of all productive factors.

[3] If the same quantity of productive effort is used more efficiently, the sacrifice of either consumption of effort will be somewhat mitigated.

[4] Since part of the money income of the beneficiaries is returned to the government in taxes and loans by war goods producers, sacrificers and beneficiaries will to some extent be the same people.

[5] E. A. J. Johnson and Herman E. Krooss, *The Origins and Development of the American Economy*, p. 147.

[6] Bureau of the Census, *Census of Manufactures, 1939*, p. 20.

[7] R. W. Hecht and G. T. Barton, *Gains in Productivity of Farm Labor*, Department of Agriculture Technical Bulletin No. 1020, December 1950, p. 102.

[8] Federal Reserve Board, *Index of Industrial Production*.

[9] *Statistical Abstract of the United States, 1924*, p. 420.

[10] Charles O. Hardy, *Wartime Control of Prices*.

[11] *Economic Almanac for 1945–46*, p. 54.

[12] Federal Reserve Board, *Banking and Monetary Statistics*, p. 544.

[13] For example, Alvin H. Hanson, *Monetary Theory and Fiscal Policy*: Kenyon E. Poole, ed., *Fiscal Policies and the American Economy*; Albert G. Hart, *Money, Debt, and Economic Activity*; Seymour E. Harris, *The National Debt and the New Economics*.

15

Evaluation of
World War I Finance

In the previous chapters the effects of the financing of the war on the banking system and on the general economy have been discussed. There now remains the problem of evaluating the war finance policies and practices.

The problem of evaluation involves comparison, which inevitably leads to the problem of selecting a standard against which such a comparison may be made. Three possibilities present themselves. First, one might compare war finance in the United States with the financing of the war by the other major belligerents. Second, there might be a comparison of World War I with other war periods in the United States. Third, one could evaluate war finance in practice as set against a background of theoretical standards. In this last step it would be necessary to consider the psychological and political aspects as well as the economic aspects for they are the all-important limiting factors.

The United States and the Other Belligerents

WAR EXPENDITURES

The war expenditures of the United States far exceeded those of any other nation. Average daily war expenditures of the United States during fiscal 1918 and 1919 amounted to $42.8 million. This was about $10 million a day greater than the war expenditures of any of the other belligerents during this period, and $32 million a day more than those of Italy, which had the lowest daily war expenditures of all. A computation of real expenditures would show an even wider difference since the wholesale price level in Great Britain, France and Italy was higher than that of the United States throughout the entire war period. The British and French expenditures are also

Table 78
Average Daily War Expenditures of Major Belligerents
(millions of dollars)

Country	Period Covered	Average Daily War Expenditure
United States	July 1, 1917–June 30, 1919	$42.8
Great Britain	April 1, 1917–March 30, 1919	32.6
France	January 1, 1917–December 31, 1917	32.4
Germany	July 1, 1917–December 31, 1918	32.2
Russia	January 1, 1916–October 31, 1918	33.1
Italy	July 1, 1917–June 30, 1918	10.4

Source: For the United States, see Table 19; for other countries, see E. R. A. Seligman, *Essays in Taxation,* pp. 753–754.

Note: An attempt has been made to compare the same general time periods wherever possible.

overstated by the amount of American loans which were never repaid.

WAR REVENUES

Despite the greater expenditures, the United States managed to raise a far greater proportion of its war expenditures from revenue sources than did any of the other belligerent nations. Excluding fiscal 1920 so as to make the data more comparable, the ratio of war revenue to war expenditures of the various nations show wide differences in accomplishment.   For the time periods covered in Table 79, the United States raised 23.3

Table 79
War Expenditures and War Revenues of Major Belligerents
(billions)

Country	Period Covered	(a) War Expenditures	(b) War Revenues	Ratio of (b) to (a)
United States (dollars)	July 1917– June 1919	32.6	7.6	.233
Great Britain (pounds)	April 1914– March 1919	8.61	1.75	.203
France (francs)	August 1914– March 1919	168.2	−1.5	−.009
Italy (lira)	May 1915– June 1918	77.6	12.6	.162
Germany (marks)	August 1914– December 1918	155.9	2.6	.017

Source: Tables 19 and 21; E. R. A. Seligman, *Essays in Taxation*, pp. 760, 762.

Note: Data on Great Britain reflect a nonwar balanced budget based on prewar (1914) expenditures. Other foreign figures reflect a nonwar balanced budget based on prewar revenues.

per cent of its war expenditures from war revenue sources. Great Britain came closest to the United States with 20.3 per cent of its war expenditures raised through war revenue. However, in the case of Great Britain, additional nontax revenues accounted for 5 per cent of the total. If these nontax revenues were to be excluded, the ratio of British war revenue to war expenditures would drop to 18.3 per cent.[1]

Ranked below Great Britain was Italy, which raised 16.2 per cent of its war expenditures by war revenues. France, struggling under invasion and occupation of its industrial areas, was faced with shrinking revenues.[2] In France it was not until 1917 that revenues again were equal to the 1913 figure, and for the period covered total revenue was 1.5 billion francs less than the assumed nonwar revenue. France, therefore, raised no revenue to pay for its war expenditures and failed even to balance its nonwar budget.

Germany did little better than France. Of 155.9 billion marks of war expenditures, all but 2.6 billion was raised by borrowing. Germany, feeling confident of victory, relied much more heavily on loans,[3] so that only 1.7 per cent of war expenditures came from revenue sources.

WAR BORROWING

The United States did its borrowing at lower interest rates than did any of the other belligerents. Great Britain sold her first war loan in March 1915 at $3\frac{1}{2}$ per cent, and her second in June 1915 at $4\frac{1}{2}$ per cent. Beginning in October 1917 a continuous issue of 4 and 5 per cent war bonds was made, the difference in the interest rate depending on a tax exemption.[4]

France issued her first war bonds at 5 per cent, but sold the bonds at a discount of $12\frac{3}{4}$ per cent. Later, 5 per cent bonds were sold as low as 70. Russia began war borrowing in September 1914 with a 5 per cent issue at 94 followed by six more issues, the

Table 80
Data on Bond Sales, Major Belligerents,
1917–1918

Country	Interest Rates	Issue Prices
United States	$3\frac{1}{2}$–$4\frac{1}{4}$	100
Great Britain	4–5	95–$100\frac{1}{2}$
France	4	68.6–70.8
Italy	5	$86\frac{1}{2}$–90
Russia	5	85
Germany	$4\frac{1}{2}$–5	95–98

Source: E. R. A. Seligman, Essays in Taxation, p. 775.

last of which was offered at 85. Italy issued a total of five loans at $4\frac{1}{2}$ to 5 per cent, none of which were issued at par and the last one offered at $86\frac{1}{2}$.

Germany relied at the beginning on long-term loans starting in September 1914 with a 5 per cent issue at $97\frac{1}{2}$. The interest rate never rose above 5 per cent and for some of the later issues dropped to $4\frac{1}{2}$ per cent. While Germany never sold any of the bond issues at par, the discount never fell below 5 per cent. So far as interest rates and issue prices of the war loans were concerned, Germany made a better showing than did any of the other belligerents except the United States and Great Britain.

World War I and Other Wars

WAR EXPENDITURES

Average daily war expenditures of $25.8 million from 1917 to 1920 were more than 12 times the average daily war expenditures of $2.1 million during the Civil War (1862–1865), and less than one-sixth of the average daily war expenditures during World War II.[5]

Table 81
War Expenditures and Gross National Product,
World Wars I and II
(billions of dollars)

Year	(a) G.N.P.	(b) War Expenditures	Ratio of (b) to (a)
World War I			
1917	$ 49.9	$ 1.34	.027
1918	61.6	13.05	.212
1919	65.7	18.21	.277
1920	82.8	5.40	.065
Total	$260.0	$ 38.00	.146
World War II			
1942	$161.6	$ 20.8	.129
1943	194.3	66.2	.341
1944	213.7	81.9	.383
1945	215.2	85.3	.396
1946	211.1	47.3	.224
Total	$995.9	$301.5	.303

Source: Table 73; U.S. Treasury Department, *Annual Report, 1949*, p. 361; Bureau of Foreign and Domestic Commerce, *National Income and Product of the United States, 1929–1950*, p. 150.

In terms of both money costs and real costs, World War II was by far the costlier war in both absolute and relative terms. War expenditures averaged $60.3 billion annually during World War II compared with an annual average war expenditure of $9.5 billion during World War I. World War II war expenditures represented 30.3 per cent of the gross national product, compared with 14.6 per cent for World War I.

Although World War II was a more expensive war by all standards, Federal expenditures relative to prewar expenditures increased at a much greater rate during World War I. Average annual expenditures of $10.25 billion from 1917 to 1920 were 13.8 times the $742 million of expenditures in 1916. World War II average annual expenditures of $71.9 billion were 7.1 times the 1940 expenditures and only 3.5 times those of 1941. From a percentage point of view, the added impact of increased expenditures during the war period was greater during World War I than during World War II.

WAR REVENUES

The ratio of war revenue to war expenditures was slightly lower in World War I than in World War II, but it was greater than the Civil War ratio. In both the Civil War and World War I

Table 82
War Expenditures and War Revenues in the United States:
Civil War, World War I, and World War II

Year	War Expenditures (a)	War Revenues (b)	Ratio of (b) to (a)
	Civil War		
	(millions of dollars)		
1862	$ 408.3	—$ 14.5	—.035
1863	648.2	46.2	.071
1864	798.8	198.1	.248
1865	1,231.1	267.2	.217
1866	454.3	491.5	1.082
Total	$3,540.7	$988.5	.279

Table 82
(continued)

Year	War Expenditures (a)	War Revenues (b)	Ratio of (b) to (a)
	World War I *(billions of dollars)*		
1917	$ 1.34	$ .38	.284
1918	13.05	3.44	.263
1919	18.21	3.91	.215
1920	5.40	5.96	1.104
Total	$ 38.00	$ 13.70	.360
	World War II *(billions of dollars)*		
1942	$ 20.8	$ 4.2	.202
1943	66.2	13.7	.207
1944	81.9	35.4	.432
1945	85.3	36.3	.426
1946	47.3	$ 31.5	.666
Total	$ 301.5	$121.1	.401

Source: Table 23; U.S. Treasury Department, *Annual Report, 1949*, pp. 358–361.

Note: The balanced budget assumption for nonwar expenditures is assumed for the three war periods.

periods, the ratios were aided considerably by a budget surplus in the last year included in the war years. If the last year were to be deleted from the computation, the ratios for the three war periods would be 16, 24, and 35 per cent for the Civil War, World War I and World War II respectively rather than the ratios of 27.9, 36, and 40.1 per cent shown in Table 82.

Unlike the experience during World War II, the ratio of war

revenue to war expenditures during World War I decreased each year except the last. This reflected the failure of taxation to increase at the same rate as the expenditures were increasing.

The taxes imposed during the war by the Revenue Acts of 1917 and 1918 were inadequate both as to amount and type. Total revenue of $16.7 billion from 1917 to 1920 was equal to only 6.4 per cent of the gross national product during the period.[6] During World War II taxation was equal to 18.8 per cent of the gross product.[7] However, the average annual receipts during World War II were only 2.4 times as large as those in the first prewar year (1941) and 4.3 times as large as those in the second prewar year (1940), whereas average annual receipts during World War I were 5.4 times as large as those in 1916 and 6 times as large as 1915 receipts. The relative increase in taxation was therefore much larger compared with the prewar period during World War I than during World War II.

WAR BORROWING

The same general pattern of war borrowing was used by the Treasury during both World Wars. The use of the banking system to provide funds for the Treasury was even more prevalent during World War II.[8] This was accomplished by a round-about method whereby the debt was sold originally to nonbank investors and repurchased by the commercial banks and the Federal Reserve banks. Of the $146.7 billion of debt sales in the seven war loans and the Victory Loan in World War II, $10.2 billion or 7 per cent was sold to commercial banks, but by February 1946 the commercial banks possessed $57.2 billion of the war debt, equal to 32 per cent. The Federal Reserve banks and the commercial banks combined held 42 per cent of the World War II increase in debt in February 1946 compared with 25 per cent of the World War I debt in June 1919, including Federal Reserve rediscounts resulting from the "borrow and buy" policy in effect during World War I. Rediscounts secured by the governments during World War II amounted to only about .1 per cent of the war debt in December 1945 and 1946.[9]

Regulation of the interest rate and the market prices of government bonds went much further during World War II than during World War I. The interest rate structure set up at the start of the second war was kept unchanged throughout the war period. The market prices of Treasury issues were supported by the open-market operations of the Federal Reserve banks, the assurance that the interest rate on later war issues would not be increased, and the "posted rate" on Treasury bills. The rate of $\frac{3}{8}$ per cent posted by the Federal Reserve banks assured bill buyers a ready market for Treasury bills at par.

Table 83
Absorption of the War Debt, World Wars I and II

June 1916–June 1919	Amount (millions)	Per Cent
Net increase in debt	$24,263.	100
To Federal Reserve banks	175.	1
To commercial banks	4,395.	18
To nonbank investors	18,119.	75
Rediscounts	1,574	6

November 1942–February 1946	Amount (billions)	Per Cent
Net increase in debt	$ 179.4	100
To Federal Reserve banks	17.5	10
To commercial banks	57.2	32
To nonbank investors	104.7	58

Source: U.S. Treasury Department, *Annual Report, 1949*, p. 397; Federal Reserve Board, *Banking and Monetary Statistics*, p. 19; Tables 58 and 63; Henry C. Murphy, *National Debt in War and Transition*, p. 162.

By the use of this policy in their own interests Treasury bills were utilized by the commercial banks as excess reserves.[10] The intensive support of governments during World War II as compared with World War I resulted in a par or better price for government issues during the second war while during the first war prices of government bonds sold below par during most of the period.[11]

From 1916 to 1920 the Federal interest-bearing debt increased from $972 million to $24,063 million, an increase of $23,091 million or 2,375 per cent. The Federal debt increase of $219.7 billion during World War II was an increase of 454 per cent.[12]

PRICES AND PRODUCTION

Wholesale prices in the United States, while far above their prewar levels, compared favorably with price rises in the other Allied nations. Where the wholesale price index in the United

Table 84

Wholesale Prices in War Periods in the United States

Civil War[a]		World War I[b]		World War II[b]	
Year	Index	Year	Index	Year	Index
1861	100	1916	100	1941	100
1862	117	1917	137	1942	113
1863	147	1918	153	1943	118
1864	189	1919	162	1944	119
1865	215	1920	181	1945	121
1866	190			1946	138

Source: (a) Bureau of the Census, *Historical Statistics of the United States, 1789–1945*, pp. 233–234. (b) Bureau of Labor Statistics, *Handbook of Labor Statistics, 1950*, p. 118.

Note: All series have been adjusted to reflect an index of 100 in each of the prewar years.

States stood at 239 in 1920 (1913 average = 100) the comparable price level in Great Britain was 310, and that of France was 512.[13]

In a comparison of domestic wholesale price movements during three war ·periods, prices advanced most during the Civil War, and least during World War II when most of the increase took place after the termination of hostilities and reached its peak in 1948.

The comparatively small rise in prices during World War II was due to several factors not present during World War I. Real gross national product increased from $115.5 billion in 1941 to $156.9 billion in 1944, in 1939 prices. Civilian production compared with World War I was far better maintained during World War II. From 1941 to 1945 civilian production fell 20

Table 85
Real Civilian Production, World Wars I and II
(billions of dollars)

Year	G.N.P.	World War II (1939 dollars)		World War I (1914 dollars)	Year
		War Expenditures	*Civilian Production*	*Civilian Production*	
1941	$115.5	—	$115.5	$ 41.3	1916
1942	129.7	$ 16.7	113.0	41.0	1917
1943	145.7	49.6	96.1	33.8	1918
1944	156.9	60.1	96.8	29.6	1919
1945	153.4	60.8	92.6	38.4	1920
1946	138.4	31.0	107.4		
1941–1946	$724.1	$218.2	$505.9	$142.8	1917–1920

Source: Tables 74 and 81; *Economic Report of the President*, July 1951, pp. 225–226.

Note: Government expenditures are deflated by the same divisor as the G. N. P. divisors; 1942—1.246; 1943—1.3333; 1944—1.362; 1945—1.403; 1946—1.525.

per cent in real terms as against 28.3 per cent from 1916 to 1919. Increased war expenditures during World War II were met by a greater increase in production, so that of the $218.2 billion of real war expenditures from 1942 to 1946, only $71.6 billion or 33 per cent came out of consumption. In the 1917–1920 period, of the $24.3 billion of real war expenditures, $22.4 billion or 92 per cent represented a consumption sacrifice.

An extremely important factor in keeping prices in line during World War II was the rate of savings. From 15.7 per cent of the G.N.P. in 1940 the rate of savings increased to 26.7 per cent in 1944, then declined to 22.5 per cent in 1945 and 13.6 per cent in 1946.[14] During World War I savings both in amount and rate declined reaching a low of 7 per cent against a prewar level of 16 per cent (Table 77).

War Finance—Success or Failure?

The questions as to whether the war finance program was a success or failure can both be answered in the affirmative. The program was successful to the extent that it did finance the war, but it was a failure in the sense that the program could have been improved upon. Success or failure therefore is a matter of degree and purpose rather than an absolute measure.

Tax measures were inadequate during World War I both quantitatively and qualitatively. Although tax receipts far exceeded those of the prewar years, they comprised only a small portion of the increased value of production due to the war. One increase took place from 1917 to 1918 but after that, with increasing war production, the percentage of war revenues declined. In a similiar fashion, the ratio of war revenue to war expenditure declined until 1920. As income rises, it becomes possible to increase tax rates, for according to the law of diminishing utility the added income will be regarded by the recipient at a lower value than the units of the preceding income. This was not achieved during the World War I period. On the contrary, the personal income tax average rate fell from 7 per cent in 1918 to 6.4 per cent in 1919 and 4.5 per cent in 1920,[15] and the ratio of war revenues to the increased value of production declined after 1918, averaging only 16 per cent for the four-year war period.

Qualitatively the emphasis on progressive taxation failed to achieve a transfer of purchasing power from spenders to the government. Instead, the purchasing power of the lower-income groups was increased at the expense of savings, which declined drastically over the war period. Although this policy may be upheld in a depression, it serves during an inflated war period with little or no increase in production only to increase price inflation still further.

No recognition was given in World War I tax policy to the use of tax provisions to increase productive resources. During World War II provision for the accelerated depreciation of war plants acted as an incentive for the construction of war facilities. During World War I this type of tax policy was not used.

Table 86
Ratio of War Revenue to War Expenditures and War Product
(in percentages)

Year	Ratio of War Revenue to War Expenditures[a]	War Product[b]
1917	.284	.060
1918	.263	.190
1919	.215	.177
1920	1.104	.152
Total	.360	.160

Source: (a) Table 82. (b) Prewar (1916) G.N.P. of $45.6 billion is subtracted from annual G.N.P. for the war years to determine war product.

Instead, the Act of 1917, providing that the 10 per cent tax on undistributed profits would not apply to profits invested in Federal obligations issued after September 1, 1917, was an incentive to buy bonds rather than build war plants.[16]

The borrowing program was equally lacking in foresight. The reliance on bank borrowing, the emphasis on low interest rates, the use of bank credit for nonbank bond purchasers, the overloading of the debt with short maturity issues, and the failure to concentrate more heavily on selling bonds to the lower-income groups made the Treasury loan program a program of expediency rather than of planning.

Selling government debt to the banking system either directly, or indirectly through the "borrow and buy" program,

Table 87
Federal Debt Maturities, 1917–1920
(millions of dollars)

Maturities	1917	1918	1919	1920
One year or less				
Amount	$ 310.3	$ 2,150.2	$ 4,590.3	$ 3,607.8
Per cent	11.5	18.0	18.2	15.0
One to five years				
Amount	63.9	—	3,467.8	4,364.9
Per cent	2.3	—	13.7	18.1
Five years and over				
Amount	2,338.3	9,835.7	17,176.4	16,088.4
Per cent	86.2	82.0	68.1	66.9
Total				
Amount	$2,712.5	$11,985.9	$25,234.5	$24,061.1
Per cent	100.0	100.0	100.0	100.0

Source: U.S. Treasury Department, *Annual Reports, 1917–1920.*

increased the money supply and so contributed to the inflationary pressures. In a similar fashion, the sale of debt to the savers of the nation rather than to the spenders failed to relieve the pressure on consumer spending, since bond buyers used savings to buy the bonds, leaving consumption purchasing power unchanged at its new high level.

The dependence by the Treasury on the certificates of indebtedness caused a continuous refunding problem. The certificates were refunded not only by the Liberty and Victory Loans, but by other certificate issues. Since the certificates carried the same and even higher interest rates than did the long-term loans, it would have been a wiser policy to have concentrated on the long-term issues.

As the war progressed a larger percentage of the debt was composed of the shorter-term issues. From June 1917 to June 1920 the percentage of the debt maturing in five years or less increased from 13.8 per cent to 33.1 per cent. On August 31, 1919 debt maturing in less than five years was 35 per cent of the total Federal indebtedness.[17] This situation also contributed to the refunding process, and caused a continuation of the refunding problem in the postwar period.

The low-interest rate policy kept the market prices of the Treasury issues below par throughout the war and pushed them even lower when the Victory notes were issued at higher rates. In order to counteract this fall in government bond prices, the Treasury gave tax concessions which in effect made the bonds taxable and tax-exempt at the same time. A better policy would have been to increase the rate during the war so as to provide an incentive for the shifting of investment funds from private to government bonds, and to decrease the rate in the postwar period so as to induce private investment. The policy of low rates during the war and higher rates in the postwar period accentuated both the war inflation and the postwar deflation.

The failure of the Treasury to provide a continuous medium

for purchase by the low-income group also contributed to the price inflation. The employee group received the largest income increases and paid very little of the war taxes. A special bond issue for this group, redeemable only at the option of the government, could have contributed in some way against the onslaught of consumer spending during the war, and would have provided added purchasing power during the postwar period.

All of the above-mentioned suggestions for a more efficient war finance program are subject to psychological and political limitations, especially the latter. During World War I legislators were most reluctant to impose taxes on their constituents. The pressures brought to bear on Congress by special-interest business groups made more excises politically impossible. Individuals would rather buy bonds than pay taxes and if the lower-income groups bought few bonds it was because the low-income groups had little with which to buy the bonds.

The problem of war finance involves a dual inconsistency. The Treasury, through taxes or borrowing, must get the funds from those who have them—the upper-income groups and the banking system. At the same time the program should make the shift of resources from nonwar to war production as painless as possible by keeping a tight control over the money supply and consumption. This involves a transfer of purchasing power from the lower-income groups to the government. Economic theory dictates a greater emphasis on the latter policy but expediency dictates the former, and in this respect war finance is and has always been a victory of expediency over economics.

NOTES

[1] E. R. A. Seligman, *Essays in Taxation*, p. 771.
[2] *Ibid.*, pp. 759–760.
[3] *Ibid.*, p. 761.

[4] Material on foreign war loans taken from Seligman, *Essays*, pp. 772–782.

[5] U.S. Treasury Department, *Annual Report, 1949*, pp. 3⁵⁰–361. Data adjusted by subtracting 1861 expenditures of $66.5 million annually from 1862–1865 expenditures, and 1941 expenditures of $13,386.6 million annually from 1942–1946 expenditures as assumed nonwar expenditures. Table 19.

[6] Tables 21 and 73.

[7] U.S. Department of Commerce, *National Income and Product of the U.S., 1929–1950*, pp. 150–154.

[8] For an extended discussion of World War II borrowing see Henry C. Murphy, *National Debt in War and Transition*, Chapter 12.

[9] Federal Reserve Board, *Annual Report, 1946*, p. 72.

[10] Murphy, *National Debt*, pp. 98–99.

[11] *Ibid.*, p. 221.

[12] U.S. Treasury Department, *Annual Report, 1949*, pp. 397–398.

[13] *Statistical Abstract of the United States, 1924*, p. 302.

[14] U.S. Department of Commerce, *National Income and Product of the U.S., 1929–1950*, p. 152.

[15] *Statistical Abstract of the United States, 1924*, p. 162.

[16] *Commercial and Financial Chronicle*, October 20, 1917, p. 1580.

[17] *Statistical Abstract of the United States, 1924*, p. 193.

Bibliography

Books and Pamphlets

ABBOT, CHARLES C. *Business Finances During the Critical Transition from War to Peace.* Harvard University Graduate School of Business Administration, Cambridge, 1944.

AMERICAN IRON AND STEEL INSTITUTE. *Annual Statistical Reports, 1914–1919.* New York.

———. *Monthly Production of Steel Ingots in the United States, 1901–1940.* New York.

ANDERSON, BENJAMIN M. *Economics and the Public Welfare; Financial and Economic History of the United States, 1914–1946.* D. Van Nostrand Co., Princeton, N.J., 1949.

———. *Effects of the War on Money, Credit, and Banking in France and the United States.* Oxford University Press, New York, 1919.

ARNETT, ALEX M. *Claude Kitchin and the Wilson War Policies.* Little, Brown and Company, Boston, 1937.

BACKMAN, JULES. *The Economics of Armament Inflation.* Rinehart and Company, New York, 1951.

BANKERS TRUST COMPANY. *The Balance Sheet of the Nations at War.* New York, 1917.

———. *Victory and Other Liberty Loan Acts.* New York, 1919.

BARRON'S. *The Dow Jones Averages.* New York.

BOGART, ERNEST L. *Direct and Indirect Costs of the Great World War.* Oxford University Press, New York, 1919.

BROWN, HARRY G. *The Economics of Taxation.* Henry Holt and Company, New York, 1924.

BURGESS, W. RANDOLPH. *The Reserve Banks and the Money Market.* Harper and Brothers, New York, 1927.

BUTTERS, JOHN K., AND JOHN LINTNER. *Effect of Federal Taxes on Growing Enterprise.* Harvard University Graduate School of Business Administration, Cambridge, 1945.

CHICAGO ASSOCIATION OF COMMERCE. *Taxation and Business.* Chicago, 1917.

CLARK, JOHN M. *The Costs of the World War to the American People.* Yale University Press, New Haven, 1931.

CLARK, LAWRENCE E. *Central Banking Under the Federal Reserve System, with Special Consideration of the Federal Reserve Bank of New York.* The Macmillan Company, New York, 1935.

CLARKSON, GROSVENOR B. *Industrial America and the World War.* Houghton Mifflin Company, Boston, 1924.

CLEVELAND, FREDERICK A., AND SAMUEL M. LINDSAY. *National Expenditures and Public Economy.* The Academy of Political Science, Columbia University, New York, 1921.

COUNCIL OF ECONOMIC ADVISORS. *The Economics of National Defense.* Government Printing Office, Washington, D.C., 1950.

CROWELL, BENEDICT, AND ROBERT F. WILSON. *The Giant Hand; Our Mobilization and Control of Industry and National Resources, 1917–1918.* Yale University Press, New Haven, 1921.

———. *Demobilization; Our Industrial and Military Demobilization After the Armistice, 1918–1920.* Yale University Press, New Haven, 1921.

CROWELL, JOHN F. *Government War Contracts.* Oxford University Press, New York, 1920.

CRUM, WILLIAM L., JOHN F. FENNELLY, AND LAWRENCE H. SELTZER. *Fiscal Planning for Total War.* National Bureau of Economic Research, New York, 1942.

DURAND, DAVID. *Basic Yields of Corporate Bonds, 1900–1942.* National Bureau of Economic Research, New York, 1942.

Economic Report of the President, July 1951. Government Printing Office, Washington, D.C., 1951.

ELLIS, PAUL W. *The World's Biggest Business, American Public Spending, 1914–1944.* National Industrial Conference Board, New York, 1944.

FEDERAL RESERVE BOARD. *Index of Industrial Production.* Washington, D.C. Annual.

———. *Annual Reports, 1914–1920, 1946,* Washington, D.C.

———. *Banking and Monetary Statistics.* Washington, D.C., 1943.

FISHER, IRVING. *The Right and Wrong Way of Financing the War.* Trust Companies, New York, 1918.

40 U.S. Statutes at Large. Government Printing Office, Washington, D.C., 1919.

GAYER, ARTHUR D. *Monetary Policy and Economic Stabilization.* A. and C. Black, London, 1935.

GLASS, CARTER. *An Adventure in Constructive Finance.* Doubleday, Page and Company, New York, 1927.

GOLDENWEISER, EMANUEL A. *Federal Reserve System in Operation.* McGraw-Hill Book Company, New York, 1925.

GROVES, HAROLD M. *Trouble Spots in Taxation.* Princeton University Press, Princeton, 1948.

GURNEY, EDMUND R. *War Time Finance.* Kline-Smith Publishing Co., Lincoln, 1917.

HANSON, ALVIN H. *Monetary Theory and Fiscal Policy.* McGraw-Hill Book Company, New York, 1949.

HARDING, WILLIAM P. G. *The Formative Period of the Federal Reserve System.* Houghton Mifflin Company, Boston, 1925.

HARDY, CHARLES O. *Credit Policies of the Federal Reserve System.* The Brookings Institution, Washington, D.C., 1932.

———. *Wartime Control of Prices.* The Brookings Institution. Washington, D.C., 1940.

HARRIS, SEYMOUR E. *The Economics of America at War.* W. W. Norton and Company, New York, 1943.

———. *The Economics of American Defense.* W. W. Norton and Company, New York, 1941.

———. *The National Debt and the New Economics.* McGraw-Hill Book Company, New York, 1947.

————. *20 Years of Federal Reserve Policy*. Harvard University Press, Cambridge, 1933.

HART, ALBERT G. *Money, Debt and Economic Activity*. Prentice-Hall, New York, 1948.

HECHT, R. W., AND G. T. BARTON. *Gains in Productivity of Farm Labor, United States Department of Agriculture Technical Bulletin No. 1020*. Washington, D.C., December 1950.

HENDRICKS, HENRY G. *The Federal Debt, 1919–1930*. Mimeoform Press, Washington, D.C., 1933.

HEPBURN, ALONZO B. *Financing the War*. Princeton University Press, Princeton, 1918.

HOLLANDER, JACOB H. *War Borrowing*. The Macmillan Company, New York, 1919.

JOHNSON, EDGAR A. J., AND HERMAN E. KROOSS. *The Origins and Development of the American Economy*. Prentice-Hall, New York, 1953.

JOINT COMMITTEE ON THE ECONOMIC REPORT. *The Economic and Political Hazards of an Inflationary Defense Economy*. Government Printing Office, Washington, D.C., 1951.

KEMMERER, EDWIN W. *The A B C of the Federal Reserve System*. Princeton University Press, Princeton, 1938.

KIMMEL, LEWIS H. *Taxes and Economic Incentives*. The Brookings Institution, Washington, D.C., 1950.

KING, CLYDE L. *Public Finance*. The Macmillan Company, New York, 1935.

KUZNETS, SIMON S. *Uses of National Income in Peace and War*. National Bureau of Economic Research, New York, 1942.

————. *National Product in Wartime*. National Bureau of Economic Research, New York, 1945.

LA FOLLETTE, ROBERT M. *War Profits Tax — Is it Disloyal to Advocate Just Taxation of War Profits and Surplus Incomes?* Government Printing Office, Washington, D.C., 1917.

————. *Vital Votes on Taxation of Incomes and War Profits*. Government Printing Office, Washington, D.C., 1917.

LEVIN. MAURICE, HAROLD G. MOULTON, AND CLARK WARBURTON. *America's Capacity to Consume*. The Brookings Institution, Washington, D.C:, 1934.

LEWIS, CLEONA. *American Stake in International Investments*. The Brookings Institution, Washington, D.C., 1938.

Liberty Loan Acts (U.S. Statutes). Government Printing Office, Washington, D.C., 1936.

LIBERTY LOAN COMMITTEE. *The Liberty Loan of 1917*. New York, 1917.

LOVE, ROBERT A. *Federal Financing*. Columbia University Press, New York, 1931.

MACAULEY, FREDERICK R. *Some Theoretical Problems Suggested by the Movements of Interest Rates, Bond Yields and Stock Prices in the United States Since 1856*. National Bureau of Economic Research, New York, 1938.

MADDEN, JOHN T., MARCUS NADLER, AND HARRY C. SAUVAIN. *America's Experience as a Creditor Nation*. Prentice-Hall, New York, 1937.

MARTIN, RICHARD F. *National Income in the United States, 1799–1938*. National Industrial Conference Board, New York, 1939.

McADOO, WILLIAM G. *The Second Liberty Loan* (Address delivered at the Annual Convention of the American Bankers' Association at Atlantic City, New Jersey, September 28, 1917). Government Printing Office, Washington, D.C., 1917.

———. *Crowded Years*. Houghton Mifflin Company, Boston, 1931.

MECHANICS AND METALS NATIONAL BANK. *The Cost of the War; a Brief Record and Analysis of the Finances*. New York, 1917.

MILLER, ADOLPH C. "Making Ready for New Financial Tests" (speech at the Bankers Club, Washington, D.C., 1917).

MOULON, HAROLD G. *War Debts and World Prosperity*. The Brookings Institution, Washington, D.C., 1932.

MOULTION, HAROLD G., AND LEO PASVOLSKY. *World War Debt Settlements*. The Macmillan Company, New York, 1926.

MURPHY, HENRY C. *National Debt in War and Transition*. McGraw-Hill Book Company, New York, 1950.

MYERS, MARGARET G. *New York Money Market*. Columbia University Press, New York, 1932.

NATIONAL BANK OF COMMERCE IN NEW YORK, *War Finance Primer*. New York, 1917.

NATIONAL BUREAU OF ECONOMIC RESEARCH, COMMITTEE ON RECENT ECONOMIC CHANGE. *Recent Economic Changes in the United States*. 2 volumes. McGraw-Hill Book Company, New York, 1929.

NATIONAL INDUSTRIAL CONFERENCE BOARD. *The International Financial Position of the United States.* New York, 1929.

––––––. *Economic Almanac for 1941–1942.* New York, 1941.

––––––. *Economic Almanac for 1945–1946.* New York, 1945.

NEW YORK STATE DEPARTMENT OF LABOR. *Bulletin No. 69. Idleness of Organized Wage Earners in 1914.* Albany, New York, 1915.

––––––. *Bulletin No. 73, Idleness of Organized Wage Earners in the First Half of 1915.* Albany, New York, 1915.

NOBLE, HENRY G. S. *The New York Stock Exchange in the Crisis of 1914.* Country Life Press, New York, 1915.

––––––. *The Stock Exchange.* Harper and Brothers, New York, 1933.

NOURSE, EDWIN G., AND ASSOCIATES. *America's Capacity to Produce.* The Brookings Institution, Washington, D.C., 1934.

NOYES, ALEXANDER D. *Financial Chapters of the War.* Charles Scribner's Sons, New York, 1916.

––––––. *The War Period of American Finance, 1908–1925.* G. P. Putnam's Sons, New York, 1926.

PIGOU, ARTHUR C. *The Political Economy of War.* Macmillan and Company, London, 1921.

POOLE, KENYON E., ed. *Fiscal Policies and the American Economy.* Prentice-Hall, New York, 1951.

RATNER, SIDNEY. *American Taxation, its History as a Force in Democracy.* W. W. Norton and Company, New York, 1942.

REED, HAROLD L. *The Development of Federal Reserve Policy.* Houghton Mifflin Company, Boston, 1922.

SAMUELSON, PAUL, AND EVERETT E. HAGEN. *After the War, 1918–1920, Military and Economic Demobilization of the United States.* Government Printing Office, Washington, D.C., 1943.

SELIGMAN, EDWIN R. A. *Essays in Taxation.* 10th ed. The Macmillan Company, New York, 1925.

SELIGMAN, EDWIN R. A. AND ROBERT M. HAIG. *How to Finance the War.* Columbia War Papers, Series 1, No. 7. Columbia University Press, New York, 1917.

SHOUP, CARL, MILTON FRIEDMAN, AND RUTH P. MACK. *Taxing to Prevent Inflation.* Columbia University Press, New York, 1943.

STAMP, SIR JOSHUA C. *Fundamental Principles of Taxation.* Macmillan and Company, London, 1921.

Bibliography 245

STUDENSKI, PAUL AND HERMAN E. KROOSS. *Financial History of the United States*. McGraw-Hill Book Company, New York, 1952.

SYNON, MARY. *McAdoo*. Bobbs-Merrill Company, Indianapolis, 1924.

TAX INSTITUTE. *Financing the War*. Philadelphia, 1942.

———. *Curbing Inflation Through Taxation*. Philadelphia, 1944.

TAUS, ESTHER R. *Central Banking Functions of the United States Treasury, 1789–1941*. Columbia University Press, New York, 1943.

39 U.S. Statutes at Large. Government Printing Office, Washington, D.C., 1917.

UNITED STATES DIVISION OF BOOKKEEPING AND WARRANTS. *Combined Statement of Receipts and Expenditures, 1914–1920*. Government Printing Office, Washington, D.C.

UNITED STATES DEPARTMENT OF COMMERCE, BUREAU OF THE CENSUS. *Census of Manufactures, 1939*. Government Printing Office, Washington, D.C., 1942.

———. *Historical Statistics of the United States, 1789–1945*. Government Printing Office, Washington, D.C., 1949.

———. *Statistical Abstract of the United States, 1924*. Government Printing Office, Washington, D.C.

UNITED STATES DEPARTMENT OF COMMERCE, BUREAU OF FOREIGN AND DOMESTIC COMMERCE. *Annual Reports, 1916–1920*. Government Printing Office, Washington, D.C.

———. *National Income and Product of the United States, 1929–1950*. Government Printing Office, Washington, D.C.

UNITED STATES CONGRESS, HOUSE WAYS AND MEANS COMMITTEE (64:1). *Report to Accompany H. R. 16763, to Increase the Revenue and for Other Purposes*. Government Printing Office, Washington, D.C., 1916.

——— (65:2). *Hearings on the Proposed Revenue Act of 1918*. Government Printing Office, Washington, D.C., 1918.

UNITED STATES CONGRESS, SENATE FINANCE COMMITTEE (64:1). *Hearings on H. R. 16763, an Act to Increase the Revenue and for Other Purposes*. Government Printing Office, Washington, D.C., 1916.

——— (65:1). *Hearings and Briefs . . . on H.R. 4280, an Act to Provide Revenue to Defray War Expenses and for Other Purposes*. Government Printing Office, Washington, D.C., 1917.

—— (65:2). *Hearings on H.R. 12863 to Provide Revenue and for Other Purposes.* Government Printing Office, Washington, D.C., 1918.

—— (65:2–3). *Hearings...on H.R. 12863 to Provide Revenue and for Other Purposes.* Government Printing Office, Washington, D.C., 1918.

UNITED STATES DEPARTMENT OF LABOR, BUREAU OF LABOR STATISTICS. *Consumer Price Index.* Washington, D.C.

——. *Handbook of Labor Statistics.* Government Printing Office, Washington, D.C., 1951.

——. *Historical Study No. 2: Labor Relations in the United States, Summary of Historical Events in the World War Period.* Washington, D.C., 1941.

——. *Index Numbers of Wholesale Prices.*

——. *Unemployment in the United States, July 1916.* Bulletin No. 195. Washington, D.C.

——. *War and Postwar Wages, Prices, and Hours, 1914–23 and 1939–44.* Bulletin No. 852. Government Printing Office, Washington, D.C., 1946.

UNITED STATES STEEL CORPORATION. *Annual Report, 1918.*

UNITED STATES TREASURY DEPARTMENT. *Annual Reports, 1914–1920, 1949.* Government Printing Office, Washington, D.C.

——. Comptroller of the Currency. *Annual Reports, 1917–1918.* Government Printing Office, Washington, D.C.

——. Internal Revenue Office. *Annual Report, 1917–1918.* Government Printing Office, Washington, D.C.

VANDERLIP, FRANK A. "The Liberty Loan, Its Economic Status and Effects" (address before a meeting of the Fifth Group, New York Bankers Association, Albany, New York, May 1917).

WARBURG, PAUL M. *The Federal Reserve System, Its Origin and Growth.* The Macmillan Company, New York, 1930.

WARREN, GEORGE F., AND FRANK A. PEARSON. *Prices.* John Wiley and Sons, New York, 1933.

WESTERFIELD, RAY B. *Banking Principles and Practices. Vol. 2.* The Ronald Press Company, New York, 1921.

——. *Our Silver Debacle.* The Ronald Press Company, New York, 1936.

WESTERN ECONOMIC SOCIETY. *Financial Mobilization for War*. University of Chicago Press, Chicago, 1917.

WILLIS, H. PARKER. *Federal Reserve System, Legislation, Organization and Operation*. The Ronald Press Company, New York, 1923.

WILLOUGHBY, WILLIAM F. *Government Organization in Wartime and After*. D. Appleton and Company, New York, 1919.

WILSON, WOODROW. *Address Delivered at a Joint Session of Congress on the Finances, May 27, 1918*. Government Printing Office, Washington, D.C., 1918.

WITHERS, WILLIAM. *Retirement of National Debts*. Columbia University Press, New York, 1932.

Articles

ADAMS, HENRY C. "Borrowing as a Phase of War Financing," *Annals of the American Academy of Political and Social Science*, January 1918.

ADAMS, THOMAS S. "Federal Taxes Upon Income and Excess Profits; with Discussion," *American Economic Review*, March 1918.

ANDERSON, FRANK F. "Fundamental Factors in War Finance," *Journal of Political Economy*, November 1917.

ARBUTHNOT, CHARLES C. "This Generation Can Not Escape Paying the Cost of the War," *Scientific Monthly*, November 1918.

BLAKEY, ROY G. "The New Revenue Act," *American Economic Review*, December 1916.

———. "The Personal Income Tax and Defense," *Annals of the American Academy of Political and Social Science*, March 1941.

———. "Shifting the War Burden Upon the Future," *Annals of the American Academy of Political and Social Science*, January 1918.

———. "The War Revenue Act of 1917," *American Economic Review*, December 1917.

———, AND GLADYS C. BLAKEY. "The Revenue Act of 1918," *American Economic Review*, June 1919.

BOWER, HOWARD R. "The Personal Income Tax and the Economy," *Annals of the American Academy of Political and Social Science*, November 1949.

BULLOCK, CHARLES J. "Financing the War," *Quarterly Journal of Economics*, May 1917.

DAVENPORT, HERBERT J. "War Finance and American Business," *Journal of Political Economy*, February 1916.

DURAND, EDWARD D. "Taxation Versus Bond Issues for Financing the War," *Journal of Political Economy*, November 1917.

FISHER, IRVING. "How the Public Should Pay for the War," *Annals of the American Academy of Political and Social Science*, July 1918.

FITZGERALD, JOHN J. "Task of Financing the War," *Annals of the American Academy of Political and Social Science*, January 1918.

FRIEDMAN, MILTON. "Price, Income, and Monetary Changes in Three Wartime Periods," *American Economic Review*, May 1952.

GROVES, HAROLD M. "Drawing on Wages and Small Incomes to Finance Defense," *Annals of the American Academy of Political and Social Science*, March 1941.

———. "A General Appraisal of the American Tax Problem," *Annals of the American Academy of Political and Social Science*, November 1949.

HAIG, ROBERT M. "Revenue Act of 1918," *Political Science Quarterly*, September 1919.

HOLLANDER, JACOB H. "Do Government Loans Cause Inflation," *Annals of the American Academy of Political and Social Science*, January 1918.

———. "Certificates of Indebtedness in Our War Financing," *Journal of Political Economy*, November 1918.

HUEBNER, SOLOMON S. "American Security Market During the War," *Annals of the American Academy of Political and Social Science*, November 1916.

KEITH, E. GORDON. "Tax Policy and Investment," *Annals of the American Academy of Political and Social Science*, November 1949.

KEYNES, JOHN M. "New Taxation in the United States," *Economic Journal*, December 1917.

MILLER, ADOLPH C. "War Finance and Inflation," *Annals of the American Academy of Political and Social Science*, January 1918.

MUSGRAVE, RICHARD A. "Fiscal and Monetary Problems in a High-Level Defense Economy: A Study in Taxable Capacity," *American Economic Review*, May 1950.

NEWCOMER, MABEL. "Taxation and the Consumer," *Annals of the American Academy of Political and Social Science,* November 1949.

NOYES, ALEXANDER D. "Economic Results of the War to the Present Date," *Scribner's,* August 1915.

———. "Argument Against Inflation from Government Loans," *Annals of the American Academy of Political and Social Science,* January 1918.

NOYES, C. REINOLD. "Fallacies of War Finance," *Yale Review,* October 1918.

PATTON, SIMON N. "The War and the Stock Market," *Moody's Magazine,* March 1915.

———. "Problems of War Finance," *Yale Review,* October 1917.

PLEHN, CARL C. "Substance and Shadow in War Finance," *American Economic Review,* September 1918.

———. "War Profits and Excess Profits Taxes," *American Economic Review,* June 1920.

PRENTIS, H. W., Jr. "Taxation and Business Initiative," *Annals of the American Academy of Political and Social Science,* November 1949.

REED, HAROLD L. "Credit Expansion Under the Federal Reserve," *American Economic Review,* June 1918.

SELIGMAN, EDWIN R. A. "The Cost of the War and How it was Met," *American Economic Review,* December 1919.

———. "Loans Versus Taxes in War Finance," *Annals of the American Academy of Political and Social Science,* January 1918.

———. "Newer Tendencies in American Taxation," *Annals of the American Academy of Political and Social Science,* March 1915.

———. "On Fiscal Policy." In *Financial Mobilization for War.* Western Economic Society, pp. 1–12. University of Chicago Press, Chicago, 1917.

———. "The War Revenue Act," *Political Science Quarterly,* March 1918.

SIMPSON, HERBERT D. "Social and Economic Implications of Taxation in the Defense Program," *Annals of the American Academy of Political and Social Science,* March 1941.

SPRAGUE, OLIVER M. W. "The Conscription of Income," *The Economic Journal,* March 1917.

———. "The Crisis of 1914 in the United States," *American Economic Review*, September 1915.

———. "Loans and Taxes in War Finance," *American Economic Review, Supplement*, March 1917.

———. "Relationship Between Loans and Taxes in War Finance," *Annals of the American Academy of Political and Social Science*, January 1918.

———. "War and the Financial Situation in the United States," *Quarterly Journal of Economics*, November 1914.

TAUSSIG, FRANK W. "War Tax Act of 1917," *Quarterly Journal of Economics*, November 1917.

"Unemployment Survey, 1914–1915." *American Labor Legislation Review*, November 1915.

WILLIS, R. PARKER. "American Finance and the European War," *Journal of Political Economy*, February 1913.

Periodicals (Various Dates)

Commercial and Financial Chronicle
Commercial and Financial Chronicle — monthly reviews, 1914–1920
Congressional Record
Federal Reserve Board — monthly bulletins, 1915–1920
The Iron Age
Monthly Labor Review, 1914–1915
The New York Times

Index

Senate Finance Committee, 84, 92,
107–109
Sherman, John, 137
Shipping Bill, 24
Shipping Board, U.S., 24, 66
short-term debt, funding of, 144-145
Simmons, Wallace D., 89, 92,
108–109
Smoot, Reed, 108
Spanish War Revenue Act, 145
Sprague, O. M. .W., 86–89, 97
Standard and Poor's Index, 37
steel production, 21–22, 34–35
stock exchanges, closing of, 14–15
stockholders, profits tax and, 62–63
stock market: boom of 1915–16,
35–38; prices (1914–16), 37
Strong, Benjamin, 128
Sunday, Billy, 121
surplus demand, borrowing and, 9
surplus income, taxation and, 6.
See also excess-profits tax

Taussig, F. W., 97
taxable capacity, defined, 6
taxation: "absolute value" in, 8;
academic controversy on, 86–88;
amount of as root of controversy,
86; as anti-inflation measure, 86;
balanced with borrowing, 12; vs.
borrowing, 3–4, 11, 87–88; business views on, 89–90; capital
replacement and, 7; on consumption, 88; Emergency Revenue Act
of 1914 and, 25–27; favored by
Wilson and McAdoo, 84; fifty per
cent plan, 85–87; inflation and,
4–5; investment incentive and, 6,
63; morale and, 8; political and
psychological limitations of, 8,
236; postwar effects of, 7; production incentives and, 5–8; progression and regression in, 58; purposes
of, 57; real output and, 6; shiftability and incidence in, 58; types

of, 58–64; war efficiency and, 87;
war financing and, 57–64; war
revenues and, 70–71. See also
corporation profits tax; excess-
profits tax; income tax; War
Revenue Act of 1917
Teeter, Lucius, 89
Third Liberty Loan anticipation
certificates, 153–155
Thomas, Charles S., 108
tobacco, tax on, 27–28, 84–85, 94
totalitarian state, vs. democracy, 2
Treasury bonds, tax increase and, 106
Treasury certificates of indebtedness.
See certificates of indebtedness
Treasury Department, U.S.: eco-
nomic expansion and, 38; export
trade and, 24–25; and House
Ways and Means Committee,
105–106; receipts and disburse-
ments (1915), 26; taxation and
borrowing by, 3–4; War Risk
Insurance Board, 24; War Savings
Certificates, 163–164
Treasury notes, increase in, 52
Treasury Savings Certificates, 166–
167
Truman, Harry S., 218
Twitchell, Herbert K., 132

Underwood, O. W., 93
unemployment: at outbreak of war,
25; postwar, 7. See also employment
unemployment assistance, 25
Union Bag and Paper Company, 141
United Kingdom: gold exchange
with, 38; trade with, 23
United Nations Organization, 217
United States: as debtor nation, 217;
war expenditures of, compared
with other belligerents, 221–224;
as world major financial power, 14
United States Chamber of Commerce, 89